JOURNAL FOR THE STUDY OF THE OLD TESTAMENT
SUPPLEMENT SERIES
215

Editors
David J.A. Clines
Philip R. Davies

Executive Editor
John Jarick

GENDER, CULTURE, THEORY
3

Editor
J. Cheryl Exum

Sheffield Academic Press

Plotted, Shot, and Painted

Cultural Representations
of Biblical Women

J. Cheryl Exum

Journal for the Study of the Old Testament
Supplement Series 215

Gender, Culture, Theory 3

for my mother
Rebecca Cockrell Exum

and my other mothers
Lucy Cockrell, in memoriam
and
Margaret L. Hines

Copyright © 1996 Sheffield Academic Press

Published by Sheffield Academic Press Ltd
Mansion House
19 Kingfield Road
Sheffield S11 9AS
England

Printed on acid-free paper in Great Britain
by Bookcraft Ltd
Midsomer Norton, Bath

British Library Cataloguing in Publication Data

A catalogue record for this book is available
from the British Library

ISBN 1-85075-592-2
ISBN 1 85075-778-X pbk

CONTENTS

PREFACE

I had originally intended to call this book *Still Amid the Alien Corn?*
In fact, it was previously announced by the publisher under that title,
with *Feminist and Cultural Studies in the Biblical Field* as its subtitle. I
liked having a question as a title, and I liked the cultural connections
Still Amid the Alien Corn? established between the biblical book of
Ruth, Keats's poem, Calderon's painting that appears on the cover,
and the question my title implied; namely, whether or not, or to
what extent, feminist criticism in the field of biblical studies is still, like
Keats's Ruth amid the alien corn,[1] considered marginal, an outsider
taking up lodging within the discipline. I had planned to begin the
book with a chapter, 'Still Standing amid the Alien Corn after All
These Years?', in which I pursued this question by playing with the
similarities and differences between the situation of feminist criticism
in the field and Ruth's inclusion, and, indeed, place of honor in
Israelite tradition as over against her coding as outsider, not simply
'Ruth' but 'Ruth the Moabite'. In the course of writing the book,
however, it became clear to me that I did not want to rehearse points
about feminist criticism that have been raised so often already.[2] I
wanted instead to pursue new ways of conceptualizing the issues and
to take the discussion in a rather different direction by extending the
scope of my inquiry beyond feminist biblical criticism into the
broader area of cultural criticism.

The present title, *Plotted, Shot, and Painted*, foregrounds the broader
cultural backdrop of my project. With its reference to the visual (shot
by the camera and painted) as well as to the textual (the narrative
plot), the book's title signals a shift in emphasis from the biblical text
and its portrayals of women to portrayals of biblical women in popular culture—in literature, art, music, and film. It is not simply a matter

---

1. But unlike Keats's Ruth not in tears at its situation.
2. See Alice Bach, 'Reading Allowed: Feminist Biblical Criticism Approaching
the Millennium', *Currents in Research: Biblical Studies* 1 (1993), pp. 191-215.

of the Bible influencing culture; the influence takes place in both directions. What many people know or think they know about the Bible often comes more from familiar representations of biblical texts and themes in the popular culture than from study of the ancient text itself. Where, I often ask my students, did they get the image of an Eve wandering around the garden in search of Adam in order to give him a bite of the forbidden fruit (which they usually visualize as an apple)? Not only will our knowledge of the biblical text influence the way we view, say, a painting of a biblical scene, our reading of the biblical text is also likely to be shaped by our recollection of that painting. Moreover, as I point out in Chapter 5, 'Is This Naomi?', when our conventional ways of viewing clash with our remembered versions of the biblical story, adjusting one to the other can prove hard to handle.

Plotted, Shot, and Painted is concerned with what happens to biblical women in their various cultural afterlives. In examining the different versions of biblical women's stories, I do not privilege the biblical text or any particular version over others. What this means in practical terms is that I am not interested in arguing for some 'correct', 'original' version of events—the biblical version—and then looking at how later versions 'got it right' or 'got it wrong'. The questions that concern me are, rather, How are these women's 'stories' altered, expanded, or invented—and to what ends? How is the gender ideology of the biblical text both reinscribed in and challenged by its cultural appropriations? How does what we think we know about biblical women, our preconceptions and assumptions shaped by our encounters with their cultural personae, affect the way we read their stories? Are women today still being given the same encoded gender messages about sexual behavior, gender roles and expectations we find inscribed in the Bible? Can women ever win, either in the biblical text or in its literary, musical, or visual afterlives? If not, why not? If so, how? In one form or another, these questions run through all the chapters of this book.

In asking questions of this kind, this study addresses all the issues with which the series, Gender, Culture, Theory, is concerned. *Plotted, Shot, and Painted* is about theory, more as applied than in the abstract; about culture, specifically cultural representations of biblical women; and first and foremost about gender, about social and cultural assumptions that cluster around sexual difference—gender roles, expectations, biases, stereotypes, etc.—and their influence on both representation and interpretation. The twin focus on representation—the way women are portrayed in biblical narratives and both the social assumptions and unconscious motivations that create such portrayals—and interpretation—the way we explain the meaning of these narratives in the light of our own attitudes and circumstances—is fundamental to this study. I am interested here, as I was in my earlier book, *Fragmented Women*, in representation, in the patriarchal ideology that motivates portrayals of women in the Bible, whether negative or positive. I assume, as I did in that study, that women in the biblical narrative are male constructs, and, as such, tell us more about the men who produced them than about actual women. Thus in Chapter 3, 'The Hand that Rocks the Cradle', I ask the question I also asked of stories about biblical women in *Fragmented Women*: what patriarchal agenda does this portrayal serve? But that is only a preliminary question.

The more interesting and important question as far as the present study is concerned is the question of gender bias in interpretation, a subject that received little attention in *Fragmented Women*. We can, to a certain extent at least, account for the gender bias in representation that privileges the male and the male point of view when telling stories about women (and in the many stories where women are absent): we can ascribe it to the culturally conditioned, or even unenlightened (if we prefer to be judgmental and anachronistic) world-view of ancient authors and editors. But what about gender bias in interpretation? How do assumptions about sex and sexual difference, ideas about gender roles, and contemporary gender expectations affect the way not only biblical commentators but, more important, readers in general respond to these ancient texts today? Can we avoid reinscribing their time- and culture-bound gender ideology? Should we bother to try? Do female and male readers read these texts differently? This last question has received little attention to date within the field of biblical studies, but it seems to me of critical importance. I raise it not in terms of what psychological or neurological factors might affect the way the sexes read but rather in terms of a practical question that can be addressed: what different claims do these texts make upon female and male readers? The question needs to be raised about visual images too, and Chapter 6, about Delilah, adds music to the cultural mix. The biblical text and its visual representations align readers with a male

subject position. Obviously this means that female readers and spectators will have to perform a different set of mental operations than
their male counterparts. As I seek to illustrate throughout this study,
adopting a male subject position most often means that women are
asked to identify against our own interests.

This quandary for the female reader in particular is crystallized, and
thus best exemplified, in texts and visual representations where sexuality
is foregrounded. Thus I treat the different potential reactions of
female and male readers or viewers most extensively in Chapter 1,
'Bathsheba Plotted, Shot, and Painted', where the female body is
positioned as the object of the male, voyeuristic gaze, and in Chapter 4,
'Prophetic Pornography', where the female body is again the object
of the look, this time a pornographic gaze, as well as the object of
sexual abuse. Chapter 6, 'Why, Why, Why, Delilah?', which deals
with the biblical character's development into one of culture's most
notorious *femmes fatales*, also interrogates the gaze or look, with
attention centered on the male reader or viewer, since the *femme fatale*
is a male problem.

Some chapters (Chapters 1, 2, 5, and 6) deal extensively with visual
images alongside textual ones. I approach the paintings discussed here
not in relation to art history but rather from a perspective that I describe as semiotic (as if, like a text, a painting has a story to tell) and
reader response: how might a reader 'read' the visual image in the
light of the biblical story, and vice versa? Similarly I discuss the biblical
films in terms of the biblical story and not in relation to the history of
cinema or what is called the cinematic apparatus (production, social
and institutional context, economic factors, etc.). I do, however,
touch on wider issues of film theory, especially feminist film theory,
in the chapter on Delilah, where the film star's positioning as erotic
icon has bearing on Delilah's image as *femme fatale*.

In presenting material from Chapter 1 to different audiences on
different occasions, I have been asked more than once why I take
only a heterosexual perspective in analyzing viewers' responses to the
visual images. The answer is twofold: because the paintings and films
I discuss represent heterosexuality as the norm and it is their constructions of gender I am analyzing, and because I cannot do
everything. I do not wish for a moment to diminish the importance
of studying the influence on interpretation of race, ethnicity, class,
sexual orientation, and the complex set of identities we all carry with

us. I am, however, uncomfortably conscious that to broaden my focus would diffuse my critique. I have not ignored some of these larger issues: I extend the scope of my analysis beyond a heterosexually-oriented analysis in Chapter 5, 'Is This Naomi?', where I discuss the cultural appropriation of the story of Ruth by what I call same-sex and opposite-sex interests.

Gender, culture, and theory converge in my view of the text as a cultural artifact that needs a reader to actualize it. The readers I speak about in this book are present-day female and male readers reading an ancient text, written, I think it is fair to say, by men for men. What happens when we actualize a text? When we look at a painting or a film? When I comment in Chapter 1 ('Bathsheba Plotted, Shot, and Painted') on 'the text's voyeuristic gaze at the naked female body', I am referring to what we, as modern readers, experience, to our reactions to the textual image of a woman bathing, and not to what some ancient author may have meant to suggest. I borrow the following example from Ann Kaplan:

> ...the sentence 'A woman is undressing', or the image of a woman undressing, cannot remain at the denotative level of factual information, but immediately is raised to the level of connotations—her sexuality, her desirability, her nakedness; she is immediately objectified in such a discourse, placed in terms of how she can be *used* for male gratification. That is how our culture *reads* such sentences and images, although these meanings are presented as *natural*, as denotative, because the layering of cultural connotation is masked, hidden.[3]

In this book I explore how our culture reads textual and visual images of biblical women. I am my main instance of how a reader or viewer responds, since I know my experience best, but interaction with other readers and viewers tells me something about their experiences also. Reading is not neutral, and images are constantly competing for our allegiance. As a woman and a feminist, I have something at stake in the cultural representations of biblical women I examine in this book. Voyeurism (Chapter 1), the positioning of the female body as object of male desire in literature, art, and film (Chapters 1 and 6), and pornography (Chapter 4) have an urgency about them for me because they relate to contemporary issues about women's rights, and

3. E. Ann Kaplan, *Women and Film: Both Sides of the Camera* (London: Routledge, 1983), p. 18.

they affect my life. In view of the past and ongoing influence of the Bible and its manifold cultural representations within Western culture, it seems to me especially important to examine the roots of these social problems there. The extent to which (male) commentators reinscribe the pornographic ideology of the prophetic texts I discuss in Chapter 4 actually came as something of a shock to me. Their influence on Bible readers frightens me, and I hope my critique might increase critical awareness of the harmful ideology they are perpetuating.

The stakes are not so high but the same set of issues is involved in Chapter 2, 'Michal at the Window, Michal at the Movies', where I consider the way readers naturalize textual events, often reducing them to the lowest common denominator in order to make them conform to their understanding of the way things 'happen'; for example, by applying their notions of chronology, causality, and coherence (not to mention their stereotypes and gender biases). Naturalization is one readerly response that concerns me in this study; appropriation is another. Readers will appropriate texts as they see fit, especially biblical texts, and thus Bible stories enter into the popular culture all the time with new meanings attached to them. This process is the subject of Chapter 5, where I discuss lesbian readings of the book of Ruth among other appropriations. There is really no point for me, as a biblical scholar, to say, 'You can't do this; that's not what the text means'. Can we say what a text meant or means? Well, yes and no. I do not dispute that authors had intentions in writing down these stories. Based on what I know about the Bible and its cultural background, I feel confident in saying the book of Ruth does not advocate lesbian relationships. Nor was the author of Ruth trying to challenge traditional gender categories. To claim that he was would be anachronistic. But the fact remains that the book does present a challenge to our way of thinking about gender, a challenge that today seems pertinent, even if it did not even a generation or two ago. The material that makes such a challenge possible is there, and we can use it creatively in contemporary interpretation and appropriation. Or if we don't, we can be sure someone will.

Four chapters in this book, those on Bathsheba, Michal, Ruth, and Delilah, deal extensively with portrayals of these biblical women in film, in addition to using examples from literature, art, and music. They reveal my particular interest in Hollywood biblical films both as commentary on the Bible and as transmitters of cultural views of women. Film, I argue, is an especially important site for studying the cultural appropriation of biblical women because of its unique combination of the narrative (its *own* narrative structure, whose deviations from the biblical narrative frequently point to particular problems or gaps in the biblical version) and the visual (What did people look like? What did they wear? Where did they live? etc.) to produce a new interpretation. Biblical blockbusters not only shape contemporary viewers' ideas about biblical women and how they lived (and about the Bible in general); viewers, as I indicated above, take impressions gained from biblical epics back with them when they read the biblical text. Surely King David must have looked something like Richard Gere; at least he does now in my mind, and I will always see Stuart Whitman when I think of Boaz, and appreciate Boaz all the more for it. And Hedy Lamarr, with all of her trappings, *is* Delilah for me. *Samson and Delilah* offers a good example of cinematic impact on the culture at large. It is not a little-known film; I have seen it at least four times on television in the UK in the past three years. With the kind of promotion television offers, De Mille's Oscar-winning epic has certainly reached more audiences than when it was first released, and through repeated television showings it continues to be influential in forming people's opinions about the biblical story. For all its hokeyness *Samson and Delilah* is a brilliant film. So, I discovered (sometimes only after several viewings), are the other films I discuss here. I could not disagree more strongly with Derek Elley's opinion that *The Story of Ruth* 'totally misses the warmth and honesty of the original's love between a poor Moabitess and a rich Israelite'.[4] Not only is he romanticizing when he assumes the book of Ruth is about love (see my discussion in Chapter 5), he is underestimating a sensitive and subtle screenplay. I consider *The Story of Ruth* to be the best of the 'sword and sandals' productions,[5] and I try to give a sense of its interpretive niceties in Chapter 5. My enthusiasm about the use of film as a resource for studying the Bible in culture will become apparent in the pages that follow, and I would be pleased if one effect of my study

4. Derek Elley, *The Epic Film: Myth and History* (London: Routledge & Kegan Paul, 1984), p. 31.

5. For a brief overview of the biblical epic, see Bruce Babington and Peter William Evans, *Biblical Epics: Sacred Narrative in the Hollywood Cinema* (Manchester: Manchester University Press, 1993), pp. 4-24.

were to increase my readers' interest in and enhance their appreciation of Hollywood's contribution to biblical studies.

Some of the chapters of this book originated as essays written for specific purposes, though the overall concept of the book was almost from the beginning in the background of my mind. Chapter 1 is based on my inaugural lecture as Professor of Biblical Studies at the University of Sheffield. It was an honor for me to deliver a somewhat different version of it in the series, 'The Bible in the 21st Century', at the 1994 Annual Meeting of the Society of Biblical Literature in Chicago, and I would like here to take the opportunity to thank the Society for the invitation.[6] Chapter 2 was originally written for a Festschrift for my colleague, John Rogerson.[7] I have revised it for this study, extending my discussion of cultural representations of Michal by looking at other visual representations besides film. Chapter 3, 'The Hand that Rocks the Cradle', originated as a response to myself that accompanied the reprinting of an article I had written many years earlier.[8] Since readers of the present book are not likely to have the original article before them, it seemed necessary to summarize its main points in this chapter. More important, I have used the opportunity of expanding my earlier response to give greater attention to postmodern issues concerning reading and the reading process, especially as they impinged upon my own reading experience. Chapter 4 was written for a Colloquium held at the University of Sheffield on 'The Bible in Ethics'.[9] It has been reworked and

6.   Due to the vagrancies of publishing, an earlier version of this chapter will be appearing about the same time as this book in an issue of *Semeia* devoted to the Bible in film, edited by Alice Bach.

7.   'Michal at the Movies', in *The Bible in Human Society: Essays in Honour of John Rogerson* (ed. M. Daniel Carroll R., David J.A. Clines and Philip R. Davies; Journal for the Study of the Old Testament Supplement Series, 200; Sheffield: Sheffield Academic Press, 1995), pp. 273-92.

8.   'Second Thoughts about Secondary Characters: Women in Exodus 1.8–2.10', in *A Feminist Companion to Exodus–Deuteronomy* (ed. Athalya Brenner; The Feminist Companion to the Bible, 6; Sheffield: Sheffield Academic Press, 1994), pp. 75-87.

9.   'The Ethics of Biblical Violence against Women', in *The Bible in Ethics: The Second Sheffield Colloquium* (ed. John W. Rogerson, Margaret Davies and M. Daniel Carroll R.; Journal for the Study of the Old Testament Supplement Series, 207; Sheffield: Sheffield Academic Press, 1995), pp. 248-71.

expanded in what I believe are important ways; in particular, it seemed necessary to engage recent objections to feminist writing on the topic of prophetic pornography, as well as to take account of some new critical responses to the problem.

Many of the ideas presented in this book were developed in connection with a course I teach on 'Bible Tales and Retellings in the Arts'; to the students in the University of Sheffield who have taken this course I would like to express my appreciation for their questions and ideas, critical feedback, stimulating group projects, and enthusiasm about exploring the Bible through film. I also want to thank members of a class on 'Women in the Bible' in the summer of 1995 at the Institute of Religious Education and Pastoral Ministry at Boston College, who looked at visual images with me, for one of the best experiences of my teaching career. I greatly appreciate the critical responses I received to portions of this study presented at the Society of Biblical Literature, the Bible and Ethics Colloquium, the Society for Old Testament Study, the American Summer Institute at the University of St Andrews, St Colm's College, the University of Glasgow, the University of Edinburgh, the University of Sheffield, and the Sheffield Theological Society; and I thank Erich Zenger for the invitation to join him and Ilse Müllner for a programme on Bathsheba at the Akademie Franz-Hitze Haus, Münster. I take this opportunity to acknowledge the British Academy for grants that helped defray my travel expenses to attend the 1994 and 1996 Annual Meetings of the Society of Biblical Literature, at which portions of this study were presented. I also gratefully acknowledge the help I received from the British Film Institute, the Witt Library of the Courtauld Institute of Art, and the Volunteer Services of the Walker Art Gallery, Liverpool.

Thanks, too, to Graham McElearney of the Teaching and Learning Development Group, for technical assistance with graphics; to Gill Fogg and Alison Bygrave of the Department of Biblical Studies for cheerfully helping in many ways; to colleagues David Clines and Philip Davies for criticism and encouragement, to Ellen van Wolde of the Tilburg Faculty of Theology for helpful comments on the chapter on Ruth; to Alice Bach of Stanford University for saying 'it doesn't have to go anywhere'; and to William Carl Ready for joining me in desperately seeking Bathsheba in museums in Vienna, Amsterdam, Stuttgart, and Munich. Finally, thanks to Sheffield

Academic Press, especially Steve Barganski, Carol Smith, Robert Knight and Jeremy Boucher, for working with me so closely on this book, and to Jean Allen, for keeping me on schedule.

*   *   *

Translations from the Hebrew are mine and transliterations are not scientific. In this book I refer to biblical narrators as 'he', since, even if some of the Bible's authors were women, the world-view of the Bible is the dominant androcentric world-view of the times. Upper case is used for 'god' only when used as if it were the proper name for the deity as a biblical character.

LIST OF FIGURES

1

Bathsheba Plotted, Shot, and Painted

> You painted a naked woman because you
> enjoyed looking at her, you put a mirror in her
> hand and you called the painting *Vanity*, thus
> morally condemning the woman whose
> nakedness you had depicted for your own
> pleasure.
>
> John Berger, *Ways of Seeing*

> To be given in free exchange, to be willingly
> kept in ocular circulation, to serve as object for
> readerly and visual reception, not to hold out on
> the viewer, is already surely an act of
> generosity, if not forced.
>
> Mary Ann Caws, 'Ladies Shot and Painted:
> Female Embodiment in Surrealist Art'

'Plotted' in the title of this chapter refers, of course, to the narrative handling of the story of David and Bathsheba in 2 Samuel 11. 'Shot' has nothing to do with Bathsheba's death, which is not recounted in the Bible, but rather invokes the camera, since I want to consider how Bathsheba is treated in movies based on the biblical story. I also want to look at some famous paintings of Bathsheba, from the fifteenth, sixteenth, and seventeenth centuries. My primary interest in the comparison between narrative, painting, and film is in the representation of the female body; specifically, I want to investigate how Bathsheba, who is a kind of paragon of sensuality, is portrayed as the object of sexual desire and aggression, and to inquire how her body is focalized, first in the text itself, and then in visual representations of it. I shall be looking, then, at women—for we are dealing with more than one Bathsheba here—as the object of the male gaze. And I shall be arguing that there is more to Bathsheba than meets the eye. Since I shall be self-consciously looking at looking, I invite the reader to join me in looking at our own gaze—at our collusion, or complicity, or resistance when faced with the exposure of female flesh for our literary or visual consumption. Surely female and male readers and viewers will react differently to the textual and visual images. The female reader or spectator, like it or not, is identified with the body observed. To the extent we view the naked woman as object, we are co-opted into objectifying our own bodies and reading the textual and visual representations against our own interests. I shall return to this point later.

Bathsheba Plotted

The biblical story of David and Bathsheba holds a place in popular imagination both as a tale of unbridled lust and also, curiously, as a famous 'love story'. It is, in fact, as a love story that producer Darryl F. Zanuck and director Henry King presented *David and Bathsheba* in the 1951 film by that name.[1] What is it about David and Bathsheba as a topos and about us as consumers of this topos that makes us so eager to imbue their encounter with feeling—with *mutual* feeling—rather than dismissing it as an isolated incident, a gratified whim of the king with disastrous consequences for him and his kingdom? The biblical version is no love story. Bathsheba, the wife of Uriah, is 'sent for' by King David, who has sex with her in a moment of passion. That brief encounter might have been the end of it but for one complication: Bathsheba becomes pregnant. Unlike King's film version, where David and Bathsheba romp about the countryside enjoying bucolic trysts, in the biblical account David and Bathsheba do not have sex again until after she has become his wife. Nor is there any evidence in the biblical version to suggest that David *wanted* Bathsheba either for his wife (as the film is at pains to show) or his paramour. On the contrary, the text makes clear that David would prefer to have Uriah assume paternity of the child and, presumably, continue in his marriage to Bathsheba as before. David has Uriah killed and then marries Bathsheba only because his ploy to get Uriah to 'go down to his house'—that is, to have sex with his wife (11.8-13)—fails.

In the biblical account, David's erotic involvement with Bathsheba occupies only one verse of narrative time.

---

1.   Twentieth Century Fox; produced by Darryl F. Zanuck; directed by Henry King; screenplay by Philip Dunne; and starring Gregory Peck and Susan Hayward.

> David sent messengers and took her. She came to him and he lay with her,
> while she was purifying herself from her uncleanness. Then she returned to
> her house (2 Sam. 11.4).

Since Bathsheba will become pregnant, the clause, 'while she was purifying herself from her uncleanness', is necessary to establish David's paternity. Apart from this essential information, only five actions—three on David's part and two on Bathsheba's—are minimally described. He sent, he took, and he lay: the verbs signify control and acquisition. In contrast, only her movement is described: she came and she returned.

This encounter is set in a narrative context of aggression and violence. 'All Israel' (2 Sam. 11.1)—that is, all the men except the king—are away at war, besieging a city, while David is at home, taking a woman.[2] Is Bathsheba, like Rabbah of the Ammonites, taken by force? We cannot be sure, for although 'sent' and 'took' indicate aggression on David's part, 'came' and 'returned', the two verbs of which Bathsheba is the subject, are not what one would expect if resistance were involved. The king sends for a subject and she obeys. Does she know for what purpose she is summoned? For news about her husband Uriah, who is away on the battlefield (which is the pretext used in the film *David and Bathsheba*)?[3] Or for sex? An actual demand for her sexual services is not necessary to make her feel she must agree to sex. David is, after all, the king, so is she free to refuse?

Both the placement of this scene within the account of the Ammonite war and its consequences suggest force. When, as part of his punishment, David's children reenact his sins, David's adultery with Bathsheba is replayed as rape, not once but twice. First Amnon rapes his sister Tamar (2 Sam. 13) and later, to signal his takeover of his father's kingdom, Absalom rapes ten of David's wives. The ten women are raped in a tent on the roof, a location which serves both

2.   See J.P. Fokkelman, *Narrative Art and Poetry in the Books of Samuel*. I. *King David* (Assen: van Gorcum, 1981), pp. 41-70, and Mieke Bal, *Lethal Love: Feminist Literary Readings of Biblical Love Stories* (Bloomington: Indiana University Press, 1987), pp. 10-36, for discussion of the combination of war, sexuality, and violence in 2 Sam. 11. For other explorations of the connection between women, war, and metaphors of sexual violence, see the essays in Claudia V. Camp and Carole R. Fontaine (eds.), *Women, War, and Metaphor: Language and Society in the Study of the Hebrew Bible* (Semeia, 61; Atlanta: Scholars Press, 1993).

3.   In the film, David tells Abishai to invite Bathsheba to dine with him so that he can reward her for Uriah's valor in battle.

to remind us of the place where David sinned and to fulfill Nathan's prophecy that God will do to David in the sight of the sun and all Israel what David had done in secret (2 Sam. 12.11-12; 16.21-22).

Whether or not David rapes Bathsheba is a moot question, and one I do not feel compelled to argue, since I am not interested in subjecting a literary creation to cross-examination.[4] What Bathsheba might have done or felt is not the point; the point is we are not allowed access to her point of view. The issue of force versus consent, which is crucial for constructing the woman's point of view, is not raised. Nor does the text describe an attempted seduction, which would give the woman a role, even if one in which she is manipulated.[5] Bathsheba's rape is semiotic; that is to say, her violation occurs not so much *in the story* as *by means of the story*. By denying her subjectivity,

4.   For an approach that attempts to flesh out female characters by giving them narrative life in the reader's consciousness, see Alice Bach, 'Signs of the Flesh: Observations on Characterization in the Bible', *Semeia* 63 (1993), pp. 61-79.

5.   On the problem with the rape–seduction opposition, see Ellen Rooney, '"A Little More than Persuading": Tess and the Subject of Sexual Violence', in *Rape and Representation* (ed. L.A. Higgins and B.R. Silver; New York: Columbia University Press, 1991), pp. 87-114. The film *David and Bathsheba* gives Bathsheba power by turning the encounter into a seduction scene. Susan Hayward holds Gregory Peck off until she gets what she wants: 'There are women you could send for and send away again. I am not one of them.' At this point, she has ceased to call him 'sire' and addresses him as 'David'. In part this portrayal is due to the fact that Zanuck and King have in Susan Hayward an important female star whom they want to showcase. They flesh out her character and show *her* desire; she acts, she is motivated, and the film evinces a 1950s concern with the woman's feelings. In the final analysis, however, the film reinscribes the gender ideology of the text according to which women are a temptation that can cause a man's downfall, women lead men astray, women are dangerous. Ironically, the 1985 film makes Bathsheba more passive, in what I take to be a backlash against feminism. Alice Krige as Bathsheba, not a star with the box-office attraction Hayward held, is rarely on screen. Krige as Bathsheba does not see her first son die, as Susan Hayward as Bathsheba does. Extremely damaging is her testimony that she would be willing to put up with physical abuse from her husband if only she could have a child—traditional female fulfillment at any price. Besides this speech, her only other spoken line in the movie is 'Let the king's wish prevail, Ahithophel', when David insists that Absalom, and not Solomon, will be king after him. Thus the film takes away from Bathsheba the active role and positive contribution the Bible has her make: her role in obtaining the kingship for her son Solomon (1 Kgs 1 and 2). Not only does Bathsheba not get her final moment, but her position is reversed and she speaks against her own interests in supporting Absalom over Solomon.

the narrator violates the character he created. By portraying Bathsheba in an ambiguous light, the narrator leaves her vulnerable, not simply to assault by David but also to misappropriation by those who come after him to spy on the bathing beauty and offer their versions of, or commentary on, the story. In particular, the withholding of Bathsheba's point of view leaves her open to the charge of seduction.

Both the 1951 film *David and Bathsheba* and the 1985 *King David*,[6] for example, are unable to resist the appeal of seduction in order to make David less guilty at Bathsheba's expense. *David and Bathsheba* is sensitive to the possibility of coercion: is Bathsheba free to say no? 'You are the king', says Bathsheba. 'What other answer can I give, sire? You have sent for me and made known to me your will, what else is there for me to say?' This response represents Bathsheba as a subject who feels she cannot refuse her king, one who yields to his authority, and at this point we may think that the film is out to restore Bathsheba's honor.[7] But pursuing this characterization of Bathsheba would cast King David in too negative a light. David therefore responds to Bathsheba's submission to his will with a long speech in which he prides himself for refusing ever to take anything by force, not even the kingdom: 'So I said nothing to you until you told me that there is no love in your marriage. Yes, you told me that, and so did Uriah...'[8] Only when he tells Bathsheba that she may leave, proving his respect for her right to refuse, does Bathsheba confess to having planned the whole thing! She watched him walking on his balcony every evening and knew she could count on his being there to see her. She had heard he had found no woman to please him. *She* wants to be the woman who will make him happy. *She* wants to be his wife.

In the 1985 film *King David*, drastic changes are made to make David look better. He sees Bathsheba bathing, but does not send for

6. Paramount Pictures; produced by Martin Elfand; directed by Bruce Beresford; and staring Richard Gere. Alice Krige has a minor role as Bathsheba. For interesting comments about his role as advisor to the film, see Jonathan Magonet, 'My Part in the Fall of "King David"—the Bible Goes to the Movies', in *A Rabbi's Bible* (London: SCM Press, 1991), pp. 73-85.

7. The fact that the film uses it at all shows, I think, how compelling an interpretation it is of the narrative silence. It also makes Bathsheba appear more manipulative: she does not yield to David until she has him where she wants him.

8. At the beginning of the film, Uriah has already indicated to David that he prefers the soldier's life to the marriage bed.

her. He has sex with her only after their marriage, which takes place after Uriah is dead (a death David arranges to rid Bathsheba of an abusive husband). As a result of these and other distortions of the story line, nothing that happens later in the film makes much sense. In particular, the disasters that befall David's house now appear arbitrary and random rather than as having some connection to his sin and his punishment in kind. Though Bathsheba is not clearly guilty of planning the affair, as in *David and Bathsheba*, she is nonetheless complicit in letting herself be seen bathing. When David first meets her face to face, he says, 'I've seen you once before', to which she responds, 'I know'.[9]

What I have described is not just a contribution of Hollywood. Biblical scholars draw similar conclusions. When commentators on 2 Samuel 11 suggest that Bathsheba shares the blame, are they picking up on a latent message in the text, or are they reading their own gender stereotypes back into it? George Nicol, for example, maintains:

> It cannot be doubted that Bathsheba's action in bathing so close to the king's residence was provocative, nor can the possibility that the provocation was deliberate be discounted. Even if it was not deliberate, Bathsheba's bathing in a place so clearly open to the king's palace can hardly indicate less than a contributory negligence on her part.[10]

Similarly, Hans Wilhelm Hertzberg, in his commentary on the books of Samuel, says, 'We must, however, ask whether Bathsheba did not count on this possibility', and then quotes Alfons Schulz— 'one cannot but blame her for bathing in a place where she could be seen'—before concluding, 'not, of course, that this possible element of *feminine flirtation* is any excuse for David's conduct'.[11] Though he

---

9.   Why Bathsheba has come to petition David is another aspect of the film that makes little sense, for, although she tells David that Uriah beats her and shows him her wounds, she reminds him that a woman has no redress against her husband. She can tolerate the beatings, she says, but she wants a child. David says she shall have one, to which she replies, 'Not while my husband lives'. The scene thus suggests that she puts the idea of killing Uriah into David's mind, and the very next shot is of Uriah's death letter being sealed.

10.   George Nicol, 'Bathsheba, a Clever Woman?', *Expository Times* 99 (1988), p. 360.

11.   Hans Wilhelm Hertzberg, *I & II Samuel* (trans. J.S. Bowden; The Old Testament Library; Philadelphia: Westminster Press, 1964), p. 309, italics mine. In the German original (*Die Samuelbücher* [Das Alte Testament Deutsch, 10; Göttingen: Vandenhoeck & Ruprecht, 2nd rev. edn, 1960], p. 254) the term is 'Koketterie'.

holds David accountable, Hertzberg manages to blame the woman also. He goes on to propose that, although we know nothing of Bathsheba's point of view, 'her consciousness of the danger into which adultery was leading her (Deut. 22.22) must have been outweighed by her realization of the honour of having attracted the king'.[12] I find it more than a little disquieting that what is arguably a violation and certainly an objectification has so easily, in the view of the conventional commentator, become an *honor*.

Why is it that (male) interpreters are so quick to blame Bathsheba for appearing on the scene in some state of undress? What about the responsibility of the narrator, who made the decision to portray her in the act of washing?[13] It is, after all, the biblical narrator who, using David as his agent, makes Bathsheba the object of the male gaze. When biblical commentators imply that Bathsheba desired the king's attentions and when popular renditions of the story attribute such motivation to her, they let the narrator off the hook at the woman's expense.

We also are involved in the narrator's pretense. By introducing Bathsheba to us through David's eyes, the biblical narrator puts us in the position of voyeurs:

> ...he saw from the roof a woman bathing, and the woman was very beautiful (2 Sam. 11.2).

I have discussed the voyeuristic nature of this scene in my book, *Fragmented Women*.[14] The narrator controls our gaze; we cannot look

12. Hertzberg, *I & II Samuel*, p. 310.

13. John Berger (*Ways of Seeing* [London: Penguin Books, 1972], p. 51) makes this point about visual art, but it applies as well to narrative: 'You painted a naked woman because you enjoyed looking at her, you put a mirror in her hand and you called the painting *Vanity*, thus morally condemning the woman whose nakedness you had depicted for your own pleasure'. To the extent that the narrator implies culpability on Bathsheba's part, he, too, is being hypocritical, morally condemning her for the nakedness he has created imaginatively for his pleasure, David's, and that of his ideal readers. He could, for example, have had David see Bathsheba in somewhat the same way that another biblical 'lover', Samson, sees the woman he wants: 'David went out in Jerusalem and he saw a woman who was the right one in his eyes'.

14. For the following discussion, see J. Cheryl Exum, *Fragmented Women: Feminist (Sub)versions of Biblical Narratives* (Journal for the Study of the Old Testament Supplement Series, 163; Sheffield: JSOT Press/Valley Forge, PA: Trinity Press International, 1993), pp. 174-75, 194-95.

away from the bathing beauty but must consider her appearance: 'very beautiful'. We presume she is naked or only partially clad, and thinking about it requires us to invade her privacy by undressing or dressing her mentally. The intimacy of washing is intensified by the fact that this is a ritual purification after her menstrual period, and this intimacy, along with the suggestion of nakedness, accentuates the body's vulnerability to David's and our shared gaze. A woman is touching herself and a man is watching. The viewing is one-sided, giving him the advantage and the position of power: he sees her but she does not see him.[15] Readers of this text are watching a man watching a woman touch herself.[16] Can male and female readers possibly react in the same way to the scene? For my part, I am uncomfortable being put in the position of voyeur, watching a naked woman being watched.

Nor are we and David the only voyeurs: 'Is this not Bathsheba, the daughter of Eliam, the wife of Uriah the Hittite?' (v. 3). It is not clear who says these words, whether David[17] or an attendant,[18] but in any event, 'Is this not Bathsheba?' suggests that someone else is looking too.

15. Looking at the female body is a cultural preoccupation for both men and women. Women look at women, as the genre of the fashion magazine—the how-to manual for capturing the gaze—well illustrates. Looking at women is an expression of male sexuality. Men are the owners of the gaze. Men look at women to assess us, to take stock of us, to decide how to treat us. Women look at women (including ourselves), among other reasons, in order to determine how to attract the gaze, or how to avoid attracting attention, in order to become like or unlike the image before us. Berger (*Ways of Seeing*, p. 46) puts it well: 'Men survey women before treating them. Consequently how a woman appears to a man can determine how she will be treated. To acquire some control over this process, women must contain it and interiorize it. That part of a woman's self which is the surveyor treats the part which is the surveyed so as to demonstrate to others how her whole self would like to be treated.'

16. If we accept the testimony of literature, art, film, and pornography, men are aroused by watching a woman touch herself. Even more arousing perhaps is the sight of another woman touching a woman, a scene exploited in the film *King David* (see below).

17. So, convincingly, Randall C. Bailey, *David in Love and War: The Pursuit of Power in 2 Samuel 10–12* (Journal for the Study of the Old Testament Supplement Series, 75; Sheffield: JSOT Press, 1990), p. 85.

18. So most commentators and most translations.

The woman is focalized through the male gaze:

> ...and he saw a woman bathing, and the woman was very beautiful.

How does David, through whose eyes we see the woman's body, react to what he sees? The sight of Bathsheba's body arouses his desire, and he acts on it: he sends for her and has sex with her. Lustful looking is the prelude to possessing. The story thus raises the question of the relationship between looking, desiring, and acting on the basis of desire.[19] Fortunately, not every voyeur acts on his lustful impulses. The text condemns David for doing so, but only because the woman is another man's property. The voyeuristic gaze at the female body that can lead to appropriation is permanently inscribed in the text, and we, its readers, are implicated in it. With all this looking, it is little wonder Bathsheba has become the quintessential object of the gaze in literature and art through the ages.[20] Her 'punishment' for being desired is to be forever visualized as the sensual woman who enflames male lust.

This is how the paintings and films I want to consider treat her, dramatically reinscribing the text's voyeuristic gaze at the naked female body. As readers or spectators, we are implicated in this gaze, but as gendered subjects, we are implicated differently. The biblical story, it is fair to say, was written by men for men. To the extent that female readers assume its male perspective, we are forced to read against our own interests: to accept the concept of woman as a source of temptation that can bring about a man's downfall. Even if we

19. My discussion of this issue owes much to Mieke Bal's analysis of the story of Susanna ('The Elders and Susanna', *Biblical Interpretation* 1 [1993], pp. 1-19).

20. The ease with which one can find paintings of the naked Bathsheba attests to the primacy of this scene in the painterly tradition. In spite of the fact that Bathsheba reappears in the biblical account, what most people remember about her is her bath and 'seduction' of David. This is overwhelmingly the answer I receive when I survey introductory students with the question, Who was Bathsheba? She is remembered for setting in motion the downfall of David's house, but not for helping to build Solomon's. The film *David and Bathsheba* ends, for example, before Solomon is born with a 'and-they-lived-happily-ever-after' ending in which David and Bathsheba walk out toward the balcony hand in hand to the strains of the twenty-third Psalm (where outside it is raining as a sign that the drought caused by David's sin is over, and symbolizing purification and a new beginning). In *King David* Bathsheba is present at the end of the film when David proclaims Solomon king, but she has nothing to do with it. She stands by silently, just as she appeared in silent roles the first two times we saw her: watching David dancing before the ark and bathing.

do not identify with Bathsheba, we cannot escape feeling included in the indictment of woman that she represents.[21] The paintings of Bathsheba are also by men[22] and for assumed male spectators and male owners. In commenting upon the Western artistic tradition, John Berger observes,

> In the average European oil painting of the nude the principal protagonist is never painted. He is the spectator in front of the picture and he is presumed to be a man. Everything is addressed to him. Everything must appear to be the result of his being there. It is for him that the figures have assumed their nudity. But he, by definition, is a stranger—with his clothes still on.[23]

Finally, the films, like most Hollywood movies, are produced and directed by men, and in spite of the fact that their audience consists of women and men, the naked female body remains focalized through the male gaze. The woman holds the look; she plays to and signifies male desire.[24] As Laura Mulvey has argued in her classic study on

21. The position of the female reader is well described by Judith Fetterley, 'Palpable Designs: An American Dream: "Rip Van Winkle"', in *Feminisms: An Anthology of Literary Theory and Criticism* (ed. R.R. Warhol and D. Price Herndl; New Brunswick, NJ: Rutgers University Press, 1991), p. 507.

22. There were not many women artists and women were not admitted to academies where nude models were used until the end of the eighteenth century according to Margaret R. Miles, *Carnal Knowing: Female Nakedness and Religious Meaning in the Christian West* (New York: Vintage Books, 1989), pp. 13-14. It is illuminating to compare Artemisia Gentileschi's 'David and Bathsheba' to the Bathshebas discussed here. Gentileschi gives us a sympathetic Bathsheba who appears to want to shield herself from the gaze.

23. Berger, *Ways of Seeing*, p. 54. Kenneth Clark's often discussed distinction between naked and nude is neither relevant for my purposes nor compelling; for critiques of the gender assumptions in Clark's discussion, see Miles, *Carnal Knowing*, pp. 13-16; Lynda Nead, *The Female Nude: Art, Obscenity and Sexuality* (London: Routledge, 1992), pp. 12-33. Nead deconstructs Clark's binary opposition between the naked and the nude, a binary opposition retained but reversed in Berger's study. As Nead (p. 16) remarks: 'The discourse on the naked and the nude, so effectively formulated by Kenneth Clark and subsequently reworked, depends upon the theoretical possibility, if not the actuality, of a physical body that is outside of representation and is then given representation, for better or for worse, through art; but even at the most basic levels the body is always produced through representation...There can be no naked "other" to the nude, for the body is always already in representation.'

24. Laura Mulvey, *Visual and Other Pleasures* (Houndmills: Macmillan, 1989), p. 19.

'Visual Pleasure and Narrative Cinema': 'In their traditional exhibitionist role women are simultaneously looked at and displayed, with their appearance coded for strong visual and erotic impact so that they can be said to connote *to-be-looked-at-ness*'.[25]

The male viewer of the paintings and the films, like the male reader of the biblical story, is invited to take David's symbolic position as the focalizer of the gaze: he can look through David's eyes; he can fantasize himself in David's place. The woman is naked for his pleasure. The female spectator's involvement is more complicated. Our position is that of both surveyor and surveyed, or, to use Mulvey's terms, we are both the image and the bearer of the look. The male spectator is invited to identify with the male protagonist and to desire the female image. The female spectator is also invited to look at the female image with the phallic power of the gaze, yet we are identified with that image as well. Identification and desire, which for the male spectator remain separate operations, are collapsed for us.[26] We might find the male perspective we are asked to assume uncomfortable, and therefore reject it and, with it, the pleasurable cinematic experience. Or we might enjoy the control and freedom of action that identification with the male protagonist gives us.[27] Either way, it would seem that it is not possible for our desire to be acknowledged.

25. Mulvey, *Visual and Other Pleasures* , p. 19, italics hers.

26. See Mary Ann Doane, *The Desire to Desire: The Woman's Film of the 1940s* (Houndmills: Macmillan, 1987), pp. 157, 168-69. As Kaplan (*Women and Film*, p. 31) notes, '...men do not simply look; their gaze carries with it the power of action and of possession which is lacking in the female gaze. Women receive and return a gaze, but cannot act upon it.' It should be obvious that I am pursuing a heterosexual reading, since the premise of the paintings is heterosexual and mainstream, classical Hollywood cinema represents heterosexuality as the norm. I hope it is equally obvious that I am not insisting that the approach taken here is the only way to look at this material; many factors will cause individual readers to react differently.

27. See Mulvey, *Visual and Other Pleasures*, pp. 29-38. The nature and the possibilities of a female gaze is a subject of debate among feminist film critics; see Kaplan, *Women and Film*, pp. 23-35, 200-206; Doane, *The Desire to Desire*, pp. 155-83; Doane, *Femmes Fatales: Feminism, Film Theory, Psychoanalysis* [London: Routledge, 1991], pp. 17-43; Kaja Silverman, *The Acoustic Mirror: The Female Voice in Psychoanalysis and Cinema* (Bloomington: Indiana University Press, 1988), pp. 187-234; and the essays in Lorraine Gamman and Margaret Marshment (eds.), *The Female Gaze: Women as Viewers of Popular Culture* (London: The Women's Press, 1988).

Bathsheba Painted

The story of David and Bathsheba provides both theme and pretext for artistic representations of a naked woman. Female nudity in the art of the Christian West, argues Margaret Miles, carries associations of shame, sin, and guilt. In the case of Bathsheba, the paintings imply what the cinematic representations will make explicit: Bathsheba's exhibitionism. But they also problematize it, and with it our voyeurism also.

I should explain briefly how I intend to 'read' the paintings discussed below. I am neither an art critic nor an art historian. I find art history somewhat like historical criticism in biblical studies: it asks questions about origins, about the artist's historical situation and influences on the artist's life, and it talks about composition and style, particularly in terms of contemporary trends and distinguishing characteristics. But it does not seem very much interested in the 'story' the picture has to tell, in what Berger calls 'the plane of lived experience'.[28] The mystification of art by art historians that Berger deplores is much like the mystification of the Bible by professional biblical scholars—how many people really care if a particular text was written by J, D, or P?

When I look at Rembrandt's famous painting of Bathsheba (fig. 1.1), I am not particularly interested in the artist's age or his financial circumstances when he painted her. It does not matter to me that the subject was probably the artist's common-law wife, Hendrickje Stoffels (though this may account for her sympathetic portrayal). Nor is my interpretation affected by the question whether the letter she holds in her hand represents Hendrickje's summons before the Dutch Reformed Church for 'living in sin with Rembrandt the painter' or whether the painting itself may have incited the church authorities to issue the

---

28. Berger's satiric critique (*Ways of Seeing*) of the mystification of art by art historians has emboldened my 'reading' of these paintings. Berger acknowledges his debt to Walter Benjamin. Benjamin's essay, 'The Work of Art in the Age of Mechanical Reproduction' (*Illuminations* [ed. with an introduction by Hannah Arendt; New York: Schocken Books, 1969], pp. 217-51), anticipates much modern art and film theory. The other important influence on my use of the visual is Mieke Bal's *Reading 'Rembrandt': Beyond the Word-Image Opposition* (Cambridge: Cambridge University Press, 1991).

Figure 1.1. Rembrandt, *Bethsabie au bain*, Louvre © Photo R.M.N.

summons.[29] This is not to say that I am not interested in what historical critics of the Bible have to say or that I do not appreciate knowing something about the background of a painting. But what I see when I view these paintings is a naked woman identified either by the painter or someone else as Bathsheba, and I cannot help reading the painting in the light of what I know of the story. What I am advocating here is a reader-response criticism of art. I intend to read the paintings semiotically, as if, like texts, they have a story to tell. In their case, the story is often compressed, with various elements of the story represented in one moment in time. More importantly, I want to raise questions about the interaction between painting and spectator similar to the questions I am asking about the interaction between text and reader.

The striking thing about Rembrandt's Bathsheba is that David is not looking, we are. We replace David as voyeur, as we view what we assume he has viewed already. This assumption is predicated on the letter summoning her to the king, which Bathsheba holds in her hand—an intertextual reference to Uriah's death letter, since in the story Bathsheba receives no letter from David. I cannot help thinking if she has had time to be seen by David and receive the letter and still has not put her clothes on, she must spend a good deal of her time naked.

The imagery is essentially frontal because the sexual protagonist is the spectator/owner who is looking at it.[30] Bathsheba's body, however, is slightly twisted, as if she were in the act of turning away, and her crossed legs are a modest gesture in relation to the spectator. The pose is ambivalent, making it difficult to decide: is she or is she not an exhibitionist? Mieke Bal, in a brilliant discussion of this painting in her book, *Reading 'Rembrandt'*, calls attention to a distortion of structure that requires explanation. The letter in Bathsheba's hand points to the locus of the distortion. Her legs are crossed, the right leg over the left leg, but her right foot remains at the right side of her knees. The distortion, Bal argues, draws attention to the artificiality of the display of the woman's body; it exposes itself as an exposure.

---

29. See the discussion of this issue in Bal, *Reading 'Rembrandt'*, pp. 224-27. The quotation is from Bal, p. 226, citing Gary Schwartz, *Rembrandt: His Life, His Paintings* (Harmondsworth: Penguin, 1985), p. 292.

30. Berger (*Ways of Seeing*, p. 56) makes this point about most post-Renaissance European painting of the nude.

The navel, the center of the body, had to be displayed so that the viewer could collude with David's voyeurism, but the display itself—its artificiality—had to be emphasized.[31]

Whereas Bathsheba's body is turned toward us, offering itself to our view, her head is turned away, indicating her reluctance to be seen. The expression on her face suggests an interiority that we cannot penetrate, a private, inner space that is hers alone. She is pensive, perhaps even melancholy. Should we interpret the look on her face as signifying resignation or hopelessness? We might read it proleptically as expressing mourning for her husband Uriah (2 Sam. 11.26) or grief for her dead child (2 Sam. 12.15-24), or, more generally, as regret over all the misfortune the letter in her hand will cause. The painter gives Bathsheba what the biblical narrator did not: a measure of subjectivity. He has managed to reveal an inwardness and an inaccessibility in the expression of her body and face. This humanizing of the female nude tells the spectator that she is not simply naked for him.[32]

In Hans Memling's fifteenth-century painting of Bathsheba, the only remaining panel of a triptych (fig. 1.2), once again we, and not David, are the voyeurs. David is in the background, in the upper left-hand corner of the painting. Given his distance from her window, he cannot see or have seen her very well. Indeed, she seems fairly well shielded from his view since her back is to him and her attendant, holding ready her dressing gown, stands between them. Clearly her nakedness is for the spectator's benefit. We—and, again, I mean specifically the male spectator—are invited to identify with David's perspective by means of the woman's body, which signifies his sexual arousal. What we see is female nakedness as the cause of male desire, with the slipper and the pot by the bed providing conventional symbols for sex.

Bathsheba has the long limbs and rounded belly that were standards of female beauty in the fifteenth century. The rounded belly also foreshadows Bathsheba's pregnancy, which will lead to David's downfall. Her naked body therefore suggests both the allure and the

31. Bal, *Reading 'Rembrandt'*, p. 244.

32. On such 'exceptional nudes' in European oil painting, see Berger, *Ways of Seeing*, pp. 60-61; but cf. the caveat of Nead, *The Female Nude*, p. 15. See also Bal's discussion of this painting (*Reading 'Rembrandt'*, pp. 219-46). Something similar to Rembrandt's humanizing of his subject occurs later in the narrative, when pregnancy gives Bathsheba power and voice (2 Sam. 11.5).

Figure 1.2. Hans Memling, *Bathseba im Bade*, Staatsgalerie Stuttgart

danger of female sexuality. Here, too, it seems to me, there is an awkwardness to the pose that draws attention to itself. The suggested movement appears unnatural: it is hard to see how she can keep her balance, and it seems rather awkward for her to be slipping into her dressing gown while still in the process of climbing out of such a high bath. The painting thus gives greater meaning to the precariousness of Bathsheba's position.

Neither Rembrandt's nor Memling's Bathsheba meets our voyeuristic gaze. Both are staring into space. Rembrandt's Bathsheba stares ahead pensively. Memling's stares vacantly as if she were a sleepwalker getting out of her bed. The fact that these Bathshebas do not acknowledge our gaze heightens the voyeuristic effect and conveys a sense of shame on their part in relation to the spectator.[33] Not looking back is what we tend to do when we are self-conscious about being observed, as if by ignoring the observer we can pretend we are not being watched. In addition, by averting their eyes from the viewers, the naked Bathshebas cannot accuse us of looking.

An alternative way of looking offers itself to us in these paintings. Both paintings show a servant attending Bathsheba. Neither looks upon her naked mistress: the old woman in the Rembrandt Bathsheba, so elaborately dressed as to make Bathsheba's nudity conspicuously artful, is absorbed in her work; Memling's servant modestly looks down from behind Bathsheba as she helps her into her robe. By looking elsewhere, these women make us aware of, and thus enable us to share in, their self-consciousness at the idea of looking. In other words, they problematize our voyeurism by drawing attention to the alternative: looking away. They invite us to look away from the naked woman even as the naked Bathshebas avoid returning our intrusive gaze.

In the painting of Bathsheba by the Dutch artist, Cornelis Cornelisz van Haarlem (1562–1638), David is absent, as in Rembrandt's Bathsheba. Here, however, there is no clue that he has seen or will soon see her (fig. 1.3). The complete absence of any reference to David in this painting (he cannot see from the roof of the castle far in

---

33. This is not to say that female subjects of voyeuristic painting do not look back at the spectators; Rembrandt's 'Susanna and the Elders' is good example. Looking back can have various meanings: accusation, appeal for help, acknowledgment of responsibility, etc.

Figure 1.3. Cornelis Cornelisz van Haarlem, *Het toilet van Bathseba*,
Rijksmuseum, Amsterdam

the background) dramatically illustrates that Bathsheba is naked for the spectator's pleasure. So too does the fact that Bathsheba's attendants are also naked and thus join her as objects of the voyeuristic gaze. Their nudity, in turn, dramatizes hers, since she alone is fully exposed (except for the translucent cloth hiding and marking the place of her genitals).

The women appear to be in a magnificent garden, and almost at the center of the painting is a tree in the middle of a landscaped area, like the tree of (sexual?) knowledge in the midst of the garden of Eden. The painting is a study in contrasts. Everything is dark or bright. Bathsheba's body and her servant's back, the blue cloth around the other servant's neck, the yellow robe in the foreground, the area around the tree, and the castle are bathed in light, whereas everything else is dark and difficult to distinguish. Light links the castle, and through metonymy David, with the edenic tree and Bathsheba, the forbidden fruit.

Bathsheba's brightly illuminated body presents a dramatic contrast to the servant at her side, whose darkness strengthens the impression of otherness and the exotic of which the woman is already an example. The black attendant is positioned as the dark place between the two pale figures. As representative of the new, mysterious dark continent that fascinated Europeans of the time, she symbolizes the dark and dangerously seductive mystery of woman. Her left arm is between Bathsheba's knees, and the effect of the shading and the shadows caused by the black arm against the black body is to give this arm the appearance of being thicker than the other (fig. 1.4). We might therefore see the arm as a fetish, a phallus substitute that serves to mitigate woman's threat. Bathsheba's gaze seems to be directed at this enlarged foreign body between her legs. Female sexuality is simultaneously displayed and rendered less threatening by means of the kitschy fountain in the form of a naked woman with water spewing asymmetrically from her breasts. The fountain serves also as a foreshadowing of Bathsheba's motherhood, which will neutralize her sexual threat.[34]

34. For further discussion of fetishism and other means of (male) escape from the threat of female sexuality, see below, Chapter 6.

Figure 1.4. Van Haarlem, detail

Particularly noteworthy are paintings of Bathsheba in which she is shown looking at her reflection in a mirror. Not only does the mirror function to accuse Bathsheba of vanity,[35] it also permits her to join her voyeurs in the act of looking. She thus not only colludes with but also participates in making herself the object of the voyeuristic gaze. This is most striking in the seventeenth-century painting by Carlo Maratti (fig. 1.5). Bathsheba gazes at herself, while King David looks on from the balcony in the background. Bathsheba's two servants look at each other, not at her. Yet again it is clear that the woman's nakedness is for the sake of the spectator, who alone is offered the full frontal view. Bathsheba's legs are parted, suggesting availability, though the traditional piece of cloth covers her genitals, and her left arm covers her left breast.

Bathsheba's reflection in the mirror is difficult to make out. Given the position of the mirror, we ought to be able to see her shoulders and arm, but all we can see is her face, the reflection of which appears reversed. In the painting by Hans van Aachen from the early seventeenth century (fig. 1.6), Bathsheba's reflection is also, and more arrestingly, reversed. This distortion, like that in Rembrandt's painting of Bathsheba, draws attention to itself, and alerts the viewer that something is awry. We might take it as foreshadowing the reversal of

35. Compare, e.g., her literary reincarnation as Bathsheba Everdene in Thomas Hardy's *Far from the Madding Crowd*. When Farmer Oak catches his first glance of Bathsheba, she is riding along on a wagon. Unaware that she is being watched, she takes out a mirror and surveys herself for no apparent reason ('woman's prescriptive infirmity had stalked into the sunlight'). To the gatekeeper at the toll bar, Oak remarks on the 'greatest' of her faults with one comment, 'vanity'.

Figure 1.5. Carlo Maratti, *David and Bathsheba*. Whereabouts unknown.
Photograph: Courtauld Institute of Art

Figure 1.6. Hans van Aachen, *David und Bathseba*,
Kunsthistorisches Museum, Vienna

the fortunes of Bathsheba, Uriah, and, of course, King David. Or, alternatively, as a hint that there is another side to the story, and even another side to Bathsheba. The image in the mirror is not an accurate reflection of the lovely face of the woman but a transformation of her almost innocent beauty, prefiguring perhaps the formidable woman she will become (1 Kings 1–2).[36] As a perversion of perspective, it calls our attention to the perversion of the voyeuristic gaze that leads in this case to appropriation.[37]

Who is the figure looking over Bathsheba's shoulder and holding the mirror? A servant? According to the description in the museum catalogue, the figure is a female servant (*Dienerin*),[38] but the features, especially the neck, are rather mannish. Could this figure represent David's voyeuristic gaze (David is barely visible in the distance, on the rooftop), so that Bathsheba looks upon herself reflected through his eyes, as it were?[39] Or is it a reminder of Uriah, who is away on the battlefield, and his claim to possession of the woman (and the gaze)? Another, earlier painting by van Aachen, dating from 1596, presents a suggestive point of comparison. In *Scherzendes Paar mit einem Spiegel (Der Künstler mit seiner Frau)* (fig. 1.7), van Aachen has painted his wife, Regina di Lasso, who served as the model for Bathsheba, looking at her reflection in a mirror. Her breasts are bared to the spectator. The artist, laughing, looks over her shoulder directly at the spectator. With one hand he holds the mirror, displaying his wife for the spectator's pleasure. His other hand rests on his wife's shoulder, and he wags his finger at the spectator in a knowing gesture, as if

36. The reflection is not as unflattering in the original painting as it appears on the reproduction, though there seems to be a distorting mark on the face from below the ear just about to the chin. A *memento mori*?

37. I have not been able to locate an explanation within art history for the complete reversal of the woman's face in the mirror. It is well established that the disparity between a beautiful face and its unflattering reflection in a mirror served as a sign of vanity, a symbol of the transitory nature of beauty and worldly pleasure, and a *memento mori*; for a useful discussion, see Jane Dillenberger, *Image and Spirit in Sacred and Secular Art* (New York: Crossroad, 1990), pp. 51–66.

38. *Eros und Mythos: Begleitheft zur Ausstellung des Kunsthistorischen Museums, Wien 1995*, p. 63.

39. As, for example, in the miniature from the Codex Germanicus 206 (c. 1454), which represents David on the roof as well as standing next to the bathing woman. A reproduction can be found in Dorothée Sölle *et al.*, *Great Women of the Bible in Art and Literature* (Grand Rapids: Eerdmans, 1994), p. 184.

playfully (or mockingly) saying, 'I am offering this to you to enjoy, but shame on you for looking'.

Figure 1.7. Hans van Aachen, *Scherzendes Paar mit einem Spiegel (Der Künstler mit seiner Frau)*, Kunsthistorisches Museum, Vienna

The similarities between this painting and *David und Bathseba* are striking. The same woman appears as the subject of both paintings. A figure stands behind her, looking over her shoulder and holding a mirror in which we see her reflection.[40] *David und Bathseba* assumes two spectators, David on the roof, who cannot see the woman very well, and the viewer of the painting, whose view is close-up and direct. *Scherzendes Paar* has only one, the viewer. The artist both invites the voyeuristic gaze by exposing the woman (his wife) and at the same time implicitly criticizes it: David ought not to be looking; the viewer of *Scherzendes Paar* is chided for it. If the figure looking over Bathsheba's shoulder is not Uriah, at the least he or she stands in the position of the husband who cooperates, even to the extent of holding the mirror, and whose presence simultaneously accuses the viewer of looking.[41] Not only is the subject (and the moral?) of the paintings similar, it is easily confused: in the museum catalogue for the 1995 exhibit, the photographs of the paintings appear on the same page with the titles reversed.

Bathsheba Shot

Our gaze does not permit the naked Bathsheba to leave her bath or the canvas. The cinematic Bathshebas, in contrast, are in motion, and our gaze at them is both guided and interrupted. We can gaze only at what the camera chooses to show us. Unlike the canvas Bathshebas, frozen in time, ever available to our intrusive gaze, these movie stars

40. The museum catalogue refers to *Scherzendes Paar* as a moralizing allegory (*Eros und Mythos,* p. 62). What looks on the reproduction like a crack in the mirror appears in the painting to be a sliver of light, a reflection of some unseen light source such as a window or door, perhaps to show that this is a mirror and not a portrait.

41. In another painting of Bathsheba with a mirror, Pieter de Grebber's *Toilet of Bathsheba* in the Rijksmuseum, Amsterdam, a child is holding the mirror. Like the artist in *Scherzendes Paar,* the child returns the spectator's gaze as if to acknowledge our joint complicity in the viewing. In this painting, the letter summoning her to the king momentarily takes Bathsheba's gaze away from her image in the mirror. De Grebber's Bathsheba is less available to the spectator than those discussed here; a translucent wrap covers much of her body, and her left arm hides her breasts. A servant points to the window, through which we can make out the faint outlines of the balcony from which we assume David will have seen her. The mirror reflects Bathsheba's hand, holding the letter, thereby calling attention to the letter's fateful consequences.

are performing for the gaze. Susan Hayward knows that theater audiences are watching along with Gregory Peck. During her bath, she looks around in all directions, making a pretense of not noticing her attendants, or David, or us, all of whom are looking at her, while coquettishly casting a glance at the camera. Alice Krige in the role of Bathsheba strikes a pose that tells us she is looking back at David, returning his and our shared gaze.

Film is by nature a voyeuristic medium: we sit passively in a darkened theater and spy on other people's lives. We watch anonymously and with impunity. The replacement of David with the viewer as voyeur is achieved in both films by means of zoom shots, overcoming a difficulty of perspective the paintings could not. The close-ups of Bathsheba bathing create the illusion that what we see is what incites David, but, of course, he is back on the roof and not in the room with the camera, the woman, and us. We are privy to more than David can see. In addition, the films contribute something lacking in the paintings, since our voyeurism includes David's response as well as Bathsheba's bath. The paintings show us Bathsheba through David's eyes but do not expose him to us, as the films do by recording on his face his reaction to what he sees (he does, of course, like Berger's spectator of the nude painting, have his clothes on).

When David spies Bathsheba bathing in the 1951 film *David and Bathsheba*, the timing of the scene and the music add to the titillation. We are watching David as the camera moves back and forth between his face, as an indicator of his arousal, and what he sees, the image that activates his lustful gaze (figs. 1.8–1.14). Through the window, we glimpse, through his eyes as it were, the woman bathing. From a distance, we watch her slip out of her robe and step behind a screen, which is where her bath will take place. Then we see David's face, attentive and interested. Next we see the woman again, through the window, which is framed and illuminated as if it were a movie screen, with David in the position of moviegoer in the shadows. Again we see his face, fixed on the screen/scene before him. He munches on grapes he has plucked from an overhanging branch, a rather obvious sign that his sexual appetite has been whetted by the sight of Bathsheba. Our next view of Bathsheba is a zoom shot into the room. Drawing on the iconographic tradition, the film shows Bathsheba attended by two servants, whose blackness, as in the painting by van Haarlem, lends a sense of otherness and the exotic. In

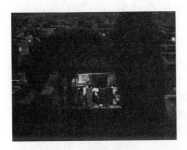

Figure 1.8

Figure 1.9

Figure 1.10

Figure 1.11

Figure 1.12

Figure 1.13

Figure 1.14

this close shot, one attendant is washing Bathsheba, but because Bathsheba is bathing behind a screen, we cannot see her hands, and so we do not see her actually touching Bathsheba. Both the hierarchy of status and the hint of intimacy between women appear calculated to intensify male arousal. David's superiority to Bathsheba is mirrored in Bathsheba's superiority to her attendants, who, however, enjoy greater access to Bathsheba's naked body than David has—at the moment—and also, at the moment, their gaze, like ours, is not from a distance, like his. Unlike David and us, they are allowed on Bathsheba's side of the screen.

In the next shot, the camera lingers on David's face for what seems to be a much longer time than it actually is. The slow pace allows the spectator to imagine, perhaps even to participate in, his arousal: when the camera shifts back to Bathsheba again, what will we see? I said earlier, with regard to the biblical text, that we cannot look away from the woman but are forced to think about her appearance. Of course, we *can* read the text without visualizing the naked woman, especially if we are casual readers. The pacing of the cinematic scene forces us to do what the text implicitly calls for: to take account of the woman's body. Since this is a 1950s movie, the answer to the question, 'What will we see?', is: not much. We are watching David's face when Bathsheba steps from behind the screen, and when we see her again, she is already pulling her robe about her and leaving the room, the outline of her body barely but tantalizingly visible through her transparent robe against the light behind her (fig. 1.14).

This scene in the film *King David* is very similar to that in *David and Bathsheba*. It begins with the same illusion, with David in the role of moviegoer and Bathsheba framed as if on a movie screen. Again the camera moves back and forth between David and Bathsheba; in this case, a total of five times as compared to four times in the 1951 film. This film uses lighting more effectively than the earlier one to create a mood of sensuality. Bathsheba is bathing in the open air (in what looks curiously like ancient ruins) and the fire that heats her water and keeps her warm represents the flame of passion. She is filmed in hues of red and orange, colors that, as in the painterly tradition, suggest sensuousness and concupiscence, while David is filmed in the cold blue of the evening. The 1980s production, however, leaves less of the erotic for the imagination. From David on the roof, the camera moves to Bathsheba bathing, seen from a distance that represents David's perspective. Then we see his face again, and a slightly closer view of her bathing. She is naked, and she is not, like Susan Hayward, bathing behind a screen. David, and we—in ever closer views he cannot share—can see her entire naked body. She has an attendant, who is not black (this is a 1980s film), and both she and her attendant are rubbing her body. Again we see David's face, the camera moving closer in on his face just as it moves in on her body. The camera now shows an even closer shot of her and her attendant running their hands over her body. Back again to his face, followed by an even closer view of her, from the waist up. She and the attendant are washing her breasts—rather thoroughly I would say. Indeed, there are suggestions of homo-eroticism and nymphomania, certainly not innocent washing, in the way Bathsheba enjoys her bath. We then have yet another close shot of David's face, followed by an even closer view of her in which her head, neck, and shoulders fill the screen. The hint of intimacy between women I mentioned in *David and Bathsheba* is even stronger here, as both Bathsheba and her attendant caress her body repeatedly. This is a performance designed to titillate male desire. No woman bathing is going to let herself be touched like this by another woman, unless they have an intimate relationship (and we need to keep in mind that this is a servant and her mistress).

Bathsheba Framed

Biblical style typically suggests a causal connection by means of simple juxtaposition:

> ...he saw from the roof a woman bathing, and the woman was very beautiful. David sent and inquired about the woman. He said, 'Is this not Bathsheba, the daughter of Eliam, the wife of Uriah the Hittite?' David sent messengers and took her.

Because Bathsheba was seen bathing, she was sent for. It is thus the woman's fault that the man's desire is aroused. Bathsheba is guilty of being desired, but the text hints that she asked for it: she *allows* herself to be seen. By having Bathsheba plan or know she is being seen, the films go beyond the biblical text in making Bathsheba's complicity in the viewing explicit. For them, David may be a voyeur, but Bathsheba is an exhibitionist. The effect is to lessen David's guilt at the woman's expense, because she *wants* to be seen. As representations of a single moment in time, the paintings stand somewhere between the biblical account and the films with regard to accusing the woman. In them, because Bathsheba's body alone (and not David's face, as in the films) communicates and explains David's desire, her nakedness becomes a sign of her guilt.[42]

It bears mentioning that, as far as the films are concerned, it is not just Bathsheba who must be made to look bad in order that David might appear in a better light; Uriah's honor has to be sacrificed, too. In *David and Bathsheba*, Uriah is not interested in Bathsheba. He is more interested in making war than in making love: during the seven months they have been married—an arranged marriage, as the film has Bathsheba disparagingly remark—they have spent six days together. In addition to preferring the battleground to the bedroom, Uriah is a heartless follower of the letter of the law, and would invoke the law to have his wife stoned if he had reason to suspect her of adultery. In *King David*, Uriah won't have sex with his wife or touch her, except with a whip. All this is in contrast to the biblical story, where Uriah's faithfulness serves to underscore David's falseness. The biblical Uriah is on the battlefield with the army, while the king, who ought to be there too, is at home, where he catches sight of Uriah's wife. Uriah's refusal to have sexual intercourse with his wife while 'my lord Joab and the servants of my lord are camping in the open field' contrasts markedly with the king's willingness to have sex with Uriah's wife in Uriah's absence. Perhaps for the cinematic versions, the duping and murder of a good man was unthinkable. In any case, Uriah, like Bathsheba, must be guilty so that David's betrayal of him is not totally undeserved.[43]

Who is guilty in this affair? If the films wrongly accuse Uriah, do they otherwise find any support in the biblical story for their portioning out of guilt? Certainly not from God, who through the mouth of his prophet Nathan condemns David alone for sin:

> Why have you despised the word of the Lord to do what is evil in his eyes? Uriah the Hittite you have slain with the sword, and his wife you have taken to be your wife, and him you have killed with the sword of

42. Miles (*Carnal Knowing*, p. 123) makes this point with regard to Susanna.

43. In *David and Bathsheba*, David has Uriah killed to save Bathsheba's life, for otherwise she would be stoned as an adulteress. Moreover, the film goes so far as to make it Uriah's idea that David should order Joab to set him at the front of the fiercest fighting!

the Ammonites. Now therefore the sword shall never depart from your house.

> Because you have despised me and have taken the wife of Uriah the Hittite to be your wife—thus says the Lord—I am raising up evil against you out of your own house, and I will take your wives before your eyes and give them to your neighbor, and he shall lie with your wives in the eyes of this sun. For you did it in secret, but I shall do this thing before all Israel and before the sun (2 Sam. 12.9-12).[44]

In the biblical account, David's crime is twofold: he had Uriah killed and he took Uriah's wife. Both are crimes against Uriah and against God. But they are not treated as crimes against Bathsheba, who is defined solely in terms of her relation to Uriah. Having sexual intercourse with Bathsheba is a crime because it violates another man's marital rights.[45] David's punishment for adultery is that *his wives* will be raped. What he did to another man will be done to him, only more so; in neither case is the women's point of view represented.

Although the story is about *David's* guilt, it does not follow that Bathsheba is blameless. When she is introduced in the story, Bathsheba is bathing. Guilty of being seen, the beautiful woman is responsible for arousing male desire. Gender is an important factor here; a man bathing would not raise the same questions about provocativeness because what is being provoked is *male* desire. Bathing is sexually suggestive in our story because a woman is doing it and because a man is affected.

In 2 Samuel 6, David exposes himself when he dances before the ark of the Lord wearing only a loincloth. The degree of exposure is ambiguous, as in Bathsheba's case, but in both instances we are led to imagine at least partial nakedness. The sight arouses a woman's anger, not her desire. When David's wife Michal criticizes him for his exhibitionism ('How the king of Israel has honored himself today, exposing himself today in the eyes of his subjects' women servants...'),

---

44. Dividing v. 10 with Fokkelman (*King David*, pp. 83-86), who makes a convincing case against the Masoretic division.

45. Adultery is always a matter of the woman's status: a married woman who has sex with a man other than her husband commits adultery; a married man who has sex with a woman other than his wife commits adultery only if that woman is another man's wife. On adultery in ancient Near Eastern law, see Raymond Westbrook, 'Adultery in Ancient Near Eastern law', *Revue Biblique* 97 (1990), pp. 542-80, and the references cited there.

he boasts of the attention he has received ('among the women servants of whom you have spoken, among them I shall be held in honor'). This situation, where a woman views a man's nakedness, is not quite the reverse of 2 Samuel 11, where a man watches a naked woman, for David is in both cases the focal character, first as exhibitionist and then as voyeur. The women are not there for themselves but for what they reveal to us about him. (In a clever twist, the film *King David* has Bathsheba watching David dancing—thus she sees his nakedness before he sees hers. She desires him before he desires her.) Male display of sexuality is active: David is dancing. It is public: he is in control, and he lets himself be seen by women and men alike. As David's response to Michal shows, he is not ashamed of his nakedness. Female 'display' of sexuality, in contrast, is passive and private: Bathsheba is observed while bathing.

This notion is reproduced in the Western artistic tradition, where, as Margaret Miles has demonstrated, the male appears as glorified nude and the female as shamefully naked. Consider Michelangelo's famous David (fig. 1.15). His pose is not modest; rather it suggests prowess and self-assurance. Not simply physical perfection but also inner strength, or divine favor, seems to be presented in this ideal specimen of masculinity. This is a young, vigorous David in, we suppose, the days God smiled upon him—more a young Richard Gere than a jaded Gregory Peck. His pose suggests activity and purpose, in contrast, for example, to the Bathshebas we looked at, who sit or stand passively, and whose shameful or frightening genitals are hidden, by crossed legs or a part of a robe or gown.

Whatever else nakedness signifies, its connection with sexuality is never far from view. In our two scenes, nakedness and sex are linked. Michal sees David's nakedness and objects to it. As a result (the causal connection is created simply by juxtaposition), she has no children. A reasonable conclusion is that David does not again have sex with her because she objected to his (public) nakedness.[46] Bathsheba is seen naked and it leads to her becoming pregnant.

The connection between the desire to see (voyeurism) and the desire to know needs to be considered in comparing these textual and visual representations of the female body. 'It is evident that sight has

46. Another possibility is that Michal refuses to have sex with David, which would not be out of character for her. Or responsibility could lie with the deity, whom the Bible describes as opening and closing the womb.

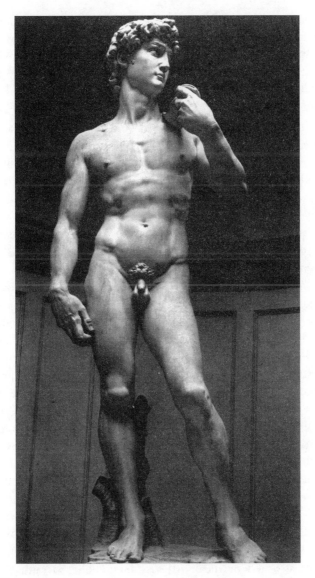

Figure 1.15. Michelangelo, *David*, Galleria dell'Accademia, Florence

always been both a central faculty and a central metaphor in the search for truth', writes Peter Brooks.[47]

47. Peter Brooks, *Body Work: Objects of Desire in Modern Narrative* (Cambridge, MA: Harvard University Press, 1993), p. 96.

> The erotic investment in seeing is from the outset inextricably bound to
> the erotic investment in knowing, in the individual's development as well
> as in the Western philosophical and literary traditions. And the value
> given to the visual in any realist tradition responds to the desire to know
> the world: it promotes the gaze as the *inspection* of reality.[48]

In the examples I have discussed, men control representation. What is
represented is the female body, seen through the male gaze. This
representation has a social function. In her analysis of film, Mulvey
discusses voyeurism as knowledge that leads to control.[49] Similarly,
Miles sees portraits of the female body in the Western artistic tradition
as attempts to capture the complexity of woman on canvas. It is a
man's way of managing the threat women pose. 'Figuration works to
displace threat in that women seem to be understood in advance of
any relationship with a real woman.'[50] In her study, *The Female
Nude*, Lynda Nead, too, argues that artistic representations of the
female nude can 'be understood as a means of containing femininity
and female sexuality'.[51] I have made similar claims about the portrayals
of women in biblical literature: they serve to define women and keep
them in their place, where their threat can be perceived as more
manageable.[52]

Just as representation is gender-determined, so too is interpretation.
Since meaning is constructed through interaction between text or
image and reader or spectator, we will decide for ourselves whether
or not we feel called upon to be voyeurs when we read the 'story of
David and Bathsheba' or view these paintings or films. Women and
men are likely to decide differently, largely but not wholly along
gender lines, based on the different demands they perceive the story
or image to be making upon them. Some of us will resist the phallocentric premises of the text and its visual representations more than
others. I have argued elsewhere that the biblical story of David and
Bathsheba invites a kind of voyeuristic complicity between the narrator and his assumed or ideal male readers.[53] The narrator not only

48. Brooks, *Body Work*, p. 99, italics his.

49. Mulvey, *Visual and Other Pleasures*, pp. 14-26; similarly, Kaplan, *Women and
Film*, pp. 23-35.

50. Miles, *Carnal Knowing*, p. 82.

51. Nead, *The Female Nude*, p. 2; see esp. her discussion, pp. 5-33.

52. Exum, *Fragmented Women*; on Bathsheba's reappearance in the story in
1 Kings 1-2, see pp. 198-200.

53. Exum, *Fragmented Women*, pp. 196-97.

controls our gaze at the naked or partially naked female body, he excuses it by letting us look without any blame being attached, which is more than he does for David. The text insinuates that David has no business looking, since it leads him to sin. He should be away at war with 'all Israel' instead of at home taking a long siesta. By setting it up so that what we see through David's eyes becomes part of our judgment against David, the narrator gives us the moral high ground. This makes it possible for readers to gaze upon the naked woman without embarrassment, or at least without feeling guilty about it. Possible, but not inevitable, and harder, I think, for women, for reasons I have tried to suggest.

The narrative strategy of allowing us to look guiltlessly and, if we wish, to blame the woman at the same time is the premise behind the story's representation in painting and film. In this chapter, I have sought to problematize our position as consumers of images, to draw attention to its gendered nature, and to make it difficult to view unreflectively both texts and images that invite our collusion in voyeurism. Resisting such textual and visual claims upon us does not mean advocating the removal of nudes from museums or the deletion of sex scenes from movies (though, personally, I would like to see more censorship of films). Nor does it mean 'cleaning up' the Bible, which, interestingly, both films I have discussed attempt to do in other respects.. Resisting, as I see it, involves interrogating these materials with the aid of an interpretive strategy that takes seriously the gender politics of both representation and interpretation. Resisting involves becoming self-conscious about what we do when we see texts and images in certain ways, recognizing what is at stake personally and culturally, and taking responsibility for our interpretations.

2

Michal at the Window, Michal in the Movies

> My tongue will tell the anger of my heart
> …I will be free
> Even to the uttermost, as I please, in words.
> Shakespeare, *The Taming of the Shrew*,
> Act IV, Scene III

Chapter 1 examined ways the quintessential biblical sex object, Bathsheba, is focalized both in the biblical text and, especially, in visual representations of her famous bath. In this chapter I want to return to the two Hollywood films discussed briefly in Chapter 1 and to inquire into the presentation of another of 'David's women', his first wife, Michal, daughter of King Saul and symbol of the unity of the two royal houses, whose elimination from the wider biblical story is both inevitable and necessary.[1] My question is, What happens to Michal when she is portrayed on the silver screen? By way of anticipation, my answer is that through the process of naturalization, with its attendant urge to offer moral evaluation, the complexity of the biblical character is lost, and the tensions she represents (which are focused in and resolved through her character) are subsumed, but not wholly erased, under the concept of woman as shrew. After discussing the films in some detail, I shall turn briefly to other visual representations, one ancient and one more recent that, to my mind, epitomize the place and role assigned to Michal, both in the biblical text and in the films (though only one of them utilizes it): the image of the woman at the window. The woman confined to the home, the woman's 'proper' place, is an image conjured up dramatically in the narrative of 2 Samuel 6, where from the window Michal watches David dancing before the ark and her ire is aroused.

My purpose in analyzing the cinematic representations of Michal is

---

1. For discussion of the necessity of Michal's elimination from the narrative, see Exum, *Fragmented Women*, pp. 16-41.

not to argue that they offer us 'bad' readings of the biblical story but
rather that their readings represent serious, if flawed, attempts to come
to terms with the very tensions that pose problems for interpreters of
the biblical text. As Jonathan Magonet, who served as advisor to the
film *King David*, puts it, the cinematic versions offer us 'yet another
attempt to get to grips with the Bible from a whole new range of
presuppositions, viewpoints and intentions. The fact of filming means
that things we might otherwise take for granted have actually to be
visualized and indeed interpreted.'[2]

The key oppositions that create tensions and complicate the portrayal of Michal in the biblical account are: the house of David versus
the house of Saul, marriage bond versus kinship, male versus female,
the political (or public) versus the domestic (or private), and, to a
certain extent, lower class versus upper class. Far from being 'bad'
readings, some of the cinematic gap-filling where Michal is concerned is both plausible and fascinating (and not vastly different from
the gap-filling one finds in biblical commentaries). Moreover, the fact
that the films reproduce the tensions in the biblical account, if only to
play them out in different ways, sometimes as dead ends, can make us
more aware of the resistance of certain problematic textual elements to
naturalization, especially in a later, vastly different culture.

The methodological standpoint adopted here refuses to privilege
either written interpretations over visual ones or the interpretations
of biblical scholars over popular culture. Whatever else they are, the
films represent *interpretations* of the biblical story. Like all readings,
they fill gaps, and they fill them according to their understanding of
the biblical story and in ways that will be comprehensible to their
audiences in terms of attitudes and values of the times. Not only do
they reflect assumptions about the Bible in their own particular social
contexts, they also influence the way Bible stories and Bible characters
are perceived in the popular culture. In the case of Michal, they make

---

2.   Magonet, 'My Part in the Fall of "King David"', pp. 84-85. That cinematic
interpretations can profitably be used to shed light on biblical texts is the premise
behind Larry J. Kreitzer's recent studies, *The New Testament in Fiction and Film: On
Reversing the Hermeneutical Flow* (The Biblical Seminar, 17; Sheffield: JSOT Press,
1993) and *The Old Testament in Fiction and Film: On Reversing the Hermeneutical Flow*
(The Biblical Seminar, 24; Sheffield: Sheffield Academic Press, 1994). See also
Bernard Brandon Scott, *Hollywood Dreams and Biblical Stories* (Minneapolis: Fortress
Press, 1994), whose project is to have the Bible and the movies 'hear different and
new intonations *in the other's voice*' (p. x, italics mine).

a minor biblical character accessible to audiences who may not even remember her from the Bible, and they give us what is probably a more striking and memorable Michal because they have simplified and compressed the plot (whereas the biblical Michal can easily get lost in the complexities of the larger story).[3] In particular, they make it more likely that audiences' lasting impression of Michal will be one of a nagging, spiteful shrew, and not—as is possible (but not inevitable, to judge from some commentators)[4] from the biblical text—a woman whose love has justifiably turned to hate. As I hope to show, an important result of the naturalization process is that viewers will end up blaming the woman. The process of naturalization and the simplification of Michal's character are not simply the product of Hollywood; these are common responses of readers when faced with the difficulty of accommodating the complexities of the text. Even biblical scholars (!) succumb to the temptation to naturalize events in order to make them intelligible and thus subject to moral judgment, as references below to the scholarly literature will show.

What's Love Got to Do with It?

Naturalization is at its strongest where love is concerned, and this is not surprising considering the strong romantic interest in the films. The romantic interest is, of course, between David and Bathsheba, not David and Michal, but, as we shall see, the films use one relationship to help explain the other. The Bible provides the catalyst for speculation on the love theme. It tells us that Michal loves David in

3.   This seems to be Clines's point, when he argues: 'But in the end, I know that I should not let my reading of David from Michal's point of view be determinative for my reading of David; I will have to end up with a reading *with* the grain, that reduces Michal back to a more proportionate size and that restores a David seen from as many different perspectives as the story offers'; see David J.A. Clines, 'The Story of Michal, Wife of David, in its Sequential Unfolding', in *Telling Queen Michal's Story: An Experiment in Comparative Interpretation* (ed. David J. A. Clines and Tamara C. Eskenazi; Journal for the Study of the Old Testament Supplement Series, 119; Sheffield: JSOT Press, 1991), p. 130 (italics his).

4.   At one extreme, for example, Alexander Whyte calls her a 'daughter of Lucifer' (Alexander Whyte, 'Michal, Saul's Daughter', in *Bible Characters: Gideon to Absalom* [London: Oliphants, c. 1898], p. 178, cited in Clines and Eskenazi [eds.], *Telling Queen Michal's Story*, p. 291). For a broad range of interpretations of Michal, see the essays in *Telling Queen Michal's Story*.

1 Sam. 18.20, and later, in 2 Sam. 6.16, it reports that 'she despised him in her heart'. How can we resist searching for clues to this remarkable transformation? There are only two major scenes in the biblical account in which Michal plays an active part. In 1 Samuel 19, she saves David's life by warning him of Saul's plan to kill him and by orchestrating his escape. We can view this as an illustration of her love. The seriousness of the risk she takes by helping David is suggested by the similarity to her brother Jonathan, who also helps David escape from Saul: Saul nearly kills Jonathan in his rage over Jonathan's support of his enemy (1 Sam. 20.33). Michal's second major scene is her quarrel with David, which is triggered by David's dancing before the ark in a grand public ceremony that she watches from the window (2 Sam. 6), and it illustrates her loathing. It is difficult to imagine that this loathing is sudden, that one moment she loves him and the next moment she sees him cavorting before the ark and starts to hate him. Thus what happens between these two scenes is important for understanding the change that takes place in Michal.

Not much takes place between these two scenes, but what does is reported (or not reported) in such a way as to fuel our curiosity. Although we are informed that Michal loved David, nothing is said about David's loving Michal. By itself, the silence is hardly remarkable, but in view of Michal's feelings and of her treatment by David, it takes on significance. After he flees Saul's court, David has two secret meetings with Jonathan but none with Michal. He finds refuge for his parents with the king of Moab, but he makes no effort either to include Michal in this arrangement or to take her with him, though he takes other wives while he is on the run (1 Sam. 25.42-43). Is it unreasonable for us to conclude that David is not particularly interested in Michal, except as a means to Saul's throne? The Bible never explicitly presents this as David's motive, but why else would Saul give Michal in marriage to another man, and why would David not seek her return to him until the issue of his kingship over the northern tribes gets raised? In the meantime, David has acquired six other wives.

The urge to look for the cause of Michal's change of heart—to familiarize it by making it conform to our expectations and common perceptions about the realm of personal relationships—is difficult to resist, given such rich and tantalizing material for musing about character development. It might be possible to explain the change in

Michal's feelings toward David as a result of feeling neglected by him, and, indeed, one of our films gives prominence to the neglect theme. Or we might decide that she is bitter over her treatment at the hands of men—her father Saul and her husband David, who use her as a pawn in their struggle over the kingship. Here again the Bible is particularly reticent. We do not know Michal's feelings about being given as a wife to Paltiel once David has fled the court (and the coup), nor about being forcibly taken from Paltiel and returned to David as a result of his negotiations with Abner over the kingdom. This is a significant gap, and the films fill it differently.

In *David and Bathsheba*, Michal loves David but he no longer loves her; in *King David*, the situation is reversed: he loves her, but she spurns him in order to return to her second husband. Either scenario is possible as a means of explaining the tension that gives rise to the rift between them. In 2 Sam. 3.16, when Michal is taken to David, her grief-stricken husband Paltiel follows in tears. Like the statements that Michal loved David and later hated him, this bit of (unnecessary) information invites our speculation. Is the biblical narrator, or are we, really interested in Paltiel? The fact that the narrator bothers to describe Paltiel's emotional response renders the silence about Michal's reaction especially significant. But what does it signify? Because nothing is said about Michal's attitude, one film can have her want the reunion with David and the other can have her oppose it.

The Biblical Confrontation Scene

Since they do not present any of the information given in 1 Sam. 25.44 or 2 Sam. 3.13-16 as action, both films resolve the love interest theme by means of a confrontation scene in which Michal and David rehearse their mutual grievances. The only place Michal and David quarrel in the Bible is 2 Samuel 6, so we can take the interpersonal dynamics and the characterization of Michal in this scene as the source for their quarrel in the films,[5] even in its altered version in *David and Bathsheba*.

> As the ark of the Lord entered the city of David, Michal the daughter of
> Saul looked down from the window and saw King David leaping and

---

5.   They are the source for the characterization of Michal, the minor character, but not for David, who is the subject of both films and whose character development is traced throughout them.

cavorting before the Lord, and she despised him in her heart . . . David
returned to bless his house, and Michal the daughter of Saul went out to
meet David. She said, 'How the king of Israel has honored himself today,
exposing himself today in the eyes of his subjects' women servants as one
of the worthless fellows flagrantly exposes himself'. David said to Michal,
'Before the Lord who chose me over your father and over all his house to
appoint me king-elect over the people of the Lord, over Israel—I will
dance before the Lord. And I shall dishonor myself even more than this
and be abased in my eyes, but among the women servants of whom you
have spoken, among them I shall be held in honor.' And Michal the
daughter of Saul had no child to the day of her death (2 Sam. 6.16, 20-23).

What triggers Michal's emotional outburst? 'Her disgust is not
aesthetic, it is sexual', says David Clines.

> She cannot bear to see the man she has loved flaunt himself as sexually
> available—presumably, that is, to anyone but her. His self-exposure earns
> the acclaim of the bystanders, but is in fact a humiliation to him, if only
> he could recognize the fact; and it is a humiliation to her as well, because
> it proclaims David's indifference in matters of sexual loyalty.[6]

Walter Brueggemann, on the other hand, finds Michal lacking in
religious sensibilities:

> David is utterly Yahweh's man, a fact Michal either cannot understand or
> refuses to acknowledge . . . In David's utter abandonment to dance and in
> his liturgic, social, royal extravagance, a new order is authorized, wrought
> out of unrestrained yielding and worship. David is freshly legitimate.[7]

6.   Clines, 'The Story of Michal, Wife of David, in its Sequential Unfolding',
p. 138. Clines disagrees with my contention that the issue here is the kingship. He
thinks that is the issue for David—the way David would like to see it—but not for
Michal. I have no quarrel with Clines's suggestion that sex is the issue for the *character*
Michal. When I say kingship is the issue, I am talking about what is at stake not for
the characters, but rather for the *narrator*. For a different kind of political interpretation of Michal's role in the account, see C.L. Seow, *Myth, Drama, and the Politics of
David's Dance* (Harvard Semitic Monographs, 44; Atlanta: Scholars Press, 1989),
pp. 129-31.

7.   Walter Brueggemann, *First and Second Samuel* (Interpretation: A Bible
Commentary for Teaching and Preaching; Louisville: John Knox Press, 1990),
pp. 252-53. Cf. R.A. Carlson, *David, the Chosen King* (Stockholm: Almqvist &
Wiksell, 1964), p. 93: 'It seems likely that this [Michal's barrenness] is to be interpreted as a punishment sent by Yahweh on account of her attitude to the Ark'. It
seems to me rather customary that when commentators cannot find any other reason
to account for negative textual evaluations of characters (i.e. when naturalization is
difficult), they resort to accusing the character of having the wrong religious attitude.

(In contrast to Michal, who presumably represents the illegitimate and stale.) But perhaps there is another reason for her vitriolic reproach.

> For Michal, the fact of exposure was less important than the humiliation—as she saw it—of cheapening himself before the masses, of descending to their level...She was the daughter of the nobility contrasted with the man she actually regarded as simple, as a boor, as one who may have taken up the reigns [sic] of government but not the grandeur of the kingship.[8]

Jan Fokkelman combines all these explanations:

> ...she is the 'daughter of Saul' and this is the way she feels: of royal blood, from a different tribe and family to David. She now looks down, in two different meanings of the word...The window symbolizes her special frame of mind, which prevents her from empathetically and joyfully taking part in the sacred festivities and everybody's rejoicing...We onlookers can take the clause [v. 20] to be a poorly-disguised sign of sexual jealousy.[9]

Sexual jealousy, lack of the proper religious enthusiasm, royal arrogance—these are all ways of naturalizing Michal's outburst, of explaining it in familiar terms based on constructions of 'reality' or literary and cultural conventions. Each of these interpretations picks up on what it perceives to be signals in the text, and in their desire to find a determinate cause to account for Michal's criticisms, they close off other ways of viewing the conflict.

Far from being a matter of simple cause and effect, Michal's outburst points to a larger textual problematic. I mentioned above some of the key oppositions that meet in Michal, making her character a suitable point for resolving a complex nexus of ideological issues. Michal belongs to both the house of Saul and the house of David; she is linked by kinship bonds to one and marriage to the other. For ideological reasons, however, the houses cannot be united, and for the threat of contamination she represents, Michal will have to be eliminated. A potential political problem—how to explain David's acquisition of Saul's throne and the suspicious elimination of rival Saulide claimants—is given theological justification: the throne is David's because God took it from Saul and gave it to him. The

---

8.   Adin Steinsaltz, *Biblical Images: Men and Women of the Book* (New York: Basic Books, 1984), p. 150; cited in Clines and Eskenazi (eds.), *Telling Queen Michal's Story*, p. 284.

9.   Jan Fokkelman, *Narrative Art and Poetry in the Books of Samuel*. III. *Throne and City* (Assen: van Gorcum, 1986), pp. 196-99.

tension surrounding the transfer of kingship from Saul to David resurfaces at various places in the narrative of 1 and 2 Samuel. In 2 Samuel 6, the political problem is displaced by playing it out as a domestic dispute, though traces of the political significance remain (as when Michal refers to David as 'the king' and he responds to her by addressing the issue of the kingship before answering her charge about his comportment). Michal goes outside to meet David; she leaves the security of the house, the woman's domain, and levels her charges at the king in the public arena. This is not, therefore, despite evidence to the contrary, merely a private matter between husband and wife. Indeed, the outcome—that Michal has no child—is not just the sign of the breakdown of the marriage bond but a solution to a political and theological problem: there will be no child of this union, no descendant of Saul who is also a descendant of David and who, as a scion of both royal houses, might claim the throne in the name of a house rejected by God.

Where one might have expected the conflict between the two royal houses to surface—between David and Saul's heir-apparent, Jonathan—there is harmony: Jonathan loves David and accepts his role as second-in-command in David's kingdom (1 Sam. 23.17), and he (conveniently) dies before this 'solution' to the Saul–David opposition is tested. Instead the conflict is played out between David and Michal, as representative of Saul's house (by referring to her as 'Saul's daughter' in 2 Sam. 6, the narrator aligns her with her father's house). In the battle between the sexes (the male versus female opposition), the woman inevitably loses. With Michal's remark about David's 'male servants' women servants', a class issue enters the picture as a final opposition. It is used not to separate Michal from David so much as to isolate her from other women, making gender solidarity impossible and effectively humiliating the woman and eliminating her from the picture.[10]

In what follows I want to show how the films pick up on and play out the central thematic oppositions of the biblical account in such a way that the love interest theme overshadows but does not totally obscure the political, theological, gender, and class issues.

10. For fuller discussion, see J. Cheryl Exum, *Tragedy and Biblical Narrative: Arrows of the Almighty* (Cambridge: Cambridge University Press, 1992), pp. 81-95; Exum, *Fragmented Women*, pp. 16-60.

The Film David and Bathsheba

Perhaps the most significant aspect of the domestic dispute between David and Michal in the film *David and Bathsheba* is that it is not occasioned by David's dancing before the ark. Instead, David has returned from fighting against the Ammonites (where, incidentally, he makes the acquaintance of Uriah) to hold court in Jerusalem. When he enters his chambers, Michal is waiting for him. She complains because he did not greet her upon his return, as he did his other wives, and he responds that he would have greeted her had she been with the others instead of remaining aloof (here we encounter Steinsaltz's aristocratic princess).

There is another important difference. Unlike the biblical version, where Michal goes *outside* to meet David, this confrontation is private. As a result, Michal's complaint loses any larger political significance. The evidence of the biblical displacement of the political and theological conflict onto the domestic plane is erased and the dispute becomes purely a matter between husband and wife in the film, where David's right to the throne is never questioned, although David questions himself and his god.[11] His self-doubt, ennui, and rejuvenation by the 'right' woman (Bathsheba) are more accessible to the twentieth-century audience than the theological and political tensions of the distant, unfamiliar biblical account.

In her first appearance in the film, Michal wears drab (blue and black), rather bulky clothing that is unflattering and a far cry from Susan Hayward's low-cut, well-fitting outfits. Her head is covered in an unbecoming way (Hayward's usually is not, and when it is, her face and hair are carefully exposed). Unlike Hayward the star, who plays Bathsheba and whose appearance is coded for visual and erotic impact,[12] Michal's appearance is coded for the opposite effect. She provides no erotic interest either for David or the (male) viewer, though she once did for David, as we later learn. The moment she opens her mouth, Michal makes a negative impression. Her tone is

11. Babington and Evans discuss David's search for himself in their chapter on 'Henry King's *David and Bathsheba* (1951)', in *Biblical Epics*, pp. 79-81. They point out the film's affinities with film noir, the 1940s melodramatic 'Woman's Picture', and the Western pastoral (pp. 74-76).

12. For discussion of this function of the female movie star, see Mulvey, *Visual and Other Pleasures*, pp. 14-26.

altogether haughty and sarcastic. She resents being ignored by David, and she is jealous: she does not want to be just one of his wives, she wants to be first. Lest we mistake Jayne Meadows's rigid demeanor for bad acting, the filmmaker takes care to have both David and Michal refer to Michal's aloofness (she says he once approved of her aloofness and he says he does not object to it now), and has David accuse her of sarcasm. Michal tries her best to start a row by insulting David and belittling him, but he tolerates her badgering in a patronizing kind of way. He is presented as the long-suffering husband who does not want to get involved in another pointless argument, and she is the aggrieved wife who has to keep picking at him to get attention (fig. 2.1). The issue of kingship gets raised, an indication the filmmaker is aware of its importance, but its significance is altered. The political issue that occupied the biblical narrator—the fact that Saul's kingdom is in David's hands—becomes a personal matter of Saul's true kingliness versus David's inadequacy: Michal calls David a fraud, in contrast to Saul, whom they agree was 'every inch a king', and David accepts her allegation. Michal's arrogance is further underscored when she introduces a class distinction: 'The shepherd's son is dismissing the daughter of Saul'. In the biblical account, however, the legitimacy of the king, not his social class, is the issue. Saul's and David's backgrounds before their anointing are not very different.

Figure 2.1. Gregory Peck and Jayne Meadows, in *David and Bathsheba*

The biblical silence surrounding David's feelings for Michal is problematic and I have proposed that it hints at his lack of interest in her. *David and Bathsheba* handles the problem by removing any suggestion that David might be at fault.[13] Thus, though the biblical account never tells us that David loved Michal, the film does, perhaps because a David who would marry for political reasons and not out of love would not be a very appealing biblical hero for a 1950s audience. When Michal asks, 'Why did you marry me, David?', he responds, 'Because I loved you'. But what about the biblical evidence: David's two meetings with Jonathan but neglect of Michal after his escape from Saul? Or his leaving Michal behind? The film fills the gaps in the biblical story by having David claim that he begged Michal on his knees to go with him into exile but she refused. It is only at this point in their conversation, when Michal challenges the genuineness of his love, that David finally loses his temper. Clearly everything is the woman's fault. Though he does not defend himself against any of Michal's other accusations, David cannot let go unchallenged the charge that he failed in love. He fights back, blaming Michal for dishonoring her marriage vows by letting herself be married off to another. When she claims that it was against her will, he responds that he 'cannot help thinking that real love would have fathered a stronger will'.

Introducing the concept of 'real love' and the notion that her will would have had anything to do with it is a clever touch with important repercussions. In the biblical account, Saul exercises his paternal right in giving his daughter in marriage, first to David and then to Paltiel. Although the latter case is admittedly unusual in that Michal is already married, it could be justified on the grounds that David's abandonment of Michal constituted divorce (cf. Judg. 15.2), or even read as an instance of the king placing himself above the law. In any event, the accusation that Michal could have resisted the remarriage but did not is a naturalization that appeals to our modern sensibilities. It also encourages us to hold Michal accountable, to see her as having control over her own life rather than as a pawn or a victim at the mercy of powerful men.

Not only is this Michal blameworthy, she is naive: surprisingly for

---

13. This is only one of the moves to make David look better at the expense of other characters: we saw in Chapter 1 how Bathsheba in particular but also Uriah get similar treatment.

a woman in her position, she does not seem to have thought of her political significance to David. Throughout the scene, she is concerned only with the way David has treated her, and she is hurt and bitter. Only at the end of the scene, when she asks David why he took her back from Paltiel, does he acknowledge his political motivation: 'You might have guessed. Without Saul's daughter at my side the northern tribes would not have acknowledged me as king. By taking you back I made Israel one.' Obviously, she had not guessed. She seems shocked and taken aback at this revelation. Politics is important, but only for exposing the woman's naiveté.

Clearly the Michal of *David and Bathsheba* is bitter, but is her bitterness justified? Has she been wronged by David? In the cinematic version, he, and not she, is the wronged party. *She* has wronged *him* ('you deserted me'), since she refused to follow him into exile when he 'begged [her] on [his] knees' and she 'even dishonored [her] vows and let [her] father marry [her] to another'. Nor does the unsympathetic picture of her stop here: the invention of two additional scenes for Michal guarantees that we will sympathize with David as the victim of her vindictiveness. After the confrontation scene, she is out for revenge. When David tries to trick Uriah into having sexual intercourse with Bathsheba in an effort to conceal their adultery, it is Michal who informs David that Uriah has not gone to his house. Once again she is waiting for David in his chambers, ready to pick a fight. She does not come straight to the point, however, but first taunts him, playing on his jealousy: 'It's a terrible thing to know that your beloved is in the arms of another'. She should know. Still the sarcastic, bitter woman, she tells David she has learned the secret of Bathsheba's pregnancy from her servants and she calls his ploy to get Uriah to assume paternity of the child a 'clever trick worthy of the son of goatherds'.

Michal is transformed from shrew to villain. She is brought on the scene a final time to accuse Bathsheba of adultery and demand her death. Whereas biblical law demands the death of both the adulterer and the adulteress, in the film only the woman's death is called for.[14]

14. In *David and Bathsheba*, the child dies before Nathan delivers his parable about the poor man's ewe lamb. After David pronounces the death sentence upon himself, Nathan tells him it is not God's will that he should die but only that he be punished. David replies that he has not escaped punishment, as his son is dead. Nathan goes on to insist that the woman must expiate her sin because she was a 'faithless wife'.

Inconsistent on this point, having repeatedly emphasized that in Israel the king is subject to the law, *David and Bathsheba* is typical of classical cinema of the forties and fifties in its need to show 'bad' women punished. The 'bad' woman is either punished and killed off or punished and redeemed, as is the case with Bathsheba.[15] In this scene, the people are afraid to condemn Bathsheba to David's face, but the prophet Nathan comes up with two surprise witnesses: Michal and David's young son Absalom (would the testimony of a woman and a child have been sufficient to convict a man of a capital crime in biblical times?). The effect of this characterization is devastating for Michal: she has become a caricature of spite and cruelty. By this point, the audience will surely have lost any sympathy they might once have had with her. But not David: 'I cannot find it in my heart to blame you for what you do', he says (naturalizing through Christianizing?). Had he responded to Michal in kind, the film's carefully cultivated picture of David as the long-suffering victim of Michal's ire would be undermined. His magnanimous gesture makes him look all the more noble, and the fact that it does not weaken her resolve shows her all the more unworthy of our respect.

The Film King David

In the film *King David*, once again we have a sympathetic David and a shrewish Michal. As in *David and Bathsheba*, her audience with the king is private, and the political importance of the conflict is undermined. Still the haughty and resentful Michal, she refers to David formally and disdainfully as 'the king', and insists that Paltiel is her husband *and* the man she loves. David, in contrast, wants her back and considers himself, and not Paltiel, her husband: 'I am your husband, your first and only husband, in the eyes of God'. The implication, I think, is that Michal is guilty of adultery (which is rather ironic, since David does not commit adultery with Bathsheba in this film).[16] Going beyond the 1951 film in affirming David's love

15. The bad woman is redeemed through the intervention of the hero; thus Bathsheba is redeemed when David prays for her and her life is spared. On the cinematic 'punishment' and 'redemption' of the 'bad woman', see below, Chapter 6.

16. Just one of the changes made by the film to make David look better; see above, Chapter 1. In *King David*, David has sex with Bathsheba only after their marriage, which takes place after Uriah is dead.

for Michal, the 1985 version has him tell her that he has never loved another woman as he once loved her. His avowal of devotion is guaranteed to melt the heart of every woman in the audience, and to make viewers, male and female, very sympathetic to David, who is spurned by the great love of his life. When David says he needs her, Michal raises the political issue, referring to herself as a 'political necessity' as symbol of the unity between the houses of David and Saul. She is thus not naive like the Michal in *David and Bathsheba*. But the political issue, having once been raised, becomes a dead end as far as this film is concerned.

Unlike the biblical account, where she is robbed of reply, Michal has the last word here. She holds a mirror before David, tells him that he has seen the king of glory face to face,[17] and declares that his other women are better able to flatter his vanity than she is. Having the last word, however, does not make much difference, since Michal disappears from the film at this point, just as she disappears from the biblical story.[18] The real difference is the picture of David at the end of the scene. The confrontation scene in 2 Samuel 6 ended with David's rebuke of Michal followed immediately by the report of Michal's childlessness. In *King David*, Michal walks out on David. Thus he is in no way responsible for her childlessness. And in the film, moreover, his vulnerability to her rejection is endearing.

King David, following the biblical account, has Michal and David's rift take place after Michal has watched David dancing before the ark from the window of his house.[19] David, and not Michal, is the one to raise the issue of the celebration of the ark's entry into Jerusalem. He upbraids her for not participating in the festivities, accusing her of insulting her god and her king by her absence. Bringing God into it makes her look irreligious as well as petty; it hints at the insensitive

17. The Michal of *David and Bathsheba* does similarly, when she says, 'You have never loved anyone but yourself. David, meaning beloved. David, the beloved of David.' Both Michals ascribe vanity to David. This opinion of David is not without biblical support, but it becomes another loose end in the films, where neither David is portrayed as particularly self-centered or self-important.

18. She appears again, if we follow the Hebrew text, in 2 Sam. 21.8-9; see below.

19. The fact that she asks why she has been brought before him suggests that she has just been brought to David from Paltiel. If this is the case, the compression serves a naturalizing function: it fills the biblical gap—how does Michal feel about the reunion?—and it explains her anger as being as much, if not more, the result of having been forcibly taken from Paltiel as of watching David's dancing display.

religious attitude that, as we saw above, troubled Brueggemann. By having her respond only to the charge of dishonoring the king, the film leaves the charge of insulting God to stand unchallenged: 'I saw no king. I saw only a dancing man flaunting his nakedness in the sight of every common whore.' If we were not quite sure what the biblical Michal thought of these women, we have no doubts here. David cuts her off, turning the quarrel into a theological dispute rather than a question of his behavior. 'In the sight of God', he says by way of correction, 'who created man in the perfection of his own image'. In the biblical account, theology and politics are inseparable, and David's rebuke of Michal is based on divine sanction of his kingship ('Before the Lord who chose me over your father and over all his house to appoint me king-elect over the people of the Lord, over Israel—I will dance before the Lord'). In the film, the theological issue is completely divorced from politics (and the problematic textual tension surrounding the divine rejection of Saul's house) by going back to creation for its reference rather than to Davidic election. David the man is certainly in God's image, but is she, the woman?

The phrase, 'every common whore', picks up on the biblical 'in the sight of his male servants' women servants' to suggest Michal's arrogance. The class issue raised in the biblical account by Michal's disparaging comment is exploited by both films to Michal's detriment. *David and Bathsheba* showed Michal's sense of superiority by having Michal say, 'I am to go and sit with the concubines', to which David responds, 'They are my wives'. In both films, as in the Bible, Michal is represented as elitist because she looks down on other women whereas David appears more democratic because his sharp rejoinder to her pejorative remark puts Michal in her place.[20] The biblical narrator uses Michal's words to isolate her from other women. In the films, her isolation is self-imposed. In *David and Bathsheba*, Michal

20. He is most clearly democratic in *David and Bathsheba*, where he corrects 'concubines' to 'wives'. In *King David*, the fact that he responds so angrily in countering 'in the sight of every common whore' with 'in the sight of God' gives the impression that he objects to her description, although he does not actually say so. In the biblical account, David calls these women '[women] servants' whereas Michal called them '[male] servants' [women] servants', and, by saying that among them he will be held in honor, he professes a kind of solidarity with them. At the same time, what gives the couple's mutual rebukes their sting in the biblical account is the imputation of inferior status to these women; he turns her pejorative remark around to shame her.

chose not to join David's other wives to greet him upon his return from Ammon; in *King David*, she did not join in the festivities as (according to David) she should have.

Whereas *David and Bathsheba* adds two extra scenes at the end to make Michal look bad, *King David* develops its negative picture of Michal by portraying her as arrogant from the beginning. In her first appearance in the film, she is watching as the victorious young hero David returns, with Jonathan, from battle. Perhaps this scene is meant to account for her love for David, which is unexplained in the Bible,[21] though the look on her face seems to me somewhat condescending. Michal's appearance in this film, unlike *David and Bathsheba*, is coded for visual appeal (and there is partial nudity)—perhaps to explain why, later on in the film, Richard Gere as David, unlike Gregory Peck as David, still loves Michal. Her next scene is the wedding. In their wedding bed, Michal says to David, 'Did I please you, my lord?'

> 'You only have to smile, then I am pleased.'
> 'Did I smile, my lord?'
> 'My name is David.'
> 'O forgive me, the confusion is easily made.'
> 'By whom?'
> 'The people worship you as their god, while as for Jonathan . . . '

Because the conversation turns into lovers' banter (and because, for the first time, she smiles), we cannot be sure how seriously we should take Michal's arrogant tone here. But when David teases her about being immodest, her response conveys her sense of superiority: 'A king's daughter has cause to be proud'.[22] In 1 Samuel 19, Michal actively saves David's life, risking her own safety in the process. The film *King David* writes her role in saving David right out of the script. Michal is still in the wedding bed when Saul bursts into the bedroom, intent on killing David. To his question, 'Where have you hidden him?', she responds, 'I don't know where he is'. When Saul retorts,

---

21. This is another place where commentators are quick to supply explanations; see David J.A. Clines, 'Michal Observed: An Introduction', in Clines and Eskenazi (eds.), *Telling Queen Michal's Story*, p. 33, and the sources to which he refers, reprinted in the volume.

22. Compare the dialogue referred to above in *David and Bathsheba*, where Michal says to David, 'There was a time when you thought well of my aloofness', and he responds, 'I make no objection to it now'.

'Don't lie to me', she says, 'When I awoke, he was gone'. There is no reason, as there is in the biblical account, to think that she is lying to her father, for we are shown David's escape, not with Michal's help but Jonathan's. And David, who has so cavalierly left Michal behind, asks Jonathan to go with him.

A Woman Wronged?

Interestingly, both films juxtapose the quarrel scene between David and Michal and the scene between David and Bathsheba, whereas in the biblical account they are separated by four chapters of narrative in which time passes and various significant events take place. In both films, no sooner have David and Michal quarreled than he walks out the door onto the balcony from which he spies Bathsheba, suggesting that if you can't get along with one woman, you can always find another. This is an appeal to male fantasy: a sensual woman is preferable to a nagging one (and Bathsheba will never antagonize David; as Susan Hayward tells Gregory Peck, 'I had heard that never had the king found a woman to please him. I dared to hope that I might be that woman'). Using the unhappy relationship with one woman as a backdrop enables the filmmakers to explain David's emotional vulnerability to Bathsheba (in the Bible, he just takes her). It makes his behavior more excusable and places him in a more favorable light at Michal's expense.

The biblical account, in contrast, leaves open the possibility that Michal has been wronged by David. As we have seen, it never states that he loves her, though it tells us she loved him. It recounts David's two secret meetings with Jonathan, but none with Michal. It mentions no attempt on his part to take her with him, though it provides the information that he arranges for his parents' safety and that he has other wives with him in the wilderness and in the land of the Philistines. After David is offered the opportunity to become king over the northern tribes, we are informed that Michal is taken by force from her husband Paltiel and returned to David. By having David rebuke Michal and then immediately reporting that Michal had no children, 2 Samuel 6 even hints that it might be David himself who, by ceasing to have sexual relations with her, is responsible for Michal's childlessness.

If the biblical text is willing to allow for bad faith toward Michal on David's part, not so the films. In order to make David look better,

Michal must look bad. In *King David*, Michal turns her back on
David. In *David and Bathsheba*, she is so obsessed with her feelings of
being slighted that she cannot take David's advice: 'We have to go
on living, Michal'. These are his final words to her in the cinematic
confrontation scene, and they offer a striking and ironic commentary
on the final words in Michal's two major scenes in the Bible, both of
which end with a reference to her *death*. In 1 Samuel 19, Michal
presented herself as a potential victim when she told Saul that David
threatened, 'Why should I kill you?'[23] The last word, *'amitek* ('kill
you'), reappears in another form as the last word of 2 Samuel 6:
'Michal Saul's daughter had no child until the day of her death'
(*motah*). In a sense, the threat imputed to David has been realized and
David is implicated, since denying offspring to Michal is a way of
killing her off. Though it might like to, the film has difficulty suggesting anything else is the case. What does 'we have to go on living,
Michal' mean, anyway? It means very different things for David,
who walks out of Michal's presence into the arms of Bathsheba, and
for Michal. In a later scene, the film acknowledges a woman's lack of
options, when David tells Uriah,

> A woman is flesh and blood, Uriah, like us—perhaps even more so
> because we give her so little to think of but matters of the flesh. In all our
> history, only a handful of women have been permitted to write their
> names beside the men: Miriam, Deborah, Jael, perhaps one or two more.
> A woman's occupation is her husband, and her life is her love. But if her
> husband rejects her love, if he puts another love before it, if he denies her
> the only meaning that her life can have, is it not understandable that she
> seeks a meaning for it elsewhere [with another man]?

Unlike David, Michal cannot go out and start a new life with someone else. She is, as David says, 'my wife', and a member of the royal
harem. So what is she to do?

Both films attribute a measure of self-determination to Michal that,
as the very arrangement of the biblical text makes clear, she does not
really possess. The biblical Michal is hemmed in. The two scenes in
which she is active, in 1 Samuel 19 and 2 Samuel 6, are framed by
scenes in which she is acted upon, first by her father Saul (1 Sam.
18.20-29; 25.44), and then by her husband David (2 Sam. 3.12-16;

23. Jan P. Fokkelman, *Narrative Art and Poetry in the Books of Samuel*. II. *The
Crossing Fates* (Assen: van Gorcum, 1986), p. 269.

21.8-9).[24] This narrative imprisonment reflects the restrictions placed upon her as a woman: her social and political confinement, her lack of autonomy, her inability to control what happens to her.[25] Whereas the biblical account invites us to see that there may be good reason for Michal to have grown bitter, the films *David and Bathsheba* and *King David* give us little, if anything, to account for her dramatic emotional reversal from a woman who risks her life out of love to a woman who hates and rebukes.[26] The films do not present us with a woman wronged, a victim of politically motivated men; rather they offer a moral evaluation: she has only herself to blame for her plight. They naturalize her outburst by stereotyping her as a shrew. She is haughty, bitter and spiteful, not for cause, but simply by nature.

The Woman at the Window

Perhaps the image that most powerfully captures Michal's predicament is presented to us in 2 Samuel 6. Michal is inside, looking out through the window as David and 'all Israel' celebrate the ark's procession into the city. As we have seen, *King David* recreates this scene, whereas *David and Bathsheba* leaves it out. Even so, Michal's confinement is quite evident in *David and Bathsheba*: she never leaves the palace.

24. On Michal's strange reappearance in 2 Sam. 21.8-9, see Exum, *Tragedy and Biblical Narrative*, p. 91.

25. In the first scene in which she is active, Michal takes her husband's part over against her father; in the second, she takes the part of her father's house over against her husband. The scene in which she is active and takes David's part is framed by scenes in which she is acted upon by her father Saul, and the scene in which she actively represents Saul's house is framed by scenes in which she is acted upon by her husband David. For elaboration of this narrative confinement, reflecting her confinement as a woman, see Exum, *Tragedy and Biblical Narrative*, pp. 81-85; Exum, *Fragmented Women*, pp. 42-46.

26. My remarks above about the complex nexus of issues resolved in the character of Michal are not meant to reduce Michal to a mere function, but only to suggest that her character is subordinated to her function. The scanty information we have about Michal hints at a person beyond her function in the text (the task of 'recovering' this character is a particular challenge). By describing the change in her feelings for David, the biblical narrator effectively calls for the involvement, if not sympathy, of the reader with Michal. The Bible gives us the potential for a fuller characterization of Michal, which the films do not pursue, as they, too, reduce Michal to a function. But a very different and greatly simplified function: to glamorize Bathsheba and to explain David's emotional vulnerability to Bathsheba, thus making David look better.

Neither film shows us the other biblical scene in which Michal is active, and which, significantly, also involves the window. In 1 Samuel 19, when she saves David's life by letting him out through the window, she effectively loses him forever. He emerges from the domesticity the woman represents to meet his destiny in the world beyond, while she remains inside, ostensibly attending to matters defined by their very nature as domestic, and thus woman's work: making the bed and tending the sick. The repetition of the phrase, 'through the window' (1 Sam. 19.12; 2 Sam. 6.16) in the only scenes where Michal takes initiative draws attention to her confinement, inside. In 2 Samuel 6, when she dares to leave the house, the woman's domain, to confront David outside, she is humiliated and eliminated.[27] In their quarrel, David has the last word, and Michal disappears from the narrative, doomed to a childless existence.

When I look at examples of a wide-spread image in ancient Near Eastern art commonly known as 'the woman at the window',[28] I see Michal (figs. 2.2 and 2.3). The examples reproduced here date from about the eighth century BCE and probably originated in Phoenicia. Although the woman at the window is obviously not Michal, they are related thematically. I do not know of any historical relation nor do I know who the woman at the window is meant to be. The goddess? The once popular theory that she represents a prostitute waiting for a client has been challenged, but her identity has not been decided. Whatever she represents, insofar as she is confined inside the house, the woman's place, she and Michal belong to the same topos.

This is an image of a woman viewed from the man's perspective. The frequency with which the woman at the window occurs testifies to a deep fascination with her. As in 2 Samuel 6, we are outside, looking at her, inside, looking out. What is she looking at or for? At the man who created her in this image and for his self-esteem, or for some sign of his need to return to her? From her proper place,

27. I discuss this as a 'literary murder' in *Fragmented Women*, pp. 16-41; for discussion of the home as woman's place and of 'the architecture of unhomeliness', see Mieke Bal, *Death and Dissymmetry: The Politics of Coherence in the Book of Judges* (Chicago: University of Chicago Press, 1988).

28. See Philip J. King, *Amos, Hosea, Micah: An Archaeological Commentary* (Philadelphia: Westminster Press, 1988), pp. 100, 146-48; I would like to thank Michal Coogan for information on this subject in an unpublished paper, 'The Woman at the Window: An Artistic and Literary Motif'.

Figure 2.2. *'Woman at the Window'*, Courtesy of the Trustees of the British Museum

Figure 2.3. *'Woman at the Window'*

her domain inside, the woman looks out the window upon the man's world to see what men have accomplished. This is the case not only with Michal, who observes David's moment of glory, but also with the other biblical examples of the woman at the window. In 2 Kings 9.30, Queen Jezebel, having painted her eyes and adorned her head, looks out the window, waiting for the bloody arrival of the usurper, Jehu, who has already killed her son, the king, and will soon kill her. Similarly, in the Song of Deborah (Judg. 5.28), Sisera's mother peers out the window, watching in vain for her son's return from battle laden with spoil. The same image is re-employed in the film *King David*, where we observe Bathsheba, and then a young Solomon, looking down from the window as David's forces go out to meet Absalom's.[29] Passive and without any real power, they can only wait to see what the outcome will be.

Another point of contact between the woman at the window and Michal is that in her representation as a confined woman there are already indications of her resistance to her confinement. The Michal of the biblical text seeks to assert her autonomy (though she ultimately fails) by siding with her husband against her father in 1 Samuel 19 and by taking up the cause of her father's house against her husband in 2 Samuel 6. In the ancient Near Eastern examples of the woman at the window, the massive window frame occupies most of the scene. Successive layers emphasize the distance between the woman and the man's world outside. But whereas the image represents confinement, it simultaneously depicts her attempt to move beyond the imposed boundary. The woman wants to know what is happening in the outside world. Her attention is directed outward, not inward to her domestic affairs. Her haunting eyes are wide open, as if seeking to take everything in, and her big ears are straining outwards to catch every sound. In figure 2.2, her head touches the top of the window frame; in figure 2.3 the top of her head extends over the innermost layer of the window frame, which cannot hold her back. Frame and image are thus in tension.

Tension between Michal's confinement and her assertiveness can also be seen in a seventeenth-century representation of the scene in 2 Samuel 6, Jan de Bray's *David Dances before the Ark of the Covenant* (fig. 2.4). Michal is relegated to a far corner of the painting, in

29. Another divergence of the film from the biblical story is that in the film David does not abandon Jerusalem to Absalom.

Figure 2.4. Jan de Bray, *David Dances before the Ark of the Covenant*,
Collection of the Evansville Museum of Arts and Science, Evansville, Indiana

keeping with the isolation of Michal that we find in the biblical
account. Nevertheless, there is a real sense in which she controls the
scene. David, the center of attention, has his attention focused on
her. There is a direct line of vision from his eyes to hers. The
painting thus prepares us for the confrontation scene between them;
indeed David's face looks apprehensive to me, as though he fears
Michal's disapproval. By painting David so well clad, the artist has
removed what Clines, as we saw above, naturalized as the cause
of Michal's hatred toward him, sexual disgust, and has left us to dwell
on the other motives seized upon by Brueggemann, Steinsaltz, and
Fokkelman—lack of proper religious enthusiasm and arrogance. As in
the ancient Near Eastern representations of the woman at the
window, there is a massive window frame, and the woman peering
out, like her ancient Near Eastern counterparts, is out of proportion
to the scene and the size of the building. Here we see the woman at
the window and what she is looking at as well. She is both object and
owner of the gaze. We look at her and strain to get a better glimpse

and to make out the details of her face amid the shadows, and David looks self-consciously at her, thereby acknowledging the power of her gaze. Unlike the bathing Bathshebas in the paintings examined in Chapter 1, she looks back at David. The tension created in this painting between Michal's isolation in the upper right-hand corner and her domination of the scene as both focalizer of David and object of his focalization represents visually the tension in the biblical text between Michal's narrative confinement and her unsuccessful attempts to assert her autonomy.

A Window on Michal

The biblical text, de Bray's painting, and the cinematic representations of Michal on the screen all provide a kind of window on Michal for the reader or viewer, for they give us the kind of view a window gives, limited in range and perspective, and we can only imagine what a fuller picture of the woman might look like. In doing so, we find that naturalizing comes naturally. We seek to bring textual events within our conceptual grasp, and we tend to apply particular notions of chronology, causality, coherence, and contiguity, as well as particular cultural generalizations or stereotypes, in order to reduce their strangeness and make them 'natural' in accordance with the ways we believe events 'happen' or people behave under certain circumstances. As Jonathan Culler observes,

> As a linguistic object the text is strange and ambiguous. We reduce its strangeness by reading it as the utterance of a particular narrator so that models of plausible human attitudes and of coherent personalities can be made operative. Moreover, extrapolating from the postulated figure, we may tell ourselves empirical stories which make elements in the text intelligible and justified: the narrator is in a particular situation and reacting to it, so that what he says may be read within a general economy of human actions and judged by the logic of those actions.[30]

The problem with naturalization lies in the tendency to reduce textual events to a kind of lowest common denominator. It can thus easily lead us to dismiss the significance of details that do not conform to our overall interpretation. It is not enough, for example, to explain Michal's emotional reaction in 2 Samuel 6 as sexual if that leaves out

---

30. Jonathan Culler, *Structuralist Poetics: Structuralism, Linguistics, and the Study of Literature* (Ithaca, NY: Cornell University Press, 1975), p. 146.

of account Michal's political function in narratively resolving the tension created by the opposition between David's house and Saul's. Nor will it do to explain it in terms of Michal's failure to appreciate David's religious insights, without taking into account the complex way in which the text's theological agenda undergirds its political agenda. Similarly, the explanation of her reaction as a sign of her aristocratic superiority needs to be combined with an appreciation of how class in this case serves gender politics, making it easier for Michal (and the Saulide claims she represents) to be dismissed by an angry husband. Portraying Michal as a shrew, as the films do, which depends upon the viewers' familiarity with the stereotype to make this characterization appear 'natural', not only ignores the way the biblical figure is hemmed in by the political maneuverings of her father and her husband but also relieves David of responsibility for her situation, in marked contrast to the Bible's frank presentation of David's negative qualities.[31]

Reducing problematic textual elements to single causes closes off interpretive options, and this happens in biblical commentary as well as in the two Hollywood films discussed here. In the case of the films, as we have seen, traces of textual tensions remain as an indication of their resistance to naturalization. Although I have not considered commentary on the biblical story in any detail, one has only to look, say, at the samples collected in *Telling Queen Michal's Story* to recognize how readily commentators foreclose interpretive possibilities by settling on a 'familiar', 'natural' explanation of textual events. Whereas the films flatten Michal's character—ignoring the clues the Bible offers for fuller character development and ultimately inviting the viewer to blame the woman—they offer, at the same time, more open-ended interpretations of the biblical story than biblical commentary does. Representing the story visually requires the films not only to fill gaps—from the crucial question, Does David love Michal?, to the more mundane, What clothes would she have worn?—but also to supply additional detail and to interpret, as Magonet says, 'things we might otherwise take for granted'. Most commentators (even those who assign recalcitrant elements to various sources) work with a model of the organic unity of the text, according to which whatever is strange or deviant is made to seem natural. As we have seen,

31. I deal with the complexity of David's character in *Tragedy and Biblical Narrative*, pp. 120-49.

although the films also naturalize events, in the act of re-presenting the story they create their own gaps and discontinuities (loose ends or even dead ends), and these remain as strangenesses and deviances that attract our attention. The films offer their own interpretations for us to interpret and thereby invite us to look at the biblical Michal again from a different perspective. This is not to say, however, that they send us back to the Bible to discover a kinder, gentler Michal. If the Bible offers a more complex, and possibly more sympathetic, Michal, it also provides the negative image that the filmmakers adopted in the first place.

3

The Hand that Rocks the Cradle

Why did Moses have a sister?
Edmund Leach

...each reading of a book, each rereading, each
memory of that rereading, reinvents the text.
Jorge Luis Borges, *Seven Nights*

This chapter is a story, somewhat autobiographical, about reading—a story about reading and rereading the account of Moses' birth, a biblical narrative in which women play a central role. The story is autobiographical because it documents one reader's changing responses to the text in the light of feminism and of the critical responses feminists have developed for dealing with androcentrism in the fundamental texts of the Western literary canon (and with the androcentric history of their interpretation). The story begins in the modulated tones of the male-defined academic discourse in which I was trained and ends (for now) also within an academic discourse, within which I of necessity of operate, but one whose terms I insist on having a role in defining.

In 1983 my article, '"You Shall Let Every Daughter Live": A Study of Exodus 1.8–2.10', appeared in an issue of *Semeia* devoted to *The Bible and Feminist Hermeneutics*.[1] I never liked the article. It would be more accurate, and more honest, to say that I never liked the text. A story of five women and a baby. Women, it is true, are very important in these opening chapters of Exodus, but the subject of their activity is a male infant, Moses, who soon takes over the story and dominates it, while women fade into the background. His

---

1. '"You Shall Let Every Daughter Live": A Study of Exodus 1:8–2:10', in *The Bible and Feminist Hermeneutics* (ed. Mary Ann Tolbert; Semeia, 28; Decatur, GA: Scholars Press, 1983), pp. 63-82; repr. in *A Feminist Companion to Exodus to Deuteronomy* (ed. Athalya Brenner; The Feminist Companion to the Bible, 6; Sheffield: Sheffield Academic Press, 1994), pp. 37-61.

mother, his sister, and the pharaoh's daughter (accompanied by women servants) are directly involved in preserving the infant Moses' life; and although the midwives do not interact with him directly, by implication they save his life when they do not obey the pharaoh's command to kill male babies. We never hear of Shiphrah, Puah, and the pharaoh's daughter again after Exodus 2, and Moses' mother appears again only in his genealogy (Exod. 6.20; Num. 26.59). Of the many active female characters in Exod. 1.8–2.10, only Moses' sister has a role in the subsequent narrative, one that, apparently, the biblical writers felt the need to suppress (cf. Exod. 15.21 with 15.1-18)[2] or discredit (Num. 12).

Exod. 1.8–2.10 was not a text that I would have chosen for analysis of my own accord. My article was a revision of a position paper that Letty Russell invited me to present in a joint symposium of the Women and Religion Section and the Liberation Theology Group of the American Academy of Religion, which took place at the 1981 Annual Meeting of the American Academy of Religion and Society of Biblical Literature. Exod. 1.8–2.10 seemed an obvious choice as one of the topics for a panel discussion of the intersecting interests of feminist and liberation theology. The existence of a special joint session called 'The Feminist Hermeneutic Project' was an indication of the attention feminist interpretation was beginning to receive in the field of Religious Studies. At that time, one of the goals of the emerging feminist biblical criticism was to uncover positive portrayals of women in the Bible—as if one could simply pluck positive images out of an admittedly androcentric text, separating literary characterizations from the androcentric interests they were created to serve.[3]

A few years later, in a short essay that discussed a number of biblical 'mothers', I turned again to Exod. 1.8–2.10, this time using the opportunity to express my dissatisfaction with my earlier work. My conclusion bears citing here as much for what it does not say as for what it does say.

> I have dealt at length in another study with the women in the prologue to the exodus…I must confess that I was never satisfied with the results. The

2. For discussion of the relation of Miriam to the song in Exod. 15, see the essays by Trible, Janzen, van Dijk-Hemmes, Meyers, and Bach in Brenner (ed.), *A Feminist Companion to Exodus to Deuteronomy*.

3. Phyllis Trible's groundbreaking *God and the Rhetoric of Sexuality* (Philadelphia: Fortress Press) appeared in 1978.

reason, I believe, has to do with disappointment that the narrative quickly
and thoroughly moves from a woman's story to a man's story. While a
feminist critique might want to seize onto the affirmative dimension of
our paradox [without Moses there would be no exodus, but without these
women there would be no Moses], accenting the important consequences
of women's actions for the divine plan, it must also acknowledge that
being mothers of heroes—albeit daring, enterprising, and tenacious
mothers—is not enough; acting behind the scenes is not enough.[4]

Whereas I recognized the limitations of the portrayal of women in
Exodus 1–2, I had nothing to offer by way of response beyond this
kind of feeble objection, and thus was left with disappointment. It
took me years to see that what was needed to move beyond this
impasse was a reading strategy that could expose and critique the
ideology that motivates the biblical presentation of women. I adopted
such a strategy in my 1993 book, *Fragmented Women* (published ten
years after the Exodus article), but I did not take up the Exodus story
again in that work. I had no intention of writing about this text
again until Athalya Brenner approached me about reprinting '"You
Shall Let Every Daughter Live"' in *A Feminist Companion to Exodus to
Deuteronomy*. I felt I could not let that article stand without some
comment about how my thinking had changed, and so I wrote a
companion piece entitled, 'Secondary Thoughts about Secondary
Characters', indicating what I would do differently if I were writing
about Exodus 1–2 in 1994 instead of 1983.[5] Even now, I have no
desire to offer another detailed study of Exod. 1.8–2.10 and other
texts related to it. I propose rather to build on my most recent contribution to the debate by indicating some of the questions I believe a
feminist critique attentive to gender politics should ask and by looking
more closely at the reader's role in producing meaning in the light of
postmodern literary theory. In doing so, I will address two major
problems with my 1983 article. Although I address them with specific
reference to my own article, they are problems that, in my opinion,

    4.   J. Cheryl Exum, '"Mother in Israel": A Familiar Figure Reconsidered', in
Feminist Interpretation of the Bible (ed. Letty M. Russell; Philadelphia: Westminster
Press, 1985), p. 82.
    5.   J. Cheryl Exum, 'Second Thoughts about Secondary Characters', in Brenner
(ed.), *A Feminist Companion to Exodus to Deuteronomy*, pp. 75-87. The reprinted
version of '"You Shall Let Every Daughter Live"' in *A Feminist Companion to
Exodus to Deuteronomy* (pp. 37-61) is incorrectly cited on p. 37 as first appearing in
1993 instead of 1983.

still characterize some of the work that goes under the rubric of feminist interpretation today.[6] The first problem is that because I used a literary method that remained within the ideology of the text, I was able only to describe the view of women expressed in the text and not to critique it. The second is that although I mentioned the problem of the absence of women in the narrative after one moves beyond the first few chapters of Exodus—an absence as striking as the presence of so many women in the first four chapters—I did not investigate the relationship of this absence to the noticeable presence of women in the opening chapters in terms of gender politics.

Literary Analysis and the Ideology of the Text

The approach I used to analyze the text in '"You Shall Let Every Daughter Live"' was essentially a form of New Criticism as biblical scholars were practicing it in the 1960s and 1970s under the names of 'close reading' and 'rhetorical criticism', an approach that 'investigates the narrative in its present form on the premise that an understanding of its literary contours will aid us in perceiving its meaning'.[7] The method led me to focus on such stylistic features as narrative arrangement, key words and phrases, the paralleling of characters, as well as tropes, such as irony, and unusual details, such as the fact that the names of the two midwives are reported. All of these devices, I argued, work together to foreground the important role of women in the story. In terms of narrative arrangement, I divided the account of Exod. 1.8–2.10 into two parts with three movements. In the first part (1.8-22), which deals with the threat to the Hebrews as a people, my analysis sought to show how the pharaoh, though he initiates the

6.   Phyllis Trible, for example, practices essentially the same close-reading approach in 'Bringing Miriam out of the Shadows' that she used in *God and the Rhetoric of Sexuality* (1978). Though appeals to the reader and comments about the suppression of a woman's story give the impression of a more postmodern stance, for Trible the task remains one of 'unearthing the fragments [of an earlier tradition in which Miriam figured importantly] and assembling them' (p. 183). The ideology that motivates the portrayal of Miriam is never questioned; it is simply assumed that later androcentric redactors have sought to discredit Miriam.

7.   '"You Shall Let Every Daughter Live"', p. 63. See, especially, James Muilenburg's now classic call for the practice of rhetorical criticism in his 1968 address to the Society of Biblical Literature, 'Form Criticism and Beyond', *Journal of Biblical Literature* 88 (1969), pp. 1-18.

action by proposing rather absurd solutions to the problem of Hebrew overpopulation, yields his narrative centrality to women, as the midwives change the course of events by defying his command to kill the Hebrew male babies. In the second part (2.1-10), which deals with the threat to one particular Hebrew, the baby Moses, many women appear but men are strikingly absent (Moses' father disappears from the story after v. 1) or passive (Moses cries, v. 6, and grows up, v. 10, but otherwise is the object of the women's actions). Thus, I argued, not only do women take over the story in Part 1, but also 'the speech and action of women shape the contours of [Part 2 of] the story'.

> Moses' mother acts but, interestingly, does not speak. In contrast, his sister and pharaoh's daughter both act and speak. The story begins with a detailed account of the action of one woman, a daughter of Levi (vv. 2-3). A small but significant role is assigned to Moses' sister (v. 4). Next we hear of considerable activity on the part of yet another woman, the daughter of pharaoh (vv. 5-6), followed by the vital speech of the sister (v. 7). Though she has little action and only one speech, the sister is crucial to the development of the story. She has the critical linking role between the two daughters (vv. 4, 7). Once all three women are involved, narrative attention moves quickly back and forth between them (vv. 7-10), until finally an unnamed daughter gives our hero his identity: 'she called his name Moses'.[8]

The three movements of the story (1.8-14; 1.15-21; 1.22–2.10)[9] are concerned with the pharaoh's three attempts to curb the growth of the Hebrew population. In the first of these, his people carry out his command to afflict the Hebrews with hard service, but this solution is unsuccessful and the Hebrews only increase all the more. The next two movements are both stories of defiance in which the pharaoh's plan to kill the Hebrew male babies, among whom the baby Moses should be numbered, is thwarted by women. The subtle defiance of

---

8.   '"You Shall Let Every Daughter Live"', pp. 75-76.

9.   Exod. 1.22 functions as the end of what I called the first part and the beginning of the third movement, producing an overlapping structure. I used Tzvetan Todorov's concept of narrative embedding to clarify its function. Exod. 1.22 supplies 'something excessive' to the story of the midwives, 'a supplement which remains outside the closed form produced by the development of the plot. At the same time, and for this very reason, this something-more, proper to the narrative, is also something-less. The supplement is also a lack; in order to supply this lack created by the supplement, another narrative is necessary' (T. Todorov, *The Poetics of Prose* [trans. Richard Howard; Ithaca, NY: Cornell University Press, 1977], p. 76).

the midwives, who act by choosing not to act in accordance with the
pharaoh's death edict, is followed by the open defiance of Moses'
mother and of the pharaoh's daughter, who, in direct opposition to
her father's command, saves the infant Moses from death by exposure
on the Nile.[10] The narrative progression, then, is from action determined by the pharaoh in the first movement (but not successfully), to
the pharaoh sharing the stage with the midwives in the second—
where the midwives, in fact, have the last word with their clever
explanation of their failure to obey the pharaoh's decree ('before the
midwife comes to [the Hebrew women] they are delivered', 1.19)—to
the third movement, where the pharaoh drops out of the story
immediately after issuing the directive to kill male babies, and the stage
is shared by a mother, a sister, and a daughter (his daughter), whose
initiatives determine the course of events. 'This increasing concentra-
tion on women', I concluded, 'invites us to consider the significance
of the fact that ancient Israelite storytellers gave women a crucial role
in the initial stages of the major event in the nation's history'.[11]

I looked not only to narrative arrangement but also to key words
for clues to the narrative emphasis on the women's important roles;
for example, the key terms 'son' (*ben*) and 'daughter' (*bat*) are strategi-
cally placed at key points in the narrative. The semantic range of *ben*
becomes increasingly narrow as the focus shifts from the '*sons* of
Israel' as a people to one particular *son*, Moses, while the occurrences
of *bat* alert us to the vital roles played by daughters in a story about a
famous son. The pharaoh's last words, 'every son that is born you
shall expose on the Nile, but every daughter you shall let live' (1.22),
are followed immediately by the introduction of a *daughter* of Levi
(2.1) and soon thereafter (2.5) by the *daughter* of the pharaoh himself,
both of whom defy his edict, with his own daughter adopting the
boy and raising him as her own. Thus the story of Moses' birth begins

---

10.   There is a nice irony here. Pharaoh commands that every newborn male baby
be exposed on the Nile; following M. Cogan ('A Technical Term for Exposure',
Journal for Near Eastern Studies 27 [1968], pp. 133-35) in rendering *hashlik* as
'abandon, expose'. Moses' mother seems to be obeying the command when she
places Moses in the Nile, but her *placing* (*wattasem*) stands in stark contrast to the
pharaoh's 'abandon, expose' (NRSV, 'throw'). Pharaoh wanted the babies exposed
on or thrown *into the Nile*; his daughter takes the baby *out of the Nile*.

11.   '"You Shall Let Every Daughter Live"', p. 68.

with the birth of a son (*ben*) to the daughter (*bat*) of Levi (2.2) and ends with his becoming a son (*ben*) to the daughter (*bat*) of the pharaoh (2.10). Aesthetically this is really nice, I thought, and, rhetorically speaking, it maintains emphasis equally on sons and daughters. Key phrases function similarly; for example, the pharaoh is identified as the source of death by means of his repeated command to kill boy babies but let the girls live (1.16, 22), while the midwives are identified as the source of life through the repetition of '[they] let the male infants live' (1.17, 18). The implication is that Moses owes his life to the midwives.

The paralleling of characters was yet another device in which I found evidence of narrative interest in the women's roles. A significant series of actions, for example, is attributed both to Moses' mother and to the pharaoh's daughter, and I interpreted these as the narrator's way not only of indicating the importance of both women but also of showing his positive assessment of the pharaoh's daughter.[12]

> At two points the narrative pace slows to describe in detail the actions of women, the daughter of Levi and the daughter of pharaoh. The attention they give to the child is comparable, and in fact some of the same terms are used (ראה [see], לקח [take]). By the end of the story, the two daughters have something more in common—a son.[13]

The daughter of the pharaoh who has compassion on the Hebrew baby and saves him by drawing him out of the Nile is also, of course, a counterfoil to her father who seeks the deaths of boy babies by means of the Nile.

These are just some of the features on the surface structure of the text that function to highlight the role of women in this account. I also might mention irony (as in the pharaoh's proposal to kill newborn sons when the logical way to control overpopulation would be to kill daughters; the serious blunder the pharaoh makes in neglecting to exclude Egyptian male babies from the command to expose 'every son' on the Nile in v. 21 of the Hebrew text;[14] the fact that daughters

---

12. Here I was taking issue with James S. Ackerman's negative assessment of the Egyptian princess in 'The Literary Context of the Moses Birth Story (Exodus 1–2)', in *Literary Interpretations of Biblical Narratives* (ed. K.R.R. Gros Louis, with J.S. Ackerman and T.S. Warshaw; Nashville: Abingdon Press), pp. 86-96.

13. '"You Shall Let Every Daughter Live"', p. 80.

14. The versions (Syriac Peshiṭta, Septuagint, Targum, Targum Jonathan) 'correct' the Masoretic text by supplying the qualifier, 'every son born to the

are the real threat in this story), and literary flourishes that put female characters in a positive light, such as the demonstration of rhetorical skill by Moses' sister (her proposal to 'call *for you* a nurse from the Hebrew women to nurse *for you* the child' both provides the idea that the princess keep the baby and creates the impression that she makes the proposal for the princess's sake), or the pun that carries with it the suggestion that the pharaoh's daughter charts Moses' destiny when she gives him a(n Egyptian) name that in Hebrew means 'the drawer out'.

I hope this brief summary of my main points in '"You Shall Let Every Daughter Live"' is sufficient to indicate that such a literary approach was, and still is, useful. I still would not question its conclusions that the women in Exodus 1 and 2 are portrayed positively, that they are active and enterprising, and that their actions are important for the future of the Israelite people. The sustained focus on women, the subtle comparisons created by paralleling characters, the ironic twists, the artistic use of the *bat/ben* contrast to make a point—all these things contribute to a striking affirmation of the role of women in the opening chapters of Exodus. Jopie Siebert-Hommes, in articles published in 1988 and 1992,[15] describes further artistic details that highlight the women's roles. When, for example, her stylistic analysis reveals that the twelve tribes owe their deliverance to *twelve daughters*, she shows that the potential of this method is far from exhausted and that it can profitably be used to gain new insights from textual details.

Siebert-Hommes's essays and mine demonstrate, quite persuasively I believe, how positively women are portrayed in Exod. 1.8–2.10. I might note, however, that even in '"You Shall Let Every Daughter Live"', I recognized the limits of the portrayal I was describing:

Hebrews'. The omission of 'born to the Hebrews' in the MT produces the comical result that in his zealousness to be 'all' inclusive ('*all* his people', '*every* son', '*every* daughter'), the pharaoh forgets to exempt Egyptian boy babies from his death edict! This is entirely in keeping with his humorous characterization as a blundering fool.

15. Jopie Siebert-Hommes, 'Twelve Women in Exodus 1 and 2: The Role of Daughters and Sons in the Stories Concerning Moses', *Amsterdamse Cahiers voor Exegese en Bijbelse Theologie* 12 (1988), pp. 47-58; Siebert-Hommes, 'Die Geburtsgeschichte des Mose innerhalb des Erzählungzusammenhangs von Exodus i und ii', *Vetus Testamentum* 42 (1992), pp. 398-403. Detailed discussion of stylistic features can be found in Gordon F. Davies, *Israel in Egypt: Reading Exodus 1–2* (Journal for the Study of the Old Testament Supplement Series, 135; Sheffield: JSOT Press, 1992), who, curiously, provides a one-half page 'Excursus' on 'Women in Exodus 1-2' in a 181-page analysis of Exod. 1 and 2 (p. 63).

> Discussion of women in Exod. 1.8–2.10 requires consideration of their
> place within the total configuration of the narrative—a narrative which
> does not become a woman's story until 1.15, and, even then, has as its
> goal the birth of a *son* who will become the leader of his people.[16]

> It is a woman's story in so far as their action determines its direction. But
> while narrative attention focuses on the activity of women, their attention
> centers on Moses. Referred to as a בֵן [son], a יֶלֶד [boy], and a נַעַר [lad], at
> the end of the story *he* is given a name. Thereafter he becomes the central
> character of the exodus.[17]

Such statements are in tension with my central thesis about the portrayal of women in this text, and considering them now, I would
want to seize upon their potential for disrupting my rather sanguine
evaluations of the important roles women play in the events preceding
the exodus.

This brings me to the problem with this kind of literary analysis: it
places logocentric constraints on feminist criticism. By focusing solely
on the surface structure of the text, on the ways literary devices and
structures serve as guides to meaning, it limits us to describing, and
thus to reinscribing, the text's gender ideology. I now see this method
as confining, and as representing, or at least serving, the phallocentric
drive to control and organize reading (and reality) into clearly defined
categories. If we read according to the ideology of the text available
to us in the surface structure, and stop there, we are left with the
ancient (male) authors' views of women, which, in the case of Exodus
1–2, happen to be affirmative. But to see how the positive portrayal
of women in Exod. 1.8–2.10 nevertheless serves male interests, we
need to interrogate the ideology that motivates it. Granted that women
are given important roles here—and, indeed, precisely because women
are given such important roles here, we need to ask, What androcentric interests does this positive presentation promote? Key questions
for a feminist critique of these chapters are, What is it about the
women in Exod. 1.8–2.10 that makes them characters with whom
women in ancient Israel might have wished to identify?[18] And what

16. '"You Shall Let Every Daughter Live"', p. 64.
17. '"You Shall Let Every Daughter Live"', p. 75.
18. I speak here of women in ancient times, for whom texts like this served as a
means of social control. To the extent that modern women might wish to identify
with these biblical models, the Bible still serves as a means of social control. As
Renita J. Weems ('The Hebrew Women Are Not like the Egyptian Women: The

is it about these female characters that makes those responsible for maintaining the social and symbolic order want to manipulate them?[19] I can only begin to address these questions here.

Stepping outside the Ideology of the Text

As feminist critics have pointed out, even though men and women share in the making of history, symbolic production has been controlled by men.[20] Even if the Bible's authors were not all males, the dominant male world-view is the world-view that finds expression in the biblical literature. I begin, therefore, with the assumption that the biblical literature was produced by and for an androcentric community. I understand women in the biblical literature as male constructs. They are the creations of androcentric (probably male) narrators, they reflect androcentric ideas about women, and they serve androcentric interests. What Esther Fuchs observes about biblical mothers applies to other female characters as well: they 'reveal more about the wishful thinking, fears, aspirations, and prejudices of their male creators than about women's authentic lives'.[21] Since as long as we remain within the androcentric ideology of the text, we can do no more than describe ancient men's views of women, a feminist critique must, of necessity, read against the grain. It must step outside the text's ideology and consider what androcentric agenda these narratives promote.

The concepts of stepping outside the ideology of the text and reading against the grain are crucial to me as a feminist reader, but require perhaps some explanation in the light of two important methodological objections. One is that texts do not have ideologies.[22] I agree

Ideology of Race, Gender and Sexual Reproduction in Exodus 1', *Semeia* 59 [1992], pp. 25-34) points out, the text does not question but only reinscribes the ideology of difference.

19. Julia Kristeva, 'Stabat Mater', in *The Female Body in Western Culture: Contemporary Perspectives* (ed. S.R. Suleiman; Cambridge, MA: Harvard University Press, 1986), pp. 113-14.

20. See, e.g., Gerda Lerner, *The Creation of Patriarchy* (New York: Oxford University Press, 1986), pp. 5-6, 199-211, 231-33 and *passim*.

21. Esther Fuchs, 'The Literary Characterization of Mothers and Sexual Politics in the Hebrew Bible', in *Feminist Perspectives on Biblical Scholarship* (ed. Adela Yarbro Collins; Chico, CA: Scholars Press, 1985), p. 118.

22. Stephen Fowl, 'Texts Don't Have Ideologies', *Biblical Interpretation* 3 (1995), pp. 15-34.

with this critical position in principle. Authors have ideologies and readers have ideologies; texts do not. But speaking of a text's ideology is nonetheless a convenient shorthand way for expressing the idea that texts arise in concrete social situations and reflect the social locations and world-views—in other words, the ideologies—of the writers who produced them. That the Bible may have a long history of transmission and redaction does not change this fact, though it may make analysis more complicated. To say that texts have ideologies is to personalize the text by projecting a reader's response—that is, a reader's perception of the ideology of its writers—onto it. I acknowledge a certain circularity in my argument about the ideology of the text: the androcentric ideology that is the subject of my critique is the one that I as a reader have identified as motivating the text. Similarly, reading against the grain involves first determining what I perceive the grain to be. For my purposes, the grain is another way of speaking about the ideology of the text.

The other objection to the concept of reading against the grain is that to describe one's reading as 'against the grain' gives the impression that it is an idiosyncratic or individualistic reading as over against the majority of readings that read with the grain. This could suggest to some that (androcentric) readings with the grain are somehow more 'accurate' interpretations of the 'meaning' of the text, what the text is 'really about', or that they are less subjective or less influenced by gender interests than feminist readings.[23] It seems to me that, in the present intellectual climate, any commentator who openly identifies her or his interests risks the charge of subjectivity from readers and critics who still believe that there is such a thing as a neutral or objective interpretation. As I argue in Chapter 1 above and, more specifically, in Chapter 4, the role gender and other interests play in the interpretive process should not be minimized. To think that interpretation can be neutral or objective would be to assume that meaning resides in the text. My position, and one borne out by the story of reading this chapter tells, is that meaning resides in the interaction between reader and text.

---

23. This is Yvonne Sherwood's point in suggesting caution in the use of this concept; *The Prostitute and the Prophet: Hosea's Marriage in Literary-Theoretical Perspective* (Journal for the Study of the Old Testament Supplement Series, 212; Gender, Culture, Theory, 2; Sheffield: Sheffield Academic Press, 1996), p. 256.

In response to these two objections to the concepts of stepping outside the ideology of the text and of reading against the grain, I appeal to certain properties of texts highlighted by recent critical practices that go under the name of deconstruction.[24] Deconstruction draws attention to the slipperiness of language and the instabilities of texts, with their infinite deferral of meaning. Because the logic of every text is non-unitary, a text inevitably undermines its main thesis. A text typically promotes or takes for granted some set of oppositions, privileging one term as prior to or positively valued over its partner; for example, good/evil, purity/pollution, rational/emotional, objective/subjective, culture/nature, or what some feminists have identified as the primary opposition, male/female.[25] Deconstruction reveals the text's inability to sustain these oppositions by exposing chinks in the text's logical premises. It does not reverse the oppositions but rather challenges the conceptual system that makes opposition possible in the first place.

Deconstruction focuses primarily on how texts work, and not on the reading process, which is what concerns me most as a feminist critic. The ideology outside of which I stand and the grain against which I speak of reading is what, in a deconstructionist mode, I would call the main thesis of the text (here I refer especially to the privileging of male over female and related oppositions).[26] I want to expose the

24. Particularly the work of its 'founder', Jacques Derrida; see, *inter alia, Of Grammatology* (trans. Gayatri Chakravorty Spivak; Baltimore: Johns Hopkins University Press, 1976); *Writing and Difference* (trans., with introduction and notes by Alan Bass; Chicago: University of Chicago Press, 1978); *Dissemination* (trans., with introduction and notes by Barbara Johnson; Chicago: University of Chicago Press, 1981); and for a helpful introduction, see Christopher Norris, *Deconstruction: Theory and Practice* (London: Metheun, 1982).

25. Hélène Cixous and Catherine Clément, *The Newly Born Woman* (trans. Betsy Wing; Minneapolis: University of Minnesota Press), pp. 63-132.

26. As I note in the Preface to this book, although I acknowledge the importance of looking beyond gender to broader issues of race, ethnicity, class, etc., my focus here is on gender. At this particular point in time I am not ready to see criticism of a specifically feminist persuasion subsumed into a larger project before it has had an opportunity to make its full impact felt. Fortunately this kind of broader analysis is being done by others; see Weems, 'The Hebrew Women Are Not like the Egyptian Women'; Ilse Müllner, 'Tödliche Differenzen: Sexuelle Gewalt als Gewalt gegen Andere in Ri 19', in *Von der Wurzel Getragen: Christlich-feministische Exegese in Auseinandersetzung mit Antijudaismus* (ed. Luise Schottroff and Marie-Theres Wacker; Leiden: Brill, 1996), pp. 81-100.

difficulty a patriarchal text like the Bible has in maintaining patriarchal authority, and to see how a focus on a (suppressed, displaced)
female version of the story can subvert the privileged male version.
Reading against the grain is not replacing one side of the hierarchy
with the other any more than deconstruction is. Its aim is not to offer
a reading in which women are privileged in place of a reading that
privileges men—for every hierarchy is vulnerable to deconstruction.
It seeks rather to subvert the shaky premises upon which the text's
androcentric main thesis rests and to offer an alternative (not opposite)
reading that gives women characters power by making them the
subjects of their own discourse.

As the terms 'suppressed' and 'displaced' above indicate, my own
reader-response approach is informed not only by deconstructive
strategies but also by insights from psychoanalytic literary criticism.[27]
Thus my critique in this chapter centers on investigating the ideology
that motivates particular portrayals of women and on looking for the
buried or encoded messages that these texts give to women. All of us,
women and men, internalize a vast number of messages about gender
roles and expectations as part of our socialization into a society built
on gender distinctions.[28] And what we learn from reading plays a
large role in this socialization process. And so, when I read Exod.
1.8–2.10, I ask, What does this text tell women about how to view
themselves and how to behave? And, What does this particular message
imply about the people who produced this text? As I indicated above,
texts like this tell us as much about the beliefs and prejudices, fears and
desires of the writers who created them as they tell us about women
in biblical times.

27. See Peter Brooks, 'The Idea of a Psychoanalytic Literary Criticism', in
Discourse in Psychoanalysis and Literature (ed. Shlomith Rimmon-Kenan; London:
Methuen, 1987), pp. 1-18.

28. To give an example from 'real life': I recently attended a picnic where there
were three small children, two girls and a boy. Many comments were made to the
little girls about their cute outfits, matching shoes, and adorable little hats. Almost
nothing was made of the boy's attire, though he was as smartly dressed as his sister. I
am sure this was not nor will be the only time these children receive this kind of well-
meaning attention from adults, through which the girls but not the boy are getting a
message about the importance of physical appearance (and nice clothes) that will have
some effect on their self-perception as they grow older. I am not saying that this
effect of this message is inescapable, but it places an extra burden upon the girls: they
will have to unlearn a message about clothes and appearance whereas the boy will not.

In 1983 I said, 'The question is not *why* does a story of daughters form the prelude to the exodus, but rather: what effect do these stories about women have on the way we read the exodus story as a whole?'[29] That I now want to ask the very question I avoided then shows how my position as a reader of the text has shifted. Why are women allowed to play such an important role in the early chapters of Exodus? A traditional way of understanding the focus on women in Exodus 1–2 is to connect it to a familiar biblical theme: God (behind the scenes, in this case) uses the weak and lowly to overcome the strong and powerful. The inferior, but clever, women successfully defy the powerful Egyptian pharaoh. If there is a positive side to this characterization, there is also a negative one. This particular pharaoh, as I argued in my 1983 article, is exceedingly foolish, so foolish that even women can outwit him![30] Another way of looking at the important role women play in these chapters is to consider it a consequence of the focus on infants: it is only natural that women should appear in an account where babies are concerned. Both these explanations appeal to women's subordinate position and traditional domestic role to account for the emphasis on women in the opening chapters of Exodus, but neither interrogates the text's androcentric motivation.

In order to maintain and perpetuate itself, patriarchy depends on women's complicity.[31] Force, threat, and fear are often relied upon to keep women in their place. But rewarding women for their complicity is one of patriarchy's most useful strategies, because it can often achieve a level of cooperation that force or threat cannot guarantee. The honor of playing a decisive role in the future deliverance of the Israelite people is the reward the women of Exodus 1–2 receive for acting in the service of male power (the real contest in Exodus is, after all, between 'males'—between the Egyptian pharaoh and the male-identified Israelite god, or between the pharaoh and Moses).

29. '"You Shall Let Every Daughter Live"', p. 82.

30. For example, his problem is overpopulation, but he fears the Israelites will leave; putting the Hebrews to hard work and killing male infants are absurd 'solutions' to the present problem; he is gullible enough to accept without question the midwives' explanation for their failure to execute his command; he orders all male babies, not just Hebrews, exposed on the Nile; and the very things he seeks to prevent come to pass—male babies, including Moses, are spared, and the Hebrews do, eventually, leave the land.

31. See Lerner, *The Creation of Patriarchy*, pp. 5-6, 233-35.

Women, Exodus 1–2 tells us, are important; without the courage and ingenuity of women, Israel might not have survived as a people. In Exod. 1.8–2.10, the women are accorded recognition as national heroes; their bravery, cleverness, and initiative are instrumental in the founding of a nation. The risks they take to preserve the lives of male babies, especially Moses,[32] guarantees that these women will be honored for generations to come; thus the names of the two midwives, Shiphrah and Puah, are recorded, and the story later supplies the names of Moses' mother Jochebed and sister Miriam.[33]

The text tells women how important mothers are and proposes that the domestic sphere can be a place of valor, where a woman's mettle is tested. Honor and status (the two are related) are rewards patriarchy grants women for assent to their subordination and cooperation in it. One of the few roles in which women can achieve status in patriarchal society is that of mother. Motherhood is not only patriarchy's highest reward for women, it is also presented as something women themselves most desire (witness the many biblical accounts of barren women who desperately desire and finally give birth to a long-awaited son). As Fuchs points out, this is a powerful ideological strategy.[34] The women in Exod. 1.8–2.10 perform traditional female, and especially

32. As I pointed out in '"You Shall Let Every Daughter Live"', the pharaoh's question to the midwives, 'Why have you done this?', takes the form of an accusation found in juridical contexts. It suggests therefore that the midwives face a serious charge, and the fact that they get away with the incredible explanation they provide shows just how foolish this pharaoh is. Moses' mother and the pharaoh's daughter take a risk by openly defying the pharaoh's command, which was publicly issued to all his people.

33. This means that only the woman who is clearly non-Israelite, Pharaoh's daughter, is not given a name. It is not entirely clear whether the midwives are Hebrew or Egyptian; the Masoretes construed the word 'Hebrew' as an adjective, but the consonantal text is ambiguous and the Septuagint and Vulgate read, 'the midwives of the Hebrews'. On the names Shiphrah and Puah, see '"You Shall Let Every Daughter Live"', pp. 70, 72. Miriam is not identified as Moses' sister in Exodus, but only as Aaron's sister; she is identified as Moses' sister in Num. 26.59 and 1 Chron. 6.3. On the unexpected appearance of a sister in Exod. 2, and different approaches available to exegetes in dealing with logical contradictions in the narrative, see Jürgen Ebach, 'Die Schwester des Mose: Anmerkungen zu einem "Widerspruch" in Exodus 2, 1-10', in *'Mit unsrer Macht ist nichts getan…': Festschrift für Dieter Schellong zum 65. Geburtstag* (ed. Jörg Mertin, Dietrich Neuhaus, and Michael Weinrich; Herchen Verlag, 1996), pp. 101-15.

34. Fuchs, 'The Literary Characterization of Mothers', p. 130.

motherly, activities, activities focused on children—though, of course, they give new meaning to their nurturing and protective roles. The midwives not only assist in birth, they save lives. As a reward for their defiance of the pharaoh's command to kill male babies, God builds them 'houses'; that is, he gives them families.[35] Figuratively speaking, the midwives, Moses's mother, Moses' sister, and the pharaoh's daughter are all mothers of the exodus.[36]

What is it about the women in Exod. 1.8–2.10 that makes them characters with whom women might wish to identify? They exhibit admirable qualities, such as heroism, fear of God (1.17), compassion (2.6), determination (2.2-4), and cleverness (2.7), and they show that women can contribute significantly to the life of their people. The story praises women in the spirit of the old adage that the hand that rocks the cradle rules the world. In essence, its message to women is: stay in your place in the domestic sphere; you can achieve important things there. The public arena belongs to men; you do not need to look beyond motherhood for fulfillment. In Exodus 1–2, Hebrew women do not need to kill Egyptians (fighting is men's work or the work of their male-identified god [Exod. 12.29; 15.24-31]) but only to keep Hebrew males alive.

Sayings like 'the hand that rocks the cradle rules the world' and 'behind every great man is a woman' are meant to make women feel important, while in reality they serve an androcentric agenda by suggesting that women should be satisfied with their power behind the scene.[37] Exod. 1.8–2.10, where women actively determine Israel's

35. See the discussion of the difficulty of v. 21 in '"You Shall Let Every Daughter Live"', p. 74.

36. Exum, '"Mother in Israel"', p. 80.

37. The sayings have something else in common with Exod. 1.8–2.10; both popular adages and text assume that women have power but they do not have authority. Power is the ability to achieve one's goals and to get others to comply with one's will; women have always had power through a variety of means. Authority, power that is recognized and legitimated by society, has traditionally been a male prerogative; see Louise Lamphere, 'Strategies, Cooperation, and Conflict among Women in Domestic Groups', in *Woman, Culture, and Society* (ed. Michelle Zimbalist Rosaldo and Louise Lamphere; Stanford: Stanford University Press, 1974), p. 99; Michelle Zimbalist Rosaldo, 'Woman, Culture, and Society: A Theoretical Overview', also in *Woman, Culture, and Society*, pp. 21-22; Carol Meyers, *Discovering Eve: Ancient Israelite Women in Context* (New York: Oxford University Press, 1988), pp. 40-44, 181-87.

future, serves a similar agenda. It compensates women on the domestic front for the role denied them in the larger story of the exodus and journey to the promised land. But like its modern counterparts in the sayings above about women's indirect power, it has something to hide: the fear of women's power that makes it important to domesticate and confine it.

The Subversive Female Presence and its Suppression

The women in Exodus 1 and 2 are literary creations, male constructs— and they are powerful. They outwit and overcome men. Precisely because women have power that they can use to subvert authority, they present a threat to patriarchal society. Having acknowledged this threat, the text must somehow circumscribe and control this female power. It is therefore in the interest of those who maintain the social and symbolic order to represent women characters as using their power in the service of patriarchy.

Historically patriarchy has relied on class divisions and ethnic divisions among women to prevent women from forming alliances that might further the cause of their sex. We saw, for example, in Chapter 2 above, how having Michal introduce a class distinction between herself and David's 'male servants' women servants' allowed the narrator to isolate her from other women at the very moment he was isolating her so effectively from David, thus making it easier for the narrator, and David, to do away with her. Women do not often interact or speak to one another in the Bible, yet here in Exodus 2 we find Moses' mother, his sister, an Egyptian princess, and the princess's women servants all engaged in protecting the infant Moses from the pharaoh's death edict. Whereas the text offers a glimpse of the formidable threat posed to male authority when women cooperate across class and ethnic lines, it co-opts women's power for its own ends: it uses an alliance between women to defy the foreign authority that oppresses the Hebrew people. Moreover, the text describes a fairly unlikely alliance. That an Egyptian princess would openly defy her father's command to expose male babies on the Nile by taking the infant out of the Nile, and that she would adopt a Hebrew baby, could be considered 'providential'. Indeed, by having the sister appear suddenly to put the idea of adopting Moses in the princess's mind, the narrator suggests that the deity, rather than any decision by women to work together, is responsible for the propitious outcome.

One way of dealing with women's power is to diffuse it. In Exodus 1–2 this is accomplished by having three (or five) 'mothers' rescue Moses, rather than one. Imagine the power one woman would have had if she alone had saved Moses.[38] Diffusing the influence of women, I believe, is also the reason Moses' mother and sister are anonymous in this account; by withholding their names until later in the narrative, the narrator accords them less recognition and renders them less imposing.

The role the women play in the birth of the nation is comparable to the role usually played by mothers in the Bible: they yield their power, and their stories, to their husbands and sons.[39] Like a child dissociating itself from its mother, Moses must separate from his 'mothers' and exchange his passive role for an active one. Thus, almost immediately after he is rescued by *daughters* (recall the meaningful use of *bat* in Exod. 1.8–2.10), Moses rescues *daughters*. In Exod. 2.16-22, Moses—who in the space of five verses has grown up, killed an Egyptian, and fled the country—delivers seven daughters from shepherds who threaten them when they come to water the flock of their father Reuel (Jethro), the Midianite priest. He marries one of these daughters and has a son of his own (the contrast between *ben*, 'son', and *bat*, 'daughter', continues throughout the chapter). But the reversal of roles is not complete. In Exod. 4.24-26, a foreign woman again saves Moses' life: Zipporah, Moses' wife, prevents the divine Father from killing her husband, through a rite of circumcision that makes him her 'bridegroom of blood'.[40] Typically, she drops out of the picture, and is not mentioned again until Exod. 18.2-5, where we learn that Moses had sent her away.[41] Perhaps we might view the reappearance of a woman to deliver Moses violently as an instance of women refusing to be written out of the text without a struggle; in other words, as a symptom of a guilty narrative conscience. In any

38. See Athalya Brenner, *The Israelite Woman: Social Role and Literary Type in Biblical Narrative* (Sheffield: JSOT Press, 1985), pp. 99-100.

39. See Exum, *Fragmented Women*, Chapter 4, 'The (M)other's Place', pp. 94-147.

40. This strange text has posed numerous problems for interpretation. It is interesting that a woman here performs the rite of circumcision. For suggestive comments on this passage, see Ilana Pardes, *Countertraditions in the Bible: A Feminist Approach* (Cambridge, MA: Harvard University Press, 1992), pp. 84-93.

41. Jethro brings her and her two sons with him to meet Moses after the exodus from Egypt, but Zipporah is not mentioned in the reconciliation scene.

event, Moses, unhampered by the woman's presence, moves on to deliver not just women again, but rather a whole people.

After Exodus 4, women are conspicuously absent in much of the narrative of the exodus and journey to the promised land in Exodus, Leviticus, Numbers, and Deuteronomy.[42] The feminine, however, resurfaces in another form. Patriarchy seeks to diffuse, or suppress, or appropriate female power, as the Bible's classic illustration of womb envy dramatically demonstrates: in Genesis 2, the creative power of women is assumed by the prototypical Man who, like Zeus who gave birth to Athena from his head, symbolically gives birth to woman with the help of the creator god (and in the absence of a creator goddess). Perhaps 'womb envy' prompts the application of female metaphors to God and Moses later in the exodus story. In Numbers 11, when the people complain to Moses about not having meat to eat, Moses complains to God about his responsibilities:

> Did I conceive all this people? Did I bring them forth, that you should say to me, 'Carry them in your bosom, as a nurse carries the sucking child, to the land which you swore to give their fathers?'...I am not able to carry all this people alone, the burden is too heavy for me (Num. 11.12-14).

Moses, cast in a nurturing, maternal role, finds it too hard, and his rhetorical questions imply that it is God who conceived the people of Israel and who is not doing an adequate job of mothering them. God and Moses are imaged as mother and midwife—roles played by *real women* in Exodus 1–2—not so much because they are better at women's roles (here they seem to have problems, but their difficulties will be resolved), but because male figures in these roles do not threaten the status quo. Applying maternal imagery to the deity and

---

42. Exodus 19 indicates that the covenant at Sinai is made with men; the people are addressed with the command, 'Do not go near a woman' (v. 15). That the ten commandments, for example, are addressed to men is clear from the second person masculine singular pronouns and a command such as, 'You shall not covet...your neighbor's wife' (v. 17); on the difficulties, see Athalya Brenner, 'An Afterword: The Decalogue—Am I an Addressee?' in Brenner (ed.), *A Feminist Companion to Exodus to Deuteronomy*, pp. 255-58; David J.A. Clines, 'The Ten Commandments, Reading from Left to Right', Chapter 2 in his *Interested Parties: The Ideology of Writers and Readers of the Hebrew Bible* (Journal for the Study of the Old Testament Supplement Series, 205; Gender, Culture, Theory, 1; Sheffield: Sheffield Academic Press, 1995), pp. 26-45. On women's general invisibility in the laws, see Phyllis Bird, 'Images of Women in the Old Testament', in *Religion and Sexism* (ed. R.R. Ruether; New York: Simon & Schuster, 1974), pp. 48-57.

the human hero of the story is a way of appropriating maternal power. Patriarchy does not have to worry that God and Moses, acting as mother and midwife, will subvert androcentric interests and undermine the social order because they are the guarantors of the patriarchal social order.

I suggested above that Exod. 1.8–2.10 serves as a kind of compensation for the fact that women are not given a larger role in the bulk of the account of the exodus and wanderings. When the one woman from Exodus 2 to reappear in an important role does speak out for herself, claiming a position of leadership, she is put in her place. In Num. 12.1-2, we learn that Miriam (and Aaron)[43] speaks out against Moses 'because of the Cushite woman he married'. It is noteworthy that here Miriam is set over against a foreign woman, whereas Exodus 1–2 showed the cooperation between women across ethnic boundaries. Perhaps it is because such a level of cooperation cannot be tolerated that Miriam is used to speak out against a foreign woman in Numbers 12. Once gender solidarity across ethnic lines has been shattered, the complaint shifts abruptly from an objection to the woman to the issue of leadership: 'Has the Lord indeed spoken only through Moses? Has he not spoken through us also?' (v. 2). The strange account has baffled commentators, not least because only Miriam is punished for challenging Moses' authority. She becomes leprous and must be 'shut up outside the camp seven days', after which she is brought in again.

It is not without significance that this story appears just after the account in which female imagery is used for Moses and God. In Num. 11.16-30 the problem of nurturing the people is resolved by allowing seventy *men*, elders of the community, to share the task. There Moses had proclaimed, 'Would that all the Lord's people were prophets'; here he denies that role to Miriam and undermines her status as prophet (Exod. 15.20). Miriam's punishment of being quarantined outside the boundary of the camp is suggestive of the position that feminist critics have argued is occupied by women in the phallocentric symbolic order.[44] Women are at the boundary of

---

43. The verb is third person feminine singular, suggesting either that Aaron is a later addition to the story (if one takes a historical-critical approach) or that the story is primarily concerned with making only Miriam look bad.

44. For this discussion, see Toril Moi, *Sexual/Textual Politics: Feminist Literary Theory* (London: Methuen, 1985), p. 167.

the symbolic order, the border between men and chaos. As borderline figures, women partake of the properties of a border: they are neither inside nor outside. When women are viewed as inside the border, they are seen to have protective qualities (as in Exod. 1 and 2); when viewed as outside, they are dangerous (as here in Num. 12). Miriam's claim to a position of authority comparable to Moses'—and the rhetorical questions imply that God has spoken through her also— threatens to blur the distinction between Moses' role and hers. It challenges male hegemony. Punishment is swift and devastating. For threatening to disrupt the social order, Miriam is put outside the boundary of patriarchal order, symbolized by the camp, where she becomes, literally, the outsider, the other—until she is allowed to come back *inside* the camp/symbolic order in her proper, submissive role. Some commentators have argued that Aaron does not share in Miriam's punishment because he is a priest, and that the Priestly writers of the Pentateuch would not have wanted to dishonor him by portraying him as leprous and having him put outside the camp. Gender politics are also at work, I suggest: as a man, Aaron poses no threat to the symbolic order. On the contrary, his proper place is inside it, and so he remains within the camp. While leaving Aaron unblemished and unpunished, Numbers 12 effectively humiliates and eliminates the woman.

The case of Miriam in Numbers 12 offers but one example of the way women's experience, in the biblical as in other patriarchal texts, is expressed but has been displaced and distorted. But in Miriam's challenge to Moses and in her insistence on speaking out against male hegemony, traces of the woman's point of view remain to unsettle patriarchal authority.

More remains to be done to provide an effective feminist critique of the exodus and wandering traditions. Attempting, as I have done here, to account for the distortion or absence or suppression of female presence after the opening stories in Exodus 1 and 2 in terms of biblical gender politics, rather than treating it as if it were unmotivated, is, I think, is a step in the right direction. It is not the last word on this text, and perhaps not even my last word on it.

4

Prophetic Pornography

If God is male, then the male is God.
Mary Daly, *Beyond God the Father*

What is an essentially simple act of identification
when the reader of the story is male becomes a
tangle of contradictions when the reader is
female.
Judith Fetterley, *The Resisting Reader*

Feminist criticism has made us more aware of the problem of the prevalence of violence against women in the Bible, from mass violence against anonymous women—as in cases of war where we frequently find the command to destroy completely entire cities, including women and children (e.g., Deut. 2.34; 7.1-5; Josh. 6.21; 8.24-25; Judg. 21.10-14; 1 Sam. 15.3) and where the rape or humiliation of captive women is taken for granted (Judg. 5.30; Lam. 5.11; Amos 4.2-3; 7.17)—to individual cases, such as the rape, murder, and dismemberment of the Levite's wife in Judges 19; the rapes of Dinah (Gen. 34), Tamar (2 Sam. 13), and ten of David's wives (2 Sam. 16.21-22); the abduction of the dancers at Shiloh (Judg. 21.19-23); the sexual appropriation and later expulsion of Hagar (Gen. 16; 21); the slaughter of Cozbi the Midianite (Num. 25). And so on.

It is not the intention of this chapter to chronicle instances of biblical violence against women. Rather I want to examine a particularly pernicious form of biblical violence against women where the perpetrator is not a collective, such as an army plundering cities, nor particular 'evil men' but the deity himself: sexual violence where God appears as the subject and the object of his abuse is personified Israel/Judah/Jerusalem.[1] The fact that this is metaphorical violence does not

---

1. I use the term 'his' for God since God is a character in these texts who is male identified, and I capitalize 'God' as though it were a proper name when referring to this character. *Foreign* cities or nations personified as women are also sexually abused

make it less criminal. Indeed, it is extremely injurious: because God is the subject, we—that is, female as well as male readers—are expected to sympathize with the divine perspective against the (personified) woman. The examples of biblical sexual violence discussed below are illustrative and representative rather than comprehensive. All of them come from the prophetic books and the book of Lamentations, where this particular kind of imagery has its locus. (What this says about prophecy and the prophets in general is a larger ethical issue.)

In dealing with the ethical problems raised by passages in which a male deity is pictured as sexually abusing a female victim, we cannot confine ourselves to the issue of gender bias in representation, which we can describe and account for as the product of an ancient patriarchal society where the subordinate position of women was taken for granted. We also need to consider gender bias in interpretation. The kinds of questions I raised in Chapter 1 about our responses when faced with the exposure of the female body for our literary and visual consumption need to be raised here in particular. How should we respond to these offensive prophetic texts, and what is our responsibility as readers and consumers of these violent images? As was the case with the textual and visual representations of Bathsheba's body,

---

by God; e.g., Nineveh in Nahum 3.5-6; Babylon in Isa. 47.1-3 (cf. 23.13-18); Edom in Lam. 4.21-22. Because in these cases the accused woman is not God's wife and there is no covenant to give him rights of ownership over her body, they raise a different set of issues from those discussed here. In some cases, the city/woman's sexuality is deliberately construed as a threat to the (male) god's male-identified people, for whose seduction she is blamed. Others represent a(n insulting) feminization of Israel's enemies, upon whom retaliation can be enjoyed and described in a sexually degrading manner. These passages share the fear of and fascination with female sexuality that motivates the passages discussed in this chapter. On the use of sexual imagery to describe military conquest in the Hebrew Bible, see Susan Brooks Thistlethwaite, '"You May Enjoy the Spoil of Your Enemies": Rape as a Biblical Metaphor for War', *Semeia* 61 (1993), pp. 59-75; Pamela Gordon and Harold C. Washington, 'Rape as a Military Metaphor in the Hebrew Bible', in *A Feminist Companion to the Latter Prophets* (ed. Athalya Brenner; The Feminist Companion to the Bible, 8; Sheffield: Sheffield Academic Press, 1995), pp. 308-25. Gordon and Washington deal specifically with the image of the conquered city as a raped woman; so also, F. Rachel Magdalene, 'Ancient Near Eastern Treaty-Curses and the Ultimate Texts of Terror: A Study of the Language of Divine Sexual Abuse in the Prophetic Corpus', in Brenner (ed.), *A Feminist Companion to the Latter Prophets*, pp. 326-52, who, while deploring its influence on contemporary readers, sheds helpful light on the ancient Near Eastern background of the rape metaphor.

these prophetic diatribes make claims upon their readers, and their claims will be experienced differently by female and male readers. Male readers (if the commentators are any example; see below) do not find it difficult to identify with the divine perspective portrayed in these texts and thus to defend a righteous and long-suffering God for punishing a wayward and headstrong nation. Female readers, on the other hand, are placed in a double bind. On the one hand we are asked to sympathize with God and identify with his point of view. To the extent we do so, we read these texts against our own interests.[2] On the other hand, by definition we are identified with the object that elicits scorn and abuse. As I observed in Bathsheba's case, this involves acceptance if not of guilt, then at least of the indictment of our sex that these texts represent.

Gender Bias in Representation

These texts contain shocking and scandalizing language. Not surprisingly, most translations tone them down. Many terms, because they are rare or because their sexual meaning is obscure or only allusive, are difficult to translate. Pinning down specific meanings for rare words, however, is not crucial for our understanding of these passages, for their misogynistic import is clear enough.[3] By way of analogy, we have only to think of the power of our own language to convey sexual innuendo and to give common words vulgar connotations to

---

2. See Fetterley, 'Palpable Designs', and the discussion of the position of the female reader/spectator in Chapter 1 above.

3. *Contra* Robert P. Carroll, *Jeremiah* (Old Testament Library; Philadelphia: Westminster Press, 1986), pp. 134, 180. Though Carroll recognizes the ideological bias of prophetic polemic and the pornographic (a term he uses) nature of this material, he cautions (p. 180) that 'biblical condemnation of sexual activity, whether real or metaphorical, is a balanced matter of condemning male as well as female behaviour (epitomized in Hos. 4.14)'. He makes similar claims in 'Desire under the Terebinths: On Pornographic Representation in the Prophets—A Response', in Brenner (ed.), *A Feminist Companion to the Latter Prophets*, pp. 275-307. To say, as Carroll does (*Jeremiah*, p. 134) that 'Without knowing the psychological make-up of the biblical writers it is not possible to evaluate the degree to which their writings may be characterized as misogynistic or otherwise' seems to me to be inquiring after the author's intention (conscious or subconscious). I am more interested in the effect on the reader, and I experience this material as defamatory, insulting, and, ultimately, misogynistic. For further discussion of these issues, see below.

recognize that the semantic field of many of these terms is broader than any one particular lexical meaning.

The first to employ the husband–wife metaphor for God's relation to his people, Hosea uses his marriage to Gomer, 'a wife of harlotry', to illustrate God's covenantal dealings with an idolatrous Israel (prominent in chs. 1–3, the harlotry theme runs through the whole book).[4] In ch. 2, the indictment of the unfaithful woman slips into an indictment of the land personified as a harlot, whom God threatens to strip naked and slay with thirst (v. 3). After a description of her shameful behavior with her lovers and his response, God describes how he will publicly humiliate her.

> 9[11]Therefore I will take back
> my grain in its time,
> and my new wine in its season;
> and I will snatch away my wool and my flax,
> which were to cover her genitals.[5]
> 10[12]Now I will expose her genitals[6]
> in the sight of her lovers
> and no one shall rescue her from my hand.

It is important to recognize that the point of view here is male. Hosea describes the nation's unfaithfulness in terms of unrestrained female sexual freedom. The woman's decision to pursue other lovers—in other words, her control of her own body—which is threatening, is visualized as rampant promiscuity, which is not tolerated. Given the carefully circumscribed social position of women in ancient Israel, it is hard to imagine a real woman getting away with such free and open behavior. I find it difficult therefore to see the bizarre exaggerated

---

4.   For a radically new and different way of looking at what is going on in Hosea 1–3 and a trenchant critique of scholarly responses to these chapters, see Sherwood, *The Prostitute and the Prophet*.

5.   The word *'erva* is a euphemism for genitals; cf. Gen. 9.22-23; on the relation of vv. 9 and 10 [Heb. 11 and 12], see the discussion in Francis I. Andersen and David Noel Freedman, *Hosea* (Anchor Bible, 24; Garden City, NY: Doubleday, 1980), pp. 246-48.

6.   The word I translate 'genitals' here is *nablut*, a hapax. For this translation, see Hans Walter Wolff, *Hosea* (trans. G. Stansell; Hermeneia; Philadelphia: Fortress Press, 1974), pp. 31, 37 n. 52. Andersen and Freedman (*Hosea*, p. 248) dispute the meaning of the Akkadian cognate cited by Wolff. They note, however, that something concrete is meant by the image and conclude that it is 'likely that the woman is to have her naked body put on display as obscene'.

sexual appetite described here as anything other than a male fantasy of female desire, a fantasy born out of fear of female sexuality and fascination with it. The punishment for sexual 'transgression' or 'wantonness' is sexual abuse, which is also crudely fantasized in terms that conjure up the atrocities inflicted upon women prisoners of war. It is the male's job to restrain the female's freedom/wantonness and to punish the woman whose behavior brings dishonor upon him.[7] God is the wronged party here; he is male-identified and portrayed as the abusive husband. Sexual abuse is presented as justified by the woman's guilt.

Isaiah too calls Jerusalem a harlot (1.21; cf. 57.3-13). Language of sexual humiliation similar to Hosea's appears in Isa. 3.16-24, where the object of God's sexual abuse is at first real women, the women of Zion (Jerusalem). The imagery in this passage is fluid,[8] and by v. 25 the daughters of Zion have become Zion herself.

> [16]Because the daughters of Zion are haughty
> and walk with outstretched necks,
> glancing provocatively with their eyes,
> tripping along as they go,
> rattling their bangles with their feet,
> [17]the Lord will make bald
> the heads of the daughters of Zion,
> and the Lord will bare their cunts.[9]

What exactly is these women's guilt? It appears that humiliation is punishment for pride and the possession of luxury items (described and stripped away in vv. 18-23). But where did the women get this finery in the first place? From their own economic endeavors, or

7.   See the discussion in Gale A. Yee, 'Hosea', in *The Women's Bible Commentary* (ed. Carol A. Newsom and Sharon H. Ringe; Louisville: Westminster/John Knox Press, 1992), pp. 197-98.

8.   Cf. Susan Ackerman, 'Isaiah', in Newsom and Ringe (eds.), *The Women's Bible Commentary*, p. 162: 'Indeed, the identification of women, in particular the women of Jerusalem/Zion, with Jerusalem/Zion itself was made so facilely that a prophet could slip almost without notice from describing one to the other'.

9.   The meaning of v. 17 is obscure and my translation conjectural. The word *pot* in 1 Kgs 7.50 refers to the sockets in which the door pivots turned (BDB, p. 834); assuming the word refers to a hollow place in which something turns, I take it as an obscene reference to the woman's vagina (cf. RSV, 'the Lord will lay bare their secret parts'); an alternative reading is 'the Lord will lay bare their foreheads'. On the difficulties, see the commentators.

from their husbands and fathers? 'The flamboyant behaviour of the women attracted the prophet's attention and indignation, when contrasted with the abject poverty that existed in the city', observes R.E. Clements.[10] But surely there must be more to their guilt than this, so Clements does what biblical commentators typically do when no clear cause for divine punishment suggests itself—he surmises that the problem lies with an improper religious attitude: 'Trust in human beauty could signify a lack of regard for God'.[11] Can behavior be the *cause* of poverty? Otto Kaiser apparently thinks so:

> The more extravagant they are, the more they lead the men on into illegal profiteering at the expense of those who are socially weaker. In various ways, either by their own attitude to the ordinary man in the street, or by the consequences for the economic behaviour of their husbands, they are undermining the internal unity and health of the people of the covenant. They are judged not because they adorn themselves, but because they break down the order of the people of God through their whole attitude.[12]

Not only are women to blame for the crimes of men, in Kaiser's view the breakdown of the entire social fabric can be attributed to these women's *attitude*!

Not what androcentric ideology considers wanton behavior but simply what it suspects as glancing provocatively or 'ogling' is sufficient to bring the most vile abuse upon these women. At whom are they glancing provocatively, and why is it threatening? The female gaze is postulated in order to be condemned, while readers are invited to assume the text's male gaze at the women's genitalia. The intrusive textual gaze remains fixed upon the female body and its humiliation in the following verses, where the images are resolved in a picture of Zion as a ravaged woman.

10. R.E. Clements, *Isaiah 1-39* (New Century Bible Commentary; Grand Rapids: Eerdmans, 1980), p. 50.

11. Clements, *Isaiah 1-39*, p. 51.

12. Otto Kaiser, *Isaiah 1-12* (trans. R.A. Wilson; Old Testament Library; Philadelphia: Westminster Press, 1972), p. 48; similarly, G.G.D. Kilpatrick, 'Exposition to the Book of Isaiah', in *The Interpreter's Bible*, V (New York: Abingdon Press, 1956), pp. 191-92: 'It may not be as obvious, but it is equally true, that a degenerate womanhood can corrupt a nation…To a degree seldom realized, the moral quality of womanhood determines the character of society. These are the mothers of men, they set the ideals of men and, by what they are, either inspire or corrupt their sons.'

[24]Instead of perfume there will be stench,
and instead of a belt, a rope,
and instead of well-set hair, baldness,
and instead of a rich robe, a girding of sackcloth,
instead of beauty, shame.[13]
[25]Your men will fall by the sword
and your heroes in battle.
[26]And her entrances will lament and mourn,
ravaged she will sit upon the ground.

Like his prophetic predecessors, Jeremiah also refers to Israel's unfaithfulness in terms of illicit female sexual activity (e.g., 4.30; 22.20-23; and 2.33–3.20, where she is even said to have taught wicked women her ways, 2.33). The irrationally jealous husband imagines that his wife will have sex with anyone.[14] Jer. 2.23-24 masks male fear of and fascination with female desire by crudely caricaturing the woman as a young camel or wild donkey in heat.[15] In Jer. 13.22, when Jerusalem questions her harsh treatment by her lord, she is told:

It is for the greatness of your iniquity
that your skirts are lifted up
and your genitals[16] are treated violently.

13. The Masoretic text lacks 'shame'; restoring *bšt* with 1QIs[a]. The Septuagint and Vulgate lack the stichos.

14. Gracia Fay Ellwood (*Batter My Heart* [Pendle Hill Pamphlet, 282; Wallingford, PA: Pendle Hill, 1988], pp. 10-11) observes that this is a trait God shares with the battering husband.

15. I am not convinced that the actual mating behavior of camels need inform the metaphor (William L. Holladay, *Jeremiah 1* [Hermeneia; Philadelphia: Fortress Press, 1986], p. 100). For discussion of the pornographic nature of this passage, see Athalya Brenner, 'On "Jeremiah" and the Poetics of (Prophetic?) Pornography', in Athalya Brenner and Fokkelien van Dijk-Hemmes, *On Gendering Texts: Female and Male Voices in the Hebrew Bible* (Biblical Interpretation Series, 1; Leiden: Brill, 1993), pp. 177-93.

16. Hebrew *'aqebayik* is literally, 'your heels'; like Hebrew *raglaim*, 'feet', it can be a euphemism for genitals; see Carroll, *Jeremiah*, p. 303; Holladay, *Jeremiah 1*, p. 414. Taking *'aqeb* in the sense of 'hinder-part, rear' (cf. BDB, p. 784), Magdalene, 'Ancient Near Eastern Treaty-Curses', pp. 328-29 and n. 4, translates 'buttocks', yielding an equally plausible, and violent, meaning. She observes, '...any violence to the buttocks because of their location may be considered sexual violence even if there is no penetration' (p. 329 n. 4).

It is the woman's fault; abuse is deserved. Jerusalem will be raped by Babylon (13.20-27), and God not only endorses it, he participates in the attack.

> And I too will lift up your skirts over your face,[17]
> and your genitals will be seen (v. 26).

Since God has seen her 'adulteries', 'neighings' (another reference to female lust as insatiable) and 'lewd harlotries', it is presented as fitting that he should repay her in kind by exposing her genitals for all to see (as in the Latin *pudenda*, the Hebrew word *qelonek*, 'disgrace, dishonor', expresses the typical view of the female sex organs as shameful).

In Ezekiel we meet the strongest, most abusive language. Ezekiel 16 presents Jerusalem as a foundling who grows up to become God's unfaithful wife.[18] Because she has given herself to her lovers, God will assemble all her former lovers and expose her naked body to their view (vv. 35-38), after which they will be given free rein to abuse her.

> [39]I will give you into their hand
> and they will throw down your mound
> and break down your high places.
> They will strip off your clothes
> and take the ornaments of your beauty
> and leave you stark naked.
> [40]They will summon a crowd against you,
> and they will stone you with stones
> and cut you to pieces[19] with their swords.

17. Literally, 'I will strip off your skirts over your face'. Carroll (*Jeremiah*, p. 303) suggests that the use of euphemisms in the passage 'may conceal an obscene practice of exposing women by drawing their legs over their heads in order to uncover their vulvas completely'.

18. See the discussion of this chapter by Mary E. Shields ('Ezekiel 16: Body Rhetoric and Gender', *Journal of Feminist Studies in Religion*, forthcoming), who, in contrast to the usual interpretation, sees no signs of divine tenderness in this text. Shields argues convincingly that the text attributes only desire, not love, to God. Jerusalem is completely dependent on God, who provides everything for her ('but never forgot that it was his property', Ellwood, *Batter My Heart*, p. 12) and who, in his anger, strips everything away.

19. Julie Galambush (*Jerusalem in the Book of Ezekiel: The City as Yahweh's Wife* [Society of Biblical Literature Dissertation Series, 130; Atlanta: Scholars Press, 1992], pp. 67, 71) suggests that the hapax *btq* might best be understood in terms of the violent phallic image of splitting the woman open by slicing her up the middle.

The prophet compares the treatment of the woman Jerusalem to the way women who commit adultery are judged (v. 38), and thus provides an implicit warning to women in general, a warning that will be made explicit in ch. 23. The punishment for adultery is death. Here the woman is raped (symbolized by the throwing down of the mound and breaking of high places)[20] and stripped naked before she is stoned to death. But this extreme abuse, apparently, is not enough, and so the woman is dismembered in order to satisfy the divine husband's wrath ('so I will satisfy my fury upon you', v. 42). Female sexuality, whose free expression is so offensive, is mutilated and its threat thereby diffused.[21] Having vented his anger on his victim, the abuser will feel better: 'I will be calm and will not be angry any more' (v. 42). The woman, of course, since she is metaphorical, will not be dead. She will live to be abused again.

And so we come to Ezekiel 23, the most pornographic example of divine violence, where the sisters Samaria and Jerusalem become God's wives (a violation of the law in Lev. 18.18). Before graphically describing the punishment that the jealous husband inflicts on his wives for voraciously chasing after other men, the male author seems to take pleasure in picturing the sexual attentions pressed upon them by 'desirable young men' (vv. 12, 23): the handling of their breasts and their defilement by their lovers' lust. He betrays a fascination with sexual prowess and an envy of other (foreign) men's endowment, fantasizing his rivals with penises the size of asses' penises and ejaculations like those of stallions.

The prophet takes advantage of two occasions to go into the sordid details of sexual abuse, for the same punishment befalls both sisters. One of God's wives, the Northern Kingdom, dies as a result of abuse. God threatens his other wife with the same treatment. Just as he gave Samaria over to men who violated her by exposing her naked body to view and then killed her (vv. 9-10), so he will rouse against Jerusalem the lovers she has spurned (vv. 22-35).

20. In 16.24 and 31 the terms *gab* (mound) and *ramah* (high place) refer to the places the woman/city built for prostitution/illicit worship. I see double-entendre in v. 39, with the destruction of these places represented as rape. Vv. 24, 25, and 31 read singular, 'height' or 'high place', and the Septuagint, Vulgate, and some Hebrew manuscripts read the singular here in v. 39.

21. The classic biblical example of the dictum, 'If the female body scares you, cut it up!', is Judges 19; see Exum, *Fragmented Women*, pp. 170-201.

[25]I will direct my jealousy against you
that they may deal with you in fury.
They will cut off your nose and your ears...
[26]They will strip off your clothes and take the ornaments of your beauty...
[28]I am delivering you into the hand of those you hate,
into the hand of those from whom your desire has turned away.
[29]They shall deal with you in hatred
and take all you have acquired,
and leave you stark naked,
so that your unfaithful genitalia[22] may be exposed.

God's anger at the woman will fuel the anger of her former lovers. She will suffer mutilation at their hands and her naked body will be exposed. In her misery and humiliation, she will be mocked and laughed at (v. 32). Finally God calls for a crowd to be summoned against the adulterous sisters to stone them, and hack them to pieces with their swords (vv. 46-47), so that, again, we have both the stoning and the mutilation we witnessed in Ezekiel 16. To bring home the lesson, the fate of the personified cities has a moral for all women, 'that all women may take warning and not commit lewdness as you have done' (v. 48). By detailing the sexual abuse of an 'unfaithful' wife, the text appeals to female fear of male violence in order to keep female sexuality in check.

In this sampling of texts we can discover some disturbing common and repeated features. One is scapegoating women. It is the woman's fault that she is sexually abused because she asked for it by deliberately flaunting her husband's will (control) and thereby antagonizing him. Sexual sin is punished sexually in the most degrading way. Related to this is the portrayal of the woman as solely responsible for the success of the relationship. The husband shares none of the blame and deserves our sympathy as the wronged party. 'God suffers under Israel's deceitful love affair', says Hans Walter Wolff.[23] But what about the woman's suffering? Even if God does suffer (and his suffering is not physical, like the woman's), that two wrongs do not make a right is a simple ethical principle. But this is what we have in these texts.

Hosea, Jeremiah, and Ezekiel present us with the abusive husband's version of events. The woman's version, her point of view, is not represented; she is called upon to accept her abuser's accusations

---

22. Following a suggestion of Galambush (*Jerusalem in the Book of Ezekiel*, p. 76); the Hebrew reads literally, 'the nakedness of your prostitutions'.

23. Wolff, *Hosea*, p. 44.

as valid and acknowledge her guilt. Lamentations goes a step further by co-opting the woman's voice to have her blame herself. In Lamentations, as elsewhere, the woman is violated because of her sexual 'infidelity':

> [8]Jerusalem sinned grievously,
> therefore she became impure.[24]
> All who honored her despise her,
> for they have seen her nakedness.
> Even she herself groans
> and turns away.
> [9]Her uncleanness was in her skirts;
> she took no thought of the consequences for her.
> She has come down extraordinarily,
> she has no comforter...
> [10]The enemy has stretched out his hand[25]
> over all her precious things;
> for she has seen the nations
> enter her sanctuary...(Lam. 1.8-10).

The rape imagery builds upon the correspondence between body and temple and between genitals and inner sanctuary.[26] Though the woman's voice breaks through momentarily in the suggestion that God has gone too far in his abuse ('you slaughtered without mercy', 2.21), she shows no anger, only remorse, and thus she remains powerless. She accepts the blame: 'the Lord is in the right, for I rebelled against his word' (1.18; cf. 1.20, 22). Is this not the dilemma

24. The term *niddah* refers to a menstruous woman (for the difference in pointing, see *Gesenius' Hebrew Grammar* [ed. E. Kautzsch; trans. A.E. Cowley] § 20 n R 1), a reading reflected in Aquila, Symmachus, and the Syriac. Delbert R. Hillars (*Lamentations* [Anchor Bible, 7A; Garden City, NY: Doubleday, 1972], pp. 9-10) prefers the translation, 'people shake their heads at her', but recognizes a word play on *niddah*. The association with 'menstruous woman' is hard to miss, especially in view of the reference to ritual uncleanness in v. 9.

25. The word *yad*, 'hand', in v. 10 is also a euphemism for 'penis'.

26. Alan Mintz, 'The Rhetoric of Lamentations and the Representation of Catastrophe', *Prooftexts* 2 (1982), p. 4. Mintz discusses the shift of speaker from female in Lam. 1–2 to male in ch. 3, suggesting that because 'a woman's voice, according to the cultural code of Lamentations, can achieve expressivity but not reflection', the male figure is introduced in order to make meaning out of the disaster. 'This is a figure whose maleness is unambiguously declared by the use of the strong word *gever* for "man" and whose preference for theologizing rather than weeping is demonstrated throughout' (p. 9).

of many women in abusive relationships?[27] Where else can she turn except to the abuser in the hope things will improve?

In these examples of biblical violence, physical abuse is God's way of reasserting his control over the woman. The prophets enjoin the sinful woman to seek forgiveness from her abusive husband. The picture they offer suggests that abuse can be instructional and that it leads to reconciliation.[28] In Isa. 54.4-10, for example, the divine husband shows compassion on the wife he had forsaken. In Hos. 2.14-15 [Heb. 16-17], God promises to speak tenderly to his wife and restore her to favor so that she will 'respond as in the days of her youth'.[29] Her life will clearly be better, but how much better? Because the marriage relationship is one of inequality, she will always be subservient and dependent on his good will. Ezek. 16.59-63 paints a more depressing picture: God will forgive all that his unfaithful wife has done, with the result that she will never open her mouth again because of her shame. In this vision of reconciliation, the woman's lot is to be submissive and silent, which keeps her in the role of victim within the marriage relationship.

The problem we face in interpreting these passages is not just the punishment/rape imagery; the problem is the ideology that informs this imagery.[30] The concept of harlotry has meaning only within an

27. Ellwood, *Batter My Heart*, pp. 8-12.

28. Ellwood (*Batter My Heart*, pp. 9-10) likens God's change of disposition in Jer. 30.17; Isa. 42.14-16; 43.1-4, 25; 49.8-26; 51.17-23; and 54.8-11 to the behavior of a battering husband who follows abuse with repentance and sincere promises to reform.

29. Gordon and Washington ('Rape as a Military Metaphor', p. 314 n. 1) translate 'submit as in the days of her youth'; cf. the Septuagint, which reads, 'she will be humbled'. See also the discussion in Andersen and Freedman, *Hosea*, pp. 276-77. If this is the meaning (and I think obedience, faithfulness, and compliance with the husband's will is fundamentally at issue), then the bleak picture corresponds closely to that of Ezek. 16.59-63.

30. The fear of women's sexuality and the perceived need to control it motivates these and other biblical portrayals of women. By this I mean not just the negative portrayals but also the seemingly positive ones. In ancient Israel, women's sexual activity was severely circumscribed. Before marriage women were under the control of their fathers or brothers, and after marriage, of their husbands. A woman who was found not to be a virgin at marriage was to be stoned (Deut. 22.20-21). The husband had exclusive rights to his wife's sexuality (the converse was not true) and any breach of fidelity or even suspected breach of fidelity on her part was a threat to his honor that called for severe punishment (Num. 5.11-31; whether or not this trial by ordeal

ideology that views women's bodies as the property of men. Only women can be harlots or whores; in Hebrew, as in English, if the terms are applied to men it is only in an extended or figurative sense.[31] This ideology gives rise to the prophetic marriage metaphor in which the unquestioned superior male position is further privileged by placing God in the husband's position. The divine husband's superiority over his nation-wife, in turn, lends legitimacy to the human husband's superiority over his wife, who, following this model, is subservient to him and totally dependent on him.[32] Through messages about gender relations encoded in these texts, men are taught to exert their authority and women are taught to submit.[33] As Drorah Setel points out in her study of Hosean pornography, the prophetic marriage metaphor creates a contrast between God's positive (male) fidelity and Israel's negative (female) harlotry.[34] God (the male) by definition cannot be unfaithful; at most he can be, as Lamentations sometimes suggests,

was ever conducted is beside the point, since in principle the law gives the husband the *right* to demand it; for discussion, see Alice Bach, 'Good to the Last Drop: Viewing the Sotah [Numbers 5.11-31] as the Glass Half Empty and Wondering How to View It Half Full', in *The New Literary Criticism and the Hebrew Bible* [Journal for the Study of the Old Testament Supplement Series, 143; ed. J. Cheryl Exum and David J.A. Clines; Sheffield: JSOT Press, 1993], pp. 26-54). Though our modern social context is very different, this ideology remains influential, both in Western culture in general and especially for people who look to the Bible for ethical principles and moral guidance.

31. For discussion of the Hebrew root *znh* and its metaphorical use by Hosea, see Phyllis Bird, ' "To Play the Harlot": An Inquiry into an Old Testament Metaphor', in *Gender and Difference in Ancient Israel* (ed. Peggy Day; Minneapolis: Fortress Press, 1989), pp. 75-94.

32. A feature of these texts I have not developed here is the picture of the woman's utter dependence upon male support; for development of this point, see T. Drorah Setel, 'Prophets and Pornography: Female Sexual Imagery in Hosea', in *Feminist Interpretation of the Bible* (ed. Letty M. Russell; Philadelphia: Westminster Press), pp. 86-95; especially p. 92; Ellwood, *Batter My Heart*, pp. 11-12. Ezek. 23 treats this dependence theme in a perverse way; see Shields, 'Ezekiel 16: Body Rhetoric and Gender'.

33. While writing this study, I happened to watch a BBC television program called 'The Hamar Trilogy' about the Hamar women of southwest Ethiopia. In this community women are ritually beaten at a young man's coming of age ceremony, and a woman interviewed explains that it shows you love him enough to suffer for him. Wife-beating is also common; a man explains that it makes him feel like a man to beat his wife.

34. Setel, 'Prophets and Pornography', p. 93.

excessive (2.2, 17, 21; 3.43). And because most readers are likely to read with the text's ideology and privilege God, the abusive husband's behavior is not open to question. 'To involve God in an image of sexual violence', observes Judith Sanderson, 'is, in a profound way, somehow to justify it and thereby to sanction it for human males who are for any reason angry with a woman'.[35]

In our prophetic examples, sin is identified with female sexuality, and specifically, with uncontrolled or unrestrained female sexuality. 'Bad' women are promiscuous and rapacious, and female desire is consuming and dangerous. And the one who suffers from it most is the woman herself. Male control, then, is seen as necessary and desirable, and sexual abuse becomes justified as a means of correction. To make matters worse, physical assault paves the way for the abused woman's reconciliation with her abusive spouse. Abuse is thus complexly and confusingly linked with love in a pattern that consistently challenges women's sense of worth and self-esteem. A depressing body of evidence demonstrates how such texts oppress women by encouraging scapegoating and reinforcing the idea that physical abuse can be an appropriate measure for men to use against women.[36]

Gender Bias in Interpretation

In describing God's treatment of his wayward wife, the prophets rely upon a rhetorical strategy that encourages the audience to identify and sympathize with a male-identified deity. This is the privileged point of view, the 'I' that condemns the 'you', the other, whose view is not represented (Lamentations is no exception, since it uses the woman's voice to express the male point of view). When readers privilege the deity, which most readers of the Bible still do, they are forced into accepting this position, for to resist would be tantamount to challenging divine authority. This is the position taken almost without exception by biblical commentators, who, until recently,

35. Judith E. Sanderson, 'Nahum', in Newsom and Ringe (eds.), *The Women's Bible Commentary*, p. 221.

36. For a compelling application of the biblical marriage metaphor to the situation of battered women, see Ellwood, *Batter My Heart*. Ellwood also shows how child battering is part of the picture. See also Susan Brooks Thistlethwaite, 'Every Two Minutes: Battered Women and Feminist Interpretation', in *Feminist Interpretation of the Bible* (ed. Letty M. Russell; Philadelphia: Westminster Press, 1985), pp. 96-107.

have been almost without exception male. Typically these commentators either ignore the difficulties posed by this divine sexual abuse or reinscribe the gender ideology of the biblical texts; usually they do both in their ceaseless efforts to justify God. Often they not only pick up on latent gender bias in the text but also read familiar stereotypes back into it. Hans Walter Wolff, for example, sympathizes with the suffering divine husband who 'would rather not' take abusive action against his unfaithful wife but 'finds it necessary', and who strips her naked to indicate his 'freedom from the obligation to clothe her',[37] as if freedom from obligation excuses cruelty. In their Anchor Bible commentary on Hosea, Francis Andersen and Noel Freedman accept the husband's 'demand for retribution' as 'legitimate' and describe the public humiliation of the woman as a 'subtle' application of the *lex talionis* (and not, for example, as an unreasonable punitive measure or as vicious and unethical behavior).[38]

We saw above how Otto Kaiser, in his discussion of Isa. 3.16-24, reinscribes with a vengeance the ideology of the text. John Bright's Anchor Bible commentary on Jeremiah, and, more recently, William Holladay's (Hermeneia) are typical of the commentaries in these series in ignoring the problems posed by the imagery of divine sexual abuse in favor of discussion of philological and historical-critical issues. Bright, for example, in his comment on Jeremiah 13, deals only with the waistcloth incident in vv. 1-11, and has nothing to say about the

37. Wolff, *Hosea*, pp. 34, 38. When Wolff explains that God 'refuses to accept as final the divorce his wife both *desired* and *initiated*'(p. 44; italics mine), he reinscribes the textual strategy of blaming the woman (divorce was not a woman's right in Israelite society). Bernhard W. Anderson (*The Eighth Century Prophets* [Proclamation Commentaries; Philadelphia: Fortress Press, 1978], p. 89) similarly invites us to sympathize with God's suffering and to view the people's suffering as cathartic.

38. Commenting upon Hos. 2.12, they note the 'poignancy' (p. 248) of the display of the woman's naked body, but they never abandon the text's male point of view: 'Why the husband should now deliberately share this privilege [viewing his wife naked] with his rivals is not clear, although in view of the context of the former's outrage and legitimate demand for retribution (cf. v. 5), it is to be seen as a form of punishment appropriate to the crime. Just as in the past the errant wife has sought out her lovers and eagerly disrobed in their presence for the purposes of sexual gratification, so now she will be forcibly exposed in the same situation, and publicly humiliated. The subtlety of the talion here is essentially that what she did secretly and for pleasure will now be done to her openly and for her disgrace' (p. 249).

salacious verses 20-27, except that they are poetry.[39] About the same
passage Holladay speaks only of the references 'to the shocking
harlotry which that city commits, harlotry which merits her public
stripping and ravishment'.[40] Moshe Greenberg's 'holistic' approach to
Ezekiel, because it seeks to encounter the prophet on his terms, also
has the effect of suppressing the woman's point of view.[41] Walther
Eichrodt, in contrast, is not content to let the prophet speak for himself.
He is concerned with God's image in ch. 23 (though apparently
more with God's image as a husband than as an *abusive* husband): 'In
view of the way in which sex-life is elsewhere completely excluded
from the divine realm, it is monstrous to find it here stated bluntly
how God contracted a marriage with a pair of harlots'.[42] He assures
us, moreover, that the abuse imagery is not to be taken seriously.

> One can see from the very beginning that the narrative in which this is
> clothed has no importance whatsoever; this is no parable story full of
> charm and poetic beauty, like ch. 16, 17 and 19. It is an allegory, which
> gives no more than the bare essentials, and applies only a few stereotyped

39. John Bright, *Jeremiah* (Anchor Bible, 21; Garden City, NY: Doubleday,
1965), pp. 95-96. I refer to the 'Comment' section; in his textual notes to v. 22,
Bright observes that 'your skirts' is 'apparently a euphemism' and 'your heels' 'is also
a euphemism', but he leaves it to the reader to decide what the terms are euphemisms
for. Of v. 27, he writes, '"Your rutting" is literally "your neighings," i.e., animal
passion, as in v 8', and he continues, 'The verse refers to practice of the cults of pagan
gods, and the immoral rites associated with them' (p. 95).

40. Holladay, *Jeremiah 1*, p. 417. Cf. the evasive treatment of this passage in a
commentary designed as a resource for preaching (R.E. Clements, *Jeremiah*
[Interpretation, A Bible Commentary for Teaching and Preaching; Louisville: John
Knox Press, 1988], p. 87): 'Pictured in the guise of a young woman who has
abandoned all moral restraints (v. 27), Jerusalem is now to be faced with the
inevitable fate of violence and rape that awaited a young woman captured as a
prisoner of war (v. 26). The language is stark and the imagery has become rather
conventional in the wake of the earlier prophecies of Hosea. There is therefore a
certain lack of originality about it.' In another series designed to keep the 'Old
Testament alive in the Church' (p. vii), Walter Brueggemann (*To Pluck Up, to Tear
Down: A Commentary on the Book of Jeremiah 1–25* [Grand Rapids: Eerdmans, 1988],
p. 127) describes the picture of 'a humiliated slave girl' in 13.26 [!] as one of 'a rich
variety of suggestive images' that convey a 'simple message'.

41. Moshe Greenberg, *Ezekiel, 1–20* (Anchor Bible, 22; Garden City, NY:
Doubleday, 1983).

42. Walther Eichrodt, *Ezekiel* (trans. C. Quin; Old Testament Library;
Philadelphia: Westminster Press, 1970), p. 320.

pictorial images to bring out the point as clearly and unmistakably as possible. *The images which it employs have no life of their own*; their only purpose is to reproduce in quite coarse terms the unspeakable event they convey.[43]

From the scandalous imagery in Ezekiel 16, he draws a moral lesson that, like the prophetic marriage metaphor, places full responsibility for the success of the relationship upon the subordinate partner.

> The way in which expressions for God's wrath and jealousy are heaped up is to denote the inexorable, yet wholly personal, manner in which he reacts against every attempt to deny or ridicule his giving of himself in fellowship. Unless this is impressed with all possible seriousness upon the conscience of the creature, its value would become doubtful, and the absolute will behind it ambiguous. What is finally at stake is whether or not we realize the existence of that divine majesty, apart from which the dignity of man is empty or non-existent.[44]

Unfortunately, the female figure in the text has no dignity left to her.

I could easily multiply examples of biblical commentators who reinscribe the text's harmful gender ideology. What worries me most about them is the influence they have on those readers who rely on their commentaries for explication of the Bible and who often grant them the kind of authority to say 'what the text means' that they do not deserve.

The contributors to *The Women's Bible Commentary* show the difference reading as a woman makes. The authors of the entries on the prophetic books all wrestle with the implications of biblical violence against women and struggle to find ways of dealing with it. Susan Ackerman looks behind the prophetic polemic for evidence of women's real religious experience.[45] Gale Yee looks to other prophetic metaphors for the divine-human relationship as alternatives to the harmful marriage metaphor.[46] Similarly, Kathleen O'Connor finds alternative, positive models for women in certain prophetic

43. Eichrodt, *Ezekiel*, pp. 320-21, italics mine.

44. Eichrodt, *Ezekiel*, pp. 209-10. The English translation 'man' does not capture the inclusiveness of German *Mensch*: 'Es geht letztlich um die Anerkennung einer göttlichen Majestät, ohne die auch der Adel des Menschen hohl und nichtig werden müßte'; *Der Prophet Hesekiel. Kapitel 1–18* (Das Alte Testament Deutsch, 22.1; Göttingen: Vandenhoeck & Ruprecht, 1965), p. 126.

45. Ackerman, 'Isaiah', p. 162.

46. Yee, 'Hosea', pp. 200, 202.

themes (such as those that express opposition to oppression and hope for a new order of social relations based on mutuality) and in scattered instances of non-patriarchal divine imagery.[47] Katheryn Darr advocates keeping harmful texts in the canon not as an affirmation of their assertions but because they force readers to confront difficult questions.[48] Judith Sanderson, perhaps the *Commentary*'s most resistant reader, relentlessly exposes the ideological prejudices that produce such negative female imagery.[49]

I mention *The Women's Bible Commentary* to draw attention to my claim that female and male readers are likely to perceive such texts as these as making different claims upon them as readers. Although the contributors to *The Women's Bible Commentary* read this material differently, like their male counterparts they still seem to have a stake either in defending the 'real god' or defending the text, either because of their own commitment to the biblical text or for the sake of the commentary's stated audience of 'laywomen, clergywomen, and students'.[50] What distinguishes their work from that of their male counterparts is their recognition of divine sexual violence as a problem and their honesty about it.[51] One looks in vain in the standard commentaries for responses like these to the violence against women in the prophetic corpus.[52]

Regardless of how we decide to respond to it, sexual violence of which God is the perpetrator and the nation personified as a woman

47. Kathleen M. O'Connor, 'Jeremiah', in Newsom and Ringe (eds.), *The Women's Bible Commentary*, pp. 173-77.

48. Katheryn Pfisterer Darr, 'Ezekiel', in Newsom and Ringe (eds.), *The Women's Bible Commentary*, p. 190; similarly in Darr, 'Ezekiel's Justifications of God: Teaching Troubling Texts', *Journal for the Study of the Old Testament* 55 (1992), pp. 97-117.

49. See Judith E. Sanderson, 'Amos', pp. 205-209; 'Micah', pp. 215-16; and 'Nahum', pp. 217-21, in Newsom and Ringe (eds.), *The Women's Bible Commentary*.

50. Newsom and Ringe , 'Introduction', *The Women's Bible Commentary*, p. xvii.

51. This is also true of the work of Renita J. Weems, 'Gomer: Victim of Violence or Victim of Metaphor?', *Semeia* 47 (1989), pp. 87-104; Weems, *Battered Love: Marriage, Sex, and Violence in the Hebrew Prophets* (Minneapolis: Fortress Press. 1995); and Tikva Frymer-Kensky, *In the Wake of the Goddesses: Women, Culture, and the Biblical Transformation of Pagan Myth* (New York: Free Press, 1992). Their critiques are greatly tempered by the privileged position they grant the deity.

52. While I do not claim to have made an exhaustive study, Carroll's is the only major commentary I know of that faces this problem squarely insofar as he consistently reveals the power of ideology to suppress competing discourses.

is the object, along with its destructive implications for gender relations, is there. It cannot be dismissed by claiming that it is only 'metaphorical', as if metaphor were some kind of container from which meaning can be extracted, or as if gender relations inscribed on a metaphorical level are somehow less problematic than on a literal level. When, for example, Bernhard Anderson assures us the point of Hosea 2 'is not to absolutize a particular understanding of masculine–feminine relations but to lift the whole discussion up to a metaphorical level',[53] he ignores what for Yee is the crucial question: 'To whose experience does the metaphor speak, and whose experience does the metaphor exclude?' Raising this question enables Yee to conclude that 'this metaphor makes its theological point at the expense of real women and children who were and still are victims of sexual violence'.[54]

Such a conclusion as Yee's is disputed by Robert Carroll, who, in response to some of the feminist claims about the pornographic character of this material, writes as if the metaphorical violence against women were canceled out by the fact that men as well as women are the objects of the prophets' abusive language:

> If the biblical writers only used negative images of women and positive images of men, then I could see the force of the objections made by feminist readers of the Bible. But that is not the case. The metaphorization processes represent negative *and* positive images both of women and men (as metaphors!) and because such representations are inevitably metaphoric their referential force is symbolic.[55]

53. Anderson, *The Eighth Century Prophets*, p. 87. The discussion on Hosea 2 appears on pp. 86-89. Joseph Blenkinsopp (*Ezekiel* [Interpretation, A Bible Commentary for Teaching and Preaching; Louisville: John Knox Press, 1990], p. 99) similarly counsels us to 'concentrate on the point of the allegory' in Ezek. 23; he does, however, in contrast to many commentators who simply gloss over the problem, acknowledge that 'We cannot, and should not, ignore the current of antifeminism in the prophetic literature and indeed in much of the literature of antiquity…The ambiguity, suspicion, and fear aroused by female allure, and even more by the biological processes connected with birth and menstruation (one thinks of Baudelaire's *la femme est naturelle, donc abominable*), may help to explain but do nothing to render these attitudes less distasteful to the enlightened modern reader.' With regard to ch. 16, he mentions its pornographic character but chooses the unfortunate title, 'the Nymphomaniac Bride' for the section 16.1-63 (p. 76).

54. Yee, 'Hosea', p. 200; on the problem of this metaphorical divine violence, see also Weems, 'Gomer: Victim of Violence or Victim of Metaphor?'

55. Carroll, 'Desire under the Terebinths', p. 279. As I understand it, Carroll's

Carroll's observation that the 'referential force [of these metaphors] is symbolic' seems to be a special form of the 'it's only a metaphor' argument. Elsewhere he makes statements such as, 'The women in the text [Ezek. 23] are metaphors, not persons',[56] without examining how the metaphor works, what gives it its sting. The point is not that the Bible uses *positive and negative* images of *women and men*—a point that could hardly be denied—but rather that it uses a particular kind of imagery. The imagery of graphic sexual violation and abuse of a woman by a theologically justified abusive husband-deity is not addressed to women. It is, as Carroll recognizes, addressed to 'essentially a male community'. For him this seems to reduce the offensiveness that the metaphors of sexual abuse hold for women;[57] in my opinion, it intensifies it. The way to insult a man is to call him a woman. You insult him more if you call him a filthy whore who is going to have her genitals exposed, which is what these prophetic accusations do. Already inscribed in the metaphors themselves is a whole range of negative views about women and about female behavior and female

argument is that (1) these are only metaphors, (2) they are not about real women, and (3) there are negative images of men as well. Whereas I agree with Carroll that the relationship between metaphoric men and women and real men and women is a complex one, I do not accept the idea that metaphor can so neatly be separated from reality; for useful discussions of this complex issue, see Claudia V. Camp, 'Metaphor in Feminist Biblical Interpretation: Theoretical Perspectives', *Semeia* 61 (1993), pp. 3-36; Mieke Bal, 'Metaphors He Lives By', *Semeia* 61 (1993), pp. 185-207. Metaphor is a process of mapping one domain of experience onto another. That metaphoric violence against women is not the same as real violence is true, but, as I argue here, it is nonetheless harmful to real women because it shapes perceptions of reality and of gender relations for men and for women.

56. 'Desire under the Terebinths', p. 285; cf. pp. 277, 279, 283, 292, 303-304.

57. 'Desire under the Terebinths', p. 292. The citation continues: 'Feminists clearly think that the terms of abuse used in that sexual rhetoric betray more than is apparent on the surface of the language'. It is not clear to me what he means. If someone less postmodern than Carroll had made that statement, I would think its meaning is something like 'the text means what it says'. But what would that be? The example Carroll gives of negative male sexual imagery is the comparison in Ezek. 23.20, where men are 'mocked in terms of having animal-sized penises' ('Desire under the Terebinths', p. 288). I cannot imagine a man being insulted by being told he has a large penis. I suggested above that the comparison is an (unconscious) expression (fantasy) of penis envy. In any event, nothing is said about the men's behavior. If the image suggests they are 'good studs', the degree to which a man would find this suggestion objectionable is open to question.

sexuality, as well as about power in gender relations: men dominate and women submit.

Carroll's argument about prophetic rhetoric is much the same in his Jeremiah commentary, where he says, 'If feminine images of sexuality appear to be more numerous, that is because it is masculine behaviour which is being condemned: "whoring after..." is a male activity'.[58] The statement ignores the question, What have feminine images of sexuality to do with male behavior? *Why* are feminine images used in the first place? They are used because the texts under discussion here rely on a rhetorical strategy of abusing men verbally in the worst possible way—by placing them in the inferior position of a humiliated female—in order to shock them into changing their behavior. This is precisely where the problem with this kind of metaphoric abuse lies. The prophetic condemnations are aimed prin-cipally at men but the use of imagery of *female sexual sin* and *female sexual abuse* as a means of representing *male social and political sins and their consequences* reflects what amounts to a devaluation and denigra-tion of women. You insult a woman by assuming that a way to insult or put down a man is to call him a woman.

Carroll appeals to the presence of positive as well as negative images of women in the biblical text as evidence that the text is not misogy-nistic or pornographic.[59] As I have indicated, I see the question as not whether the images are positive or negative (a binary opposition I would like to avoid anyway) but how they function. The 'positive' opposite of the adulterous wife metaphor, imaging the people as God's *faithful* wife, does not exalt women, for it relies upon the same patriarchal hierarchy in which the woman remains as the subordinate, inferior member in the relationship.[60] Likewise the prospect these

58. Carroll, *Jeremiah*, p. 180; cf. 'Desire under the Terebinths', pp. 277, 279, 283.

59. Apparently it is these two terms in particular that raise Carroll's critical ire. They are, as he says, anachronistic if applied to the way ancient men viewed women. I find them nonetheless suitably descriptive of what I perceive, from my twentieth-century vantage point, as going on in the text.

60. Similarly, I do not think that offering positive images to counterbalance the negative images, as, for example, Weems (*Battered Love*) and Helen Schüngel-Straumann ('God as Mother in Hosea 11', in Brenner [ed.], *A Feminist Companion to the Latter Prophets*, pp. 194-219) do gets us very far. Reading texts against them-selves and against other texts is worth pursuing, but what is needed is something more along the lines of the analysis offered by Mieke Bal (*Death and Dissymmetry*), who finds in Yael, the Woman-with-the-Millstone, and Delilah the (missing)

texts hold out of reconciliation following punishment provides no solution to the problem posed by the imagery of sexual abuse because it is part of the pattern. It reinforces the harmful ideology of abuse as something for the victim's own good and makes acceptance of blame and submission the price of forgiveness. It leaves the woman powerless.

Claiming that there is a suffering and loving god behind this imagery will not make it go away either. For some readers of the Bible creating a canon within the canon, in which texts that are injurious are excluded, is one way of dealing with this offensive material. I prefer doing away with the notions of canon and biblical authority altogether. Because the Bible is an important part of our cultural heritage, it would be presumptuous to suggest that we can casually dispense with it. But I see no reason to privilege it. And, I would add, I think it important to recognize that God is a character in the biblical narrative (as much a male construct as the women in biblical literature) and thus not to be confused with any one's notion of a 'real' god. Increasingly, as investigation into the gender-determined nature of biblical discourse becomes more sophisticated, biblical interpreters will have to come to terms with this fact.

The problematic nature of biblical texts in which the deity violently abuses a nation metaphorically cast as a woman is gaining attention in the scholarly literature.[61] I have no solution to the problem of prophetic pornography any more than I have a solution to the problem of pornography in general. But recent work on this topic does suggest that a practical approach can yield important results, and so I would like to conclude this chapter by describing a fourfold interpretive strategy that seems to me especially promising as a response to the prophetic rhetoric of sexual abuse.

1. *Attention to the differing claims these texts make upon their male and female readers.* Readers of these texts are asked to make a dual identification—with God and with Israel—and for both sexes this involves

avenging mothers of Bath (Judg. 11), Kallah (Judg. 14), and Beth (Judg. 19); or the deconstructive reading of Sherwood, *The Prostitute and the Prophet*. Weems advocates a dual hermeneutic: 'one that helps a reader to resist the ways in which texts subjugate aspects of a reader's identity, and another that allows a reader to appreciate those aspects of texts that nurture and authorize them in their struggle for personhood' (*Battered Love*, p. 100). This hermeneutical stance serves a theological agenda; one could hardly imagine such an approach to, say, Shakespeare or Jane Austen.

61. For a variety of perspectives, see the essays in Brenner (ed.), *A Feminist Companion to the Latter Prophets*.

taking the subject position of the other sex. But pressures to identify with a particular subject position pull male and female readers in different directions. Personified Israel, whose covenant infidelity is described as harlotry, is composed of women and men (indeed, male citizens would have been the primary audience of this material). Male readers are thus placed in the subject position of women and, worse, of harlotrous, defiled, and sexually humiliated women. They are required to see themselves in the wrong and to repent and change their behavior, and because a female identification is not 'natural' for them and identification with a debased woman is shocking and repulsive, they will be anxious to cast it off. The metaphor offers them another role with which they can more readily identify, that of the faithful husband, whose point of view they are already encouraged to identify with by the prophetic rhetoric. Female readers are also called upon to adopt the divine point of view, but in our case the identification is not 'natural' because God is identified metaphorically with the male. Our 'natural' identification lies with the sinful, humiliated woman. This situation, as I said at the beginning of this chapter, forces women readers to read against our own interests and to accept the indictment of our sex encoded in these texts. Male readers, in contrast, are not reading against their interests when they adopt God's point of view toward the sinful woman. On the contrary, it is against their interests to stay in the humiliating female subject position.[62]

Recognizing how shifting subject positions function rhetorically to manipulate readers' responses along gender lines and how such rhetorical strategies affect what is at stake for female and male readers may help us all to become resisting readers. I wonder, for example,

---

62. Galambush (*Jerusalem in the Book of Ezekiel*, p. 161) describes an important effect of this rhetorical strategy on the male audience of Ezekiel: 'The depiction of Yahweh expunging his own shame by punishing (including shaming) the unfaithful Jerusalem thus serves to reinterpret the destruction of the city as a *positive* event, one that reestablishes the honor and potency of Yahweh. This metaphoric refurbishment of Yahweh's honor not only would have allowed Ezekiel's readers to avoid the shame of acknowledging their god's humiliation and defeat, but also would have allowed male Judeans to expunge their own shame by transferring it to the personified woman, Jerusalem. As men in solidarity with a divine, punishing husband, male Judeans could, at least momentarily, have seen Jerusalem (and her shame) as "other," a woman justly shamed. The humiliation of personified Jerusalem would thus paradoxically serve to recapture a sense of power and control for the militarily humiliated male residents of the city.'

how often it is the case that the imagery of female harlotry is used to describe sin but a shift occurs to male imagery (e.g., faithful sons) when reconciliation is envisioned.[63]

2. *Exposing prophetic pornography for what it is.* The prophetic texts I have cited as examples of God's sexual abuse of a nation personified as a woman contain violent representations that involve, among other atrocities, exposing the woman's genitals to view: to the view of a hostile audience posited in the text and to our, the readers', view. We are asked to adopt, and approve, the pornographic gaze at the naked and physically abused female body—pornographic because it involves objectification, domination, pain, and degradation. Doubtlessly female violation is described in such brutal detail for its shock value, but is there also some righteous satisfaction or perverse pleasure in writing about it? In reading about it, we are complicit. What do we think we are doing when we read prophetic pornography? Can we allow ourselves the moral high ground because the violence is metaphoric and presented with a theological justification; in other words, because we are reading the Bible? Can we afford to ignore the implications this imagery has for readers of the Bible, or to minimize the significance of its presence in the Bible? As Susan Griffin has shown in her subtle and compelling study, *Pornography and Silence*, it would be naive to think that pornography can be contained in such a way that it does not affect all of us. We cannot, she argues, overestimate the effect of images on our lives.

> For social science itself tells us that images shape human behavior. And thus, if the social scientist makes the argument that pornography has no effect on human behavior, we are faced with a strange and mysterious phenomenon. For in order to argue that pornography does not reach into the lives of the audience and change their behavior, we would have to say that pornographic images are different from all other images, both actual and cultural, and that the mind, when confronted with the pornographic image, suddenly acts differently than it does when confronted with any other image.[64]

63. As Mary E. Shields ('Circumcision of the Prostitute: Gender, Sexuality and the Call to Repentance in Jer. 3.1–4.4', *Biblical Interpretation* 3 [1995], pp. 61-74) shows, this is the case in Jer. 3.1–4.4. See also Shields, 'Ezekiel 16', on Ezek. 16. Galambush (*Jerusalem in the Book of Ezekiel*) documents a similar shift in imagery in Ezekiel, from the city as God's unfaithful wife to the faithful city no longer personified as a wife; threatening female elements are excluded from the vision of restoration.

64. Susan Griffin, *Pornography and Silence: Culture's Revenge against Nature* (New

Would not the ethical response to these prophetic texts be to acknowledge what it is we are reading and to take responsibility for doing something about it?[65]

3. *Looking for competing discourse(s)*. It is fair to say that female experience is denied or misnamed[66] in these examples of prophetic pornography. By asking what is the 'other' discourse with which the vituperative prophetic discourse is competing we may be able to uncover evidence of the woman's suppressed point of view in these texts. This involves looking for places where attempts to silence or

York: Harper & Row, 1981), p. 105. Further, p. 119: 'It is not in the nature of a being, a thought, or an image to be confined...The pornographic image has a life like the life of a sound wave. Set in motion in one place in a city, it affects a man walking through this part of the city. He begins to resonate with its frequency. He carries the ugliness of pornography outside this neighborhood. Let us say an image of a man beating a woman makes him more ready to strike a woman he knows. Or if this is not the case, let us say simply that he carries this image of a man striking a woman with him in his mind. Unless he repudiates this image, argues with it, decides definitely that it is not part of his nature, and rejects it, it becomes part of him. And inside his soul a man beats a woman. But this is not all. The images we carry in our minds make us into who we are...Thus, in some way, this man comes to be like the image of a man beating a woman. Perhaps he becomes more callous. Perhaps he becomes cruel to his own softness. And now we, who have not walked in the neighborhood where pornography lives, see this man, we sense his brutality, his violence... Finally, pornography has succeeded in reaching us; it has even penetrated our notion of reality.'

65. I am sure there are readers who will resist the designation 'pornographic' for this literature, and it is not my intention here to enter into a discussion of the complicated question, Exactly what constitutes pornography? For a discussion of prophetic pornography and its damaging effects, see Brenner and van Dijk-Hemmes, *On Gendering Texts*, pp. 167-95; Gordon and Washington, 'Rape as a Military Metaphor'. On Ezek. 16 and 23 as pornographic, see Galambush, *Jerusalem in the Book of Ezekiel*, pp. 124-25, 161-63 and *passim*. In a polemical exercise of his own ('Desire under the Terebinths'), Robert Carroll takes exception to Brenner's and van Dijk-Hemmes's ideological stance and their resultant interpretive claims about prophetic pornography; see the discussion above. For Brenner's latest statement, which appeared after I had completed this study, see Athalya Brenner, 'Pornoprophetics Revisited: Some Additional Reflections', *Journal for the Study of the Old Testament* 70 (1996), pp. 63-86.

66. On this phenomenon, see Setel, 'Prophets and Pornography', and van Dijk-Hemmes, 'The Metaphorization of Woman in Prophetic Speech: An Analysis of Ezekiel 23', in Brenner and van Dijk-Hemmes, *On Gendering Texts*, pp. 167-76.

suppress the woman's rival discourse, a discourse that threatens to subvert the dominant prophetic patriarchal discourse, are not completely successful.[67] For example, we can read Jer. 2.31 ('We are free; we will come no more to you') as the woman's claim to autonomy in the face of overweening possessiveness supported by patriarchal constraints; or Jer. 13.22 ('Why have these things come upon me?') as her unwillingness to accept blame. The recent studies of Fokkelien van Dijk-Hemmes and of Pete Diamond and Kathleen O'Connor profitably employ this reading strategy to challenge the dominant male discourse of Ezekiel 23 and Jeremiah 2–3 respectively. Van Dijk-Hemmes notes that the harlotrous activities of the sisters in Ezekiel 23 are described not with active verbs but in the passive: 'There their breasts were squeezed/There the teats of their maidenhood were pressed'. 'It would have been more adequate', she observes,

> to describe the events during the sisters' youth in the following manner: 'They were sexually molested in Egypt, in their youth they were sexually abused.' This way, justice would have been done to the fate of these metaphorical women, and the audience would not have been seduced into viewing women or girls as responsible for and even guilty of their own violation.[68]

Diamond and O'Connor conclude their study of Jeremiah 2–3 with similar observations:

> What would happen if female Israel told the story? Would she tell of her husband's verbal abuse, his foolish jealousy, his despicable exaggerations, his claims to have 'planted her as a choice vine' (2:21), his continual distrust of her and her sexuality? Would she recount how loving he had been and tell how he had become more and more controlling and demanding? We cannot know, of course, because in this case the husband is God, and not such a nice god, even if broken-hearted. What we do know about this metaphorical woman, though, is that she makes a moral and religious choice. She does not return to him despite the safety and social status a return might provide. She refuses to speak the words he demands of her:

---

67. For further discussion and demonstration of this approach, applied to Proverbs, see Carol A. Newsom, 'Woman and the Discourse of Patriarchal Wisdom: A Study of Proverbs 1–9', in *Gender and Difference in Ancient Israel* (ed. Peggy Day; Minneapolis: Fortress Press, 1992), pp. 142-60; for applications to prophetic texts, see Shields, 'Circumcision of the Prostitute' and 'Ezekiel 16'.

68. Van Dijk-Hemmes, 'The Metaphorization of Woman', pp. 172-73; the citation is from p. 173.

'Only acknowledge your guilt...' (3:13). She will not accept blame for the failure of the marriage, and she will not reject the gods and goddesses whom she loves. She accepts the price of her autonomy.[69]

4. *A systematic deconstructive reading of the texts in question.* Such a reading of Hosea 1–3 is offered by Yvonne Sherwood, who shows how the text contradicts its main thesis and subverts the very distinctions it makes between such 'violent hierarchies' as innocence and deviance, Yhwh and Baal, love and hate.[70] 'The text simultaneously pursues one kind of action (blessing, reconciliation) and its opposite (denunciation, violence, imprisonment and curse)', Sherwood observes.[71] God's argument that Israel loved him and betrayed him is subverted by a metaphor in which the wife is already a harlot at the point of marriage.[72] In Hos. 2.3 [Heb. v. 5] God threatens to strip the woman naked as in the day of her birth. The nakedness of the woman/land is simultaneously both infant purity, the innocence of beginning, and titillation, cruelty, and pornography.[73] It is never purely one or the other. Like the scholars mentioned above who search for the suppressed woman's competing discourse, Sherwood argues that the woman's point of view deconstructs the text's main argument, for the fact that Yhwh's wife has left him suggests some lack or inadequacy in his own character. If he is such a good husband and provider, why would she seek another? Yhwh is, moreover, tainted by and implicated in the very portrait of Baal that he so vehemently opposes.

> The text's argument depends on the premise that Yhwh is original, in both senses of the word—he is Israel's 'first husband' and he can be clearly distinguished from his rival—yet far from emphasizing Yhwh's autonomy and individuality, the text remakes him in the image of Baal. Baal is

69. A.R. Pete Diamond and Kathleen M. O'Connor, 'Unfaithful Passions: Coding Women Coding Men in Jeremiah 2–3 (4.2)', *Biblical Interpretation* 4 (1996), forthcoming.

70. *The Prostitute and the Prophet*, esp. pp. 203-53. Carroll observes that Ezek. 23 deconstructs itself but he does not show how ('Desire under the Terebinths', pp. 282-83). For some of the ethical issues raised by deconstruction, see David J.A. Clines, 'Ethics as Deconstruction, and, the Ethics of Deconstruction', in *The Bible in Ethics: The Second Sheffield Colloquium* (ed. John W. Rogerson, Margaret Davies and M. Daniel Carroll R.; Journal for the Study of the Old Testament Supplement Series, 207; Sheffield: Sheffield Academic Press, 1995), pp. 77-106.

71. *The Prostitute and the Prophet*, p. 252.

72. *The Prostitute and the Prophet*, p. 210.

73. *The Prostitute and the Prophet*, p. 211.

perceived by the woman as lover and provider, and to reclaim her
affections, Yhwh describes himself in precisely the same terms. He depicts
himself as giver of grain, wine and oil (precisely the same items attributed
to Baal) and pledges to 'seduce' the woman and to become, effectively, no
longer stern husband but rival lover…The text rejects Baal's name but
not his function: in 2.14 Yhwh pledges to lay waster her lovers' vines and
fig trees, and in 2.17 he promises to give her his own. Ironically, before he
can give, Yhwh must clear the ground of the previous giving, and the god
who claims he is original promises to repeat Baal's act of provision under
a different name.[74]

Deconstruction questions the fundamental logic of binary opposition (male/female, culture/nature, rational/emotional, objective/
subjective) and staunchly refuses to privilege *either* side of an opposition, or violent hierarchy, over its opposite. As the example from
Hosea illustrates, it unsettles the position, held by biblical narrators and
critical commentators alike, that the divine husband is in the right and
his wife is in the wrong by showing that the text cannot maintain this
distinction. Reading deconstructively offers a way of moving beyond
an either/or approach that would have us either affirm biblical portrayals of women as positive or reject them as hopelessly negative.[75]
By foregrounding what is repressed, displaced, and undecidable, it
draws attention to the inevitable traces of the woman's point of view
in male-authored texts, traces that subvert the texts' patriarchal
authority. If the voice of the other is always already inscribed within
patriarchal discourse, then women are not simply its objects, and by
taking a subject position of their own (no less shifting and unstable
than the male subject position), they cease to be powerless.

Though I have listed them separately for the purposes of discussion,
these various ways of dealing with gender-biased prophetic rhetoric
overlap, and the important work currently being done on this topic
draws on all of them.[76] Taken together they constitute not a solution
to the ethical problem of biblical violence against women but an
important rhetorical counter-strategy for dealing with it.

74. *The Prostitute and the Prophet*, p. 224.

75. See David Rutledge, 'Faithful Reading: Poststructuralism and the Sacred',
Biblical Interpretation, forthcoming.

76. Especially the studies mentioned above by Shields, Brenner and van Dijk-
Hemmes, Gordon and Washington, Diamond and O'Connor, and Sherwood.

5

Is This Naomi?

When they came to Bethlehem, the whole town
was stirred because of them, and the women said,
'Is this Naomi?'
Ruth 1.19

Influence, as I conceive it, means that there are
no texts, but only relationships *between* texts.
These relationships depend upon a critical act, a
misreading or misprision, that one poet performs
upon another, and that does not differ in kind
from the necessary critical acts performed by
every strong reader upon every text he [*sic*]
encounters.
Harold Bloom, *A Map of Misreading*

A painting by Philip Hermogenes Calderon (1833–1898), in the
Walker Art Gallery in Liverpool, is my point of departure for this
chapter (fig. 5.1).[1] When I first saw this painting, I knew only that its
subject was the book of Ruth, and I must admit that it took me a
moment to make the connection between the painting and the biblical story. Clearly the woman in white was Ruth. But who was she
embracing? The pose struck me as romantic, even erotic, and to this
day the figure clasped in Ruth's arms looks to me like Rudolph
Valentino. Upon reflection, it seemed evident that the figure must be
Naomi and that, if the painting is meant to represent some episode in
the book of Ruth, it can only be Naomi's leave-taking of her
daughters-in-law and Ruth's dramatic display of loyalty.

But is the identification so straightforward? Is this Naomi? (I take
the question from the women of Bethlehem, who, in Ruth 1.19,
have difficulty recognizing Naomi too.) I have shown this painting
to friends, colleagues, students in class, and to anyone I can persuade

1.   I wish to thank Anna Piskorowski of the Department of Biblical Studies,
University of Sheffield, for bringing this painting to my attention.

Figure 5.1. Philip Hermogenes Calderon, *Ruth and Naomi*, The Board of Trustees of the National Museums & Galleries on Merseyside, Walker Art Gallery, Liverpool

to look at it, giving them only the same initial information I had: the painting's subject is the book of Ruth. So far, opinion is fairly evenly divided between those who think the figures embracing each other are Ruth and Naomi and those who identify them as Ruth and Boaz. In favor of the identification of the figure in black as Boaz are the facts that he is significantly taller than Ruth; his clothing, both the long-sleeved robe and the more elaborate headdress, is different from the women's; and—the strongest argument—the figures appear to be locked in a romantic embrace. Indeed, Ruth, who is dressed in white like a bride, has what could be called a look of rapture upon her face. Who, then, is the figure in blue to the side? A servant? She alone carries what appear to be provisions. Is *this* Naomi? 'Naomi' was the answer I most often received from viewers who take the central figures to be Ruth and Boaz. Naomi, who observes the match she has made, is now tangential, if not quite left out of the picture. This answer and its implications, I think, are suggestive, though if one looks at the original painting and not a reproduction, this woman seems rather young to be the other's mother-in-law. Another possibility is that she is Boaz's wife—thus filling a gap already perceived by the rabbis and echoed in modern commentary. No wife is mentioned in the story, but is it likely that Boaz would be unmarried? Is his wife dead? (According to one midrashic source, Boaz's wife died the day Ruth arrived in Bethlehem.)[2]

Those who see the figures as Ruth and Naomi argue along the lines indicated above: there is no other scene in the book that fits this picture. In Ruth 1.8-18, the widowed Naomi urges her two recently widowed daughters-in-law to return to their mothers' houses, with the hope that they still might be able to find husbands.[3] In an emotional scene, where twice they burst into tears, she kisses them and bids them farewell. Orpah follows Naomi's advice and returns to her own people, but Ruth clings to her and makes her famous vow of loyalty, 'Where you go I will go, where you lodge I will lodge, your people shall be my people and your god my god...' (v. 16). Only this scene can account for the young woman in blue in the painting, looking on, with a bundle of possessions under her arm: she is Orpah, preparing to return home, while Ruth clings to her mother-in-law. In the biblical account, in contrast, Ruth never openly embraces Boaz. Her one intimate scene with Boaz is on the threshing floor at night, not in the desert in broad daylight—and not with someone watching.

What interests me about the conflicting identifications of this couple is not which is right and which is wrong, but the fact that

---

2.   *B. Bat.* 91a. As Jack M. Sasson (*Ruth: A New Translation with a Philological Commentary and a Formalist-Folklorist Interpretation* [Baltimore: Johns Hopkins University Press, 1979], p. 81) points out, 'In a polygamous society, however, such a coincidence would not be necessary'. It would be odd for the story not to mention it if Boaz had another wife. Most readers assume he did not, and as Francis Landy ('Ruth and the Romance of Realism, or Deconstructing History', *Journal of the American Academy of Religion* 62 [1994], p. 289) observes, it 'indeed makes a better story'. If we take the woman in the painting as Boaz's wife, living or dead, she is on her way out, so to speak.

3.   On the mother's house and its role in making marriage arrangements, see Carol Meyers, ' "To Her Mother's House": Considering a Counterpart to the Israelite *Bet 'ab*', in *The Bible and the Politics of Exegesis: Essays in Honor of Norman K. Gottwald on His Sixty-fifth Birthday* (ed. D. Jobling, P.L. Day and G.T. Sheppard; Cleveland: Pilgrim Press, 1991), pp. 39-51.

opinion is so clearly and strongly divided, and the arguments each side brings forward in favor of its view. If viewers cannot agree on the sex of the person in black, then clearly there is something androgynous about this figure. I suspect that if the picture were cropped to show only the embracing couple (fig. 5.2), and no clue as to who they might be were provided, most people would say they are a man and a woman.

Now one could argue that literary and artistic competence will settle the issue. Above I used the terms 'evident' and 'it can only be' in identifying the scene painted by Calderon as Naomi's taking leave of her daughters-in-law. These terms invoke a certain kind of competence that is required to make this identification; specifically, sufficient knowledge of the painting's source text to identify the event represented in the painting with a particular event in the story. Familiarity with High Victorian painting and its conventions, especially the Classical revival of the 1860s, will also help (Calderon's painting was voted the best religious picture of the 1886 Royal Academy Exhibition). But as Mieke Bal demonstrates so forcefully in her study, *Reading 'Rembrandt'*, this kind of competence, while offering a powerful interpretive tool, also exercises a powerful control over

Figure 5.2. *Calderon, detail*

interpretation. By providing a programme of how to analyze a work of art, it encourages us to interpret within established parameters and thus can prevent us from noticing details that don't fit and from exploring alternative interpretations.[4] Certainly the scene from the book of Ruth in which Ruth 'clave unto' her mother-in-law, as the King James Version has it, is well-known enough, and a competent reading will recognize it as Calderon's source. But such a competent reading is likely to ignore the mannish appearance of the figure in black and to suppress the erotic element in the painting. Thus a good case can be made for misreading. Every reading is in some sense a misreading, as Harold Bloom has helped us to appreciate.[5] Identifying the figure in black with Boaz opens new possibilities for interpretation. The question is not just one of competence, but of the implicit sexual character of the scene and the sexually ambivalent nature of the figure in black. Unlike Ruth and Orpah, this figure is almost totally covered by clothing. We cannot see the arms or hands (though the part of one hand visible around Ruth's waist looks rather large for a woman— but then, so does Orpah's hand). The features, in profile, are not soft, but neither are they harsh. The person has no beard, which suggests she might be a woman, but this does not rule out the possibility that he is a man.

The dual identifications of the embracing couple as Ruth and Naomi and Ruth and Boaz are, in fact, both based on knowledge of the biblical book. Each fastens upon a moment of intimacy in the book of Ruth to supply the context for its interpretation. There are two deeply personal and compelling encounters described in the biblical story. The one between Ruth and Naomi is straightforwardly

---

4.   Bal, *Reading 'Rembrandt'*, esp. pp. 177-215.

5.   See Harold Bloom, *The Anxiety of Influence: A Theory of Poetry* (New York: Oxford University Press, 1973) and *A Map of Misreading* (New York: Oxford University Press, 1975). I do not mean to indicate a wholesale agreement with Bloom's theory of the anxiety of influence, which focuses primarily upon authorship and by extension upon criticism; for one thing, feminist scholars have criticized its gender blindness; see, e.g., Sandra M. Gilbert and Susan Gubar, *The Madwoman in the Attic: The Woman Writer and the Nineteenth-Century Literary Imagination* (New Haven: Yale University Press, 1979), pp. 46-92; Annette Kolodny, 'A Map for Rereading: Gender and the Interpretation of Literary Texts', in *The New Feminist Criticism: Essays on Women, Literature, and Theory* (ed. Elaine Showalter; New York: Pantheon Books, 1985), pp. 46-62.

told, but still gapped[6] (*why* would Ruth make such a choice?); the other, that between Ruth and Boaz, is related more cryptically and suggestively (the conundrum, what happened between them on the threshing floor?). These scenes have become focal points of critical interpretation, where comments about the 'radicality of Ruth's act'[7] and Ruth's 'extraordinary attachment to her mother-in-law'[8] 'contre toute raison'[9] have become critical commonplaces and discussion of what did or did not transpire on the threshing floor fills pages of commentary. These scenes are also focal points of appropriation by same-sex and opposite-sex interests.

Under the category of same-sex relationships, I am concerned not simply with sexual orientation but with accounts of the strong bond between two women that range from deep and abiding friendship to lesbianism. By opposite sex interests, I refer to interpretations influenced by the (not necessarily conscious) desire to foreground the

6.   For a classic discussion of gapping, which has become rather controversial, see Meir Sternberg, *The Poetics of Biblical Narrative: Ideological Literature and the Drama of Reading* (Bloomington: Indiana University Press, 1985), pp. 186-229. For some of the controversy, see Danna Nolan Fewell and David M. Gunn, 'Tipping the Balance: Sternberg's Reader and the Rape of Dinah', *Journal of Biblical Literature* 110 (1991), pp. 193-211; Meir Sternberg, 'Biblical Poetics and Sexual Politics: From Reading to Counterreading', *Journal of Biblical Literature* 111 (1992), pp. 463-88. See also the criticisms of gap-filling hypotheses in Bal, *Lethal Love*, pp. 10-36.

7.   James G. Williams, *Women Recounted: Narrative Thinking and the God of Israel* (Sheffield: Almond Press, 1982), p. 86.

8.   André LaCocque, *The Feminine Unconventional: Four Subversive Figures in Israel's Tradition* (Minneapolis: Fortress Press, 1990), pp. 105-106. LaCocque also refers to Ruth's 'fidelity that transcends all other considerations' (p. 105) and 'total relinquishment of her self ' (p. 106); similarly, D. Harvey ('Ruth', *The Interpreter's Dictionary of the Bible*, IV) speaks of the 'unselfish devotion of Ruth to Naomi' (p. 133) and 'a tale of human kindness and devotion transcending the limits of national- or self-interest' (p. 131). Cf. also Paul Joüon, *Ruth: Commentaire philologique et exégétique* (Subsidia Biblica, 9; Rome: Biblical Institute Press, 2nd edn, 1986), p. 2: '[Ruth] est admirable dan son dévoûment pour sa belle-mère...'; Leon Morris, *Ruth* (Tyndale Old Testament Commentaries; London: Tyndale Press, 1968), p. 314: 'The love of Ruth for her mother-in-law shines through this book...'; Erich Zenger, *Das Buch Ruth* (Zürcher Bibelkommentare AT, 8; Zürich: Theologischer Verlag, 1986), p. 41: 'eine grenzenlose Solidarität'; Johanna W.H. Bos, 'Out of the Shadows: Genesis 38; Judges 4:17-22; Ruth 3', *Semeia* 42 (1988), p. 64: 'what an alliance between women can accomplish'.

9.   Kirsten Nielsen, 'La choix contre de droit dans le livre de Ruth: De l'aire de battage au tribunal', *Vetus Testamentum* 35 (1985), p. 204.

heterosexual relationship at the expense of the bond between women, which results in a romanticizing of the relationship between Ruth and Boaz. It is not a question of the existence of the heterosexual bond but of its intensity. Again, the issue is not which side is 'right', but the fact that advocates for both same-sex and opposite-sex relationships can and do lay claim to this text. The problematic I want to examine can be illustrated by Ruth's famous oath of loyalty in ch. 1:

> Entreat me not to leave you[10]
> or to return from following you,
> for where you go, I will go,
> where you lodge, I will lodge;
> your people shall be my people,
> and your god, my god.[11]
> Where you die, I will die,
> and there I will be buried.
> May Yahweh do to me and more also
> if even death parts me from you (Ruth 1.16-17).

This supreme statement of commitment has a life outside the text. As Elizabeth Cady Stanton observes, 'Her expressions of steadfast friendship in making her decision were so tender and sincere that they have become household words'.[12] In a striking cultural transformation, this oath of loyalty spoken by one woman to another has been taken over as part of the traditional wedding vow, where its application to heterosexual marriage has the effect of erasing the bond between women, especially for people who do not know its original

---

10. The Hebrew is stronger: Edward F. Campbell, Jr (*Ruth* [Anchor Bible, 7; Garden City, NY: Doubleday, 1975], p. 61) translates, 'Do not press me to abandon you', but I have followed the more beautiful and familiar 'entreat me not'. 'Leave' (*'azab*), something Ruth will not do, is the term in Gen. 2.24, where a man leaves his mother and father to cleave to his wife, as Ruth does to Naomi; see below.

11. Literally, 'your people, my people; your god, my god'. We could read this phrase, or part of it, as present tense; cf. Campbell, *Ruth*, p. 62: 'Your people become my people;/ Your God is now my God'.

12. Elizabeth Cady Stanton, 'The Book of Ruth', in *A Feminist Companion to Ruth* (ed. Athalya Brenner; Sheffield: Sheffield Academic Press, 1993), p. 21. Cf. Hans Wilhelm Hertzberg, *Die Bücher Josua, Richter, Ruth* [Das Alte Testament Deutsch, 9; Göttingen: Vandenhoeck & Ruprecht, 1969], p. 264), who says of Ruth's motivation, 'sie folgt einfach dem Zuge des Herzens', but of her oath observes, '…der etwas sentimentale Gebrauch, der bei uns mitunter von ihnen gemacht wird, entspricht nicht der Meinung des Buches Ruth'.

context.[13] It thus exemplifies the kind of gender blurring or exchange of gender positions I examine below as taking place within the book of Ruth itself.

My subject, then, is relationships—same-sex and opposite-sex relationships in the book of Ruth as they are commented on or transformed through cultural appropriation—and I shall use both nonliterary and literary metatexts as examples. Calderon's painting is my primary metatext, because it so vividly problematizes the issue of bonding by giving us an androgynous subject, and I will return to it repeatedly in the course of my discussion. My other visual metatext is the 1960 Hollywood film, *The Story of Ruth*. The literary metatexts I draw on are poems by Victor Hugo, Else Lasker-Schüler, and Maureen Duffy, and two novels, Thomas Hardy's *Far from the Madding Crowd*, and Fannie Flagg's *Fried Green Tomatoes at the Whistle Stop Cafe*.[14] Biblical commentary provides a range of scholarly metatexts, while Gerry Brenner's fictitious interview with the biblical Ruth and essays from a recent collection of reflections on the book of Ruth, *Reading Ruth: Contemporary Women Reclaim a Sacred Story*, offer popular interpretations. Without privileging any of these metatexts, I want to see how they respond to the questions about bonding raised by Calderon's painting. The arbitrariness of my choices is offset by the fact that they are meant to be illustrative; other examples of readings that advocate same-sex and opposite-sex relationships could easily be supplied. After considering how the book of Ruth lends itself to appropriation in support of same-sex and opposite-sex bonding, I shall come back to

13.   I am aware of the custom of using these verses from Ruth as part of the wedding vow in the USA, UK, Germany, and the Netherlands.

14.   Although I do not use it as one of my metatextual examples, Amos Oz's short story, 'The Hill of Evil Counsel' deserves mention because of its provocative inversions and reworkings of themes from the book of Ruth. For perceptive comments on the relationship, see Nehama Aschkenasy, *Eve's Journey: Feminine Images in Hebraic Literary Tradition* (Philadelphia: University of Pennsylvania Press, 1986), pp. 85-92; see also, for a feminist critique of the portrayal of women in Oz's fiction, Esther Fuchs, *Israeli Mythogynies: Women in Contemporary Hebrew Fiction* (Albany: State University of New York Press, 1987), pp. 59-85. For comments on another group of metatexts, see Eve Walsh Stoddard, 'The Genealogy of Ruth: From Harvester to Fallen Woman in Nineteenth-Century England', in *Old Testament Women in Western Literature* (ed. Raymond-Jean Frontain and Jan Wojcik; Conway, AR: UCA Press), pp. 205-36.

the book of Ruth and pursue the problem raised by the book and by Calderon's painting: the problem of the third person.

Ruth and Naomi

In the previous sentence I used the phrase, 'lends itself to', almost personifying the book of Ruth as if it had the power to encourage certain readings. It is generally accepted in criticism today that gender, race, ethnicity, social location, and a range of other factors influence the way we read. Indeed, there is nothing to stop readers reading as they please, finding in texts the meanings they are looking for. But the text does play a role in the reading process. Texts need readers to actualize them, but readers need texts to actualize. 'Reading' implies reading something. To use a musical analogy, if reading is performance and not composition, it needs a score (though performances may vary greatly). Where matters sexual are involved, as in the case of Ruth, there is more at stake, and reading tends to become emotionally charged.

So what features of the book of Ruth do readers latch onto to produce readings that affirm same-sex relationships? First and foremost, Ruth's stirring oath of loyalty to Naomi, one of the most beautiful and profound expressions of attachment of one human being to another in literature.[15] What Ruth gives up for Naomi's sake is no small matter: she turns her back on her homeland, her people, her god, and in their place adopts Naomi's. '[N]ot even Abraham's leap of faith surpasses this decision of Ruth's. And there is more. Not only has Ruth broken with family, country, and faith, but she has also reversed sexual allegiance...One female has chosen another female in a world where life depends upon men. There is no more radical decision in all the memories of Israel', writes Phyllis Trible eulogistically.[16] The last part of Ruth's speech, which I translated above as 'if even

15.   Cf. Sasson, *Ruth*, p. 28: 'one of literature's most poignant declarations of affection and love'. This is a commonly expressed opinion.

16.   Trible, *God and the Rhetoric of Sexuality*, p. 173. Cf. Zenger, *Das Buch Ruth*, p. 41: 'In ihrer Liebe bindet Ruth sich an all Dimensionen der sozialen und religiösen Existenz der Naemi: Sie läßt ihren eigenen Ursprung und ihre bisherigen Bindungen zurück, doch in ihrer Lebensgemeinschaft mit Naemi wird ihr ein neues Gottesverhältnis und eine neue soziale Heimat geschenkt. Das ist die Paradoxie der Liebe: Wer sich dem anderen vorbehaltlos hingibt, findet sich selbst in seiner Hingabe neu wieder.'

death parts me from you' is translated by Edward Campbell as, 'If even death will separate/Me from you'. Campbell argues that Ruth here accepts Israelite burial custom: her bones will be interred with Naomi's and thus even death will not separate them.[17] Whether or not burial in the same ancestral tomb is the issue,[18] it is clear that this is a lifelong commitment; Ruth swears that nothing will ever separate them. What would happen, for example, if Ruth were to marry not (as it turns out) someone related to Naomi, but rather a stranger? Clearly, she would not enter the household of a new husband if it meant that she would have to forsake Naomi. She vows by Naomi's and her god that this bond will not be broken.

In addition to Ruth's speech, other language in the book suggests the intensity of her devotion to Naomi. Ruth 'left [her] father and mother' (2.11) and 'cleaved (*dabeqah*) to her' (1.14). This is the language used of the first couple in Eden: 'Therefore a man leaves his father and his mother and cleaves (*dabaq*) to his wife' (Gen. 2.24). The appearance of terminology commonly understood to represent the marriage bond and its use (whether deliberate or not) to describe a bond between women sets the stage for the appropriation of the book for same-sex relationships.

The book of Ruth does not explicitly state that Naomi returns Ruth's affection. The question is, What, if any, significance should we attach to this fact? In ch. 1, Naomi displays concern for the welfare of her daughters-in-law when she urges them to return to their mothers' houses. Although she ignores Ruth's presence at the end of that chapter (v. 21, 'the Lord has brought me back empty'), by ch. 2 she has acknowledged their familial bond in speaking of 'a relative of *ours*' and 'one of *our* redeemers'. 'Relinquishing isolation, the mother-in-law embraces the daughter-in-law who has already embraced her', comments Trible.[19] But one can find signs of her

---

17. Campbell, *Ruth*, pp. 74-75; similarly, Trible, *God and the Rhetoric of Sexuality*, p. 173: 'not "until death us do part" but beyond death'.

18. Against Campbell, see Sasson, *Ruth*, p. 31, for defense of the traditional understanding, 'if anything but death parts us' (his translation, p. 28); see also Zenger, *Das Buch Ruth*, p. 42.

19. Trible, *God and the Rhetoric of Sexuality*, p. 179; see also Bos, 'Out of the Shadows', pp. 58-64. Bos observes, 'Not until the alliance becomes reciprocal can Ruth make her final and best move' (p. 64). On indirect narrator's texts as clues to the transformation of Naomi's state of mind, see Ellen van Wolde, 'Texts in Dialogue

feelings for Ruth even before the story actually gets underway. 'Naomi had already proved the strength of her love by her acceptance of Ruth throughout Ruth's barrenness, her desire for grandchildren and descendants notwithstanding', write psychiatrists Roberta Apfel and Lise Grondahl.[20] This sentiment is echoed in an essay in the same collection by Ruth Anna Putnam:

> How can we say, then, that Naomi gave nothing to Ruth or that Ruth did not accept what was given to her? Naomi, by accepting Ruth and Orpah as daughters-in-law, by treating them with respect and love rather than disdain and resentment, taught Ruth to be the kind of friend she was to become. Again, when Naomi warned Ruth against accompanying her to the land of Judah, when she was prepared to give up her last tenuous connection to her dead son for the sake of an easier life for Ruth, was she not offering up everything she had? Finally, though the risk in going to the threshing floor appeared to be all Ruth's, must we not recognize that if the plan had failed Ruth might have had no choice but to return to Moab, that is, to leave Naomi utterly alone? What we learn, I think, is that friendship indeed involves an equal giving and receiving, but that the equality need not be apparent at first glance.[21]

Clearly, the narrator does not have to attest directly to Naomi's affection for Ruth for readers to find in her behavior a genuine solicitude for her daughter-in-law, or a 'parable of friendship'.[22] Indeed, few have questioned this as a tale of *mutual* concern and loyalty (*ḥesed*).[23]

with Texts: Intertextuality in the Ruth and Tamar Narratives', *Biblical Interpretation*, forthcoming.

20.   Roberta Apfel and Lise Grondahl, 'Feminine Plurals', in *Reading Ruth: Contemporary Women Reclaim a Sacred Story* (ed. Judith A. Kates and Gail Twersky Reimer; New York: Ballantine Books, 1994), p. 59.

21.   Ruth Anna Putnam, 'Friendship', in Kates and Reimer (eds.), *Reading Ruth: Contemporary Women Reclaim a Sacred Story*, p. 52. Cf. Morris, *Ruth*, p. 241: 'The book is a book about friendship. The devotion that Ruth shows to Naomi and the care that Naomi exercises towards Ruth run through the book.'

22.   Gloria Goldreich, 'Ruth, Naomi, and Orpah: A Parable of Friendship', in Kates and Reimer (eds.), *Reading Ruth: Contemporary Women Reclaim a Sacred Story*, pp. 33-43.

23.   For readings that pursue the possibility that the women are not deeply devoted to each other, see Danna Nolan Fewell and David Miller Gunn, *Compromising Redemption: Relating Characters in the Book of Ruth* (Louisville: Westminster/John Knox Press, 1990); Gerry Brenner, 'Readers Responding: An Interview with Biblical Ruth', *Soundings* 73 (1990), pp. 233-55; and contrast the more traditional view expressed by Campbell, *Ruth*, and Robert L. Hubbard, *The Book of Ruth*

Judith Ochshorn has only good things to say about this book in which 'the central result—the birth of David's ancestor—issues from the love of women for each other'.[24]

As a matter of fact, the biblical narrator does not state that Ruth loved Naomi either. That statement is found in the mouth of other characters in the story. The women of Bethlehem tell Naomi that the son born to Ruth and Boaz will be a restorer of life for her and nourisher of her old age, 'for', they add, 'your daughter-in-law who loves you, who is more to you than seven sons, has borne him' (Ruth 4.15). While we might question their reliability,[25] we could also attach significance to the fact that others in the story world recognize Ruth's *love*, and that these characters give us their perspective on Naomi's point of view: 'more *to you* than seven sons'. Seven was the 'Israelite ideal number of sons' and 'to say that one woman was worth seven men was the ultimate tribute—particularly in a story so absorbed with having a son!'[26]

Whereas biblical commentators generally acknowledge the strong commitment of the two women to each other, more radical appropriation of the Ruth–Naomi bond for same-sex relationships takes place, not surprisingly, outside of scholarly works. This may be due largely to the scholarly concern with the book's original meaning or

(Grand Rapids: Eerdmans, 1988) that the major characters all exemplify *ḥesed* in their relationships with one another. Fewell and Gunn see Naomi as self-centered, if not selfishly motivated, throughout—a refreshing alternative to the uncomplicated readings of, e.g., Campbell, *Ruth*; Trible, *God and the Rhetoric of Sexuality*; and Katherine Doob Sakenfeld, *Faithfulness in Action* (Philadelphia: Fortress Press, 1985), pp. 32-35.

24.   Judith Ochshorn, *The Female Experience and the Nature of the Divine* (Bloomington: Indiana University Press, 1981), p. 187.

25.   Wilhelm Rudolph, for example (*Das Buch Ruth, Das Hohe Lied, Die Klagelieder* [Kommentar zum Alten Testament XVII, 1-3; Gütersloh: Gerd Mohn, 1962], p. 70), assumes the women exaggerate when they declare Ruth worth more than seven sons: 'wie die Frauen übertreibend sagen'. In Robert Alter's classic description of narrative reliability, we should give most weight to what the narrator says, then to what characters say, and next to what they do (*The Art of Biblical Narrative* [New York: Basic Books, 1981], pp. 114-30). See also Adele Berlin, *Poetics and Interpretation of Biblical Narrative* (Sheffield: Almond Press, 1983), pp. 97-98. Berlin (p. 88) translates, 'is better for you than seven sons'; that is, Ruth has done for Naomi what her sons did not (but then why seven?). Similarly, Hubbard, *The Book of Ruth*, p. 273: Ruth has proved better than seven sons.

26.   Hubbard, *The Book of Ruth*, p. 273, expresses here a common interpretation.

canonical context, but it also, I suspect, reflects scholarship's hetero-sexist bias.[27] In this case scholars do not, as so often elsewhere, engage in speculative gap filling, or 'read between the lines'.[28] Other readers, however, have been less hampered by convention. Maureen Duffy, in her poem, 'Mother and the Girl', picks up on the textual gaps surrounding Naomi's feelings for Ruth when she describes Naomi as not understanding the nature of Ruth's devotion. True, Naomi appreciates the solicitude of a daughter-in-law who always welcomed her, gave her the 'best stool' and 'hottest dish' and asked 'if she was comfortable', and who, after Mahlon's death, 'organized everything'. But to Naomi, Ruth 'had always been such a strange girl', and 'she could never decide whether she'd really loved her son'. With regard to Ruth, Duffy also exploits textual gaps when she hints at lesbian desire on Ruth's part. The strongest intimations appear at the end of the poem, after Ruth has asked Naomi's advice about Boaz's proposal:

> And Naomi said, 'He's a good catch.
> Land him,' as if her son had never
> been born. Ruth wept a night
> and in the morning told him
> thinking how the sun
> fell through Naomi's hair
> and played on her shoulders
> and breasts as she splashed
> them with water and that
> Judah hadn't been that hospitable
> they weren't that over the moon
> to see her back. 'Listen,'
> she said to Boaz. 'Your kinsman's
> widow, she's been like a second
> mother to me. I couldn't

27. For a telling critique of this bias as it affects scholarly treatments of Paul's discussion of homosexuality in Rom. 1, where the stakes are particularly high and thus interests are jealously guarded, see Dale B. Martin, 'Heterosexism and the Interpretation of Romans 1.18-32', *Biblical Interpretation* 3 (1995), pp. 332-55. With Martin, I use 'heterosexist' in the sense of a bias regarding sexual orientation that takes heterosexuality as the norm.

28. I refer here to the way Rebecca Alpert ('Finding Our Past: A Lesbian Interpretation of the Book of Ruth', in Kates and Reimer [eds.], *Reading Ruth: Contemporary Women Reclaim a Sacred Story*, pp. 91-96) describes lesbian feminist reading; see below.

> just walk out and leave her.'
> And he looking at her rich
> pastures said: 'Fine, bring
> the old lady if you want her.'
> And Ruth said: 'I do, I do.'

Duffy does not explain Ruth's weeping for us, allowing us to imagine more than one cause: tears for Mahlon, tears over Naomi's insensitivity, tears at the thought that her life together with Naomi would be disrupted by the presence of a third person, a man. If the thought of the sun falling on Naomi's hair and playing on her shoulders is suggestive of this last possibility, the inclusion of 'breasts' in Ruth's reverie invites an interpretation in terms of erotic desire. This impression is strengthened by Duffy's appropriation and emphatic repetition of the words, 'I do', which call to mind the wedding vow. Not only has the poet followed the precedent set by the biblical narrator who used language reminiscent of Gen. 2.24 in describing Ruth's commitment to Naomi, she also turns the tables on those who have incorporated the words of Ruth 1.16-17 in traditional heterosexual marriage ceremonies.

In Fannie Flagg's novel, *Fried Green Tomatoes at the Whistle Stop Cafe*, the lesbian relationship between Ruth and Idgie is more explicitly developed than in the popular Hollywood film based on the book. Well before Ruth is married it is evident that Ruth and Idgie love each other. When Ruth decides to leave her abusive marriage, the text of Ruth 1.16-20, the biblical Ruth's stirring oath of loyalty to another woman, is the sole content of the letter her modern namesake sends to Idgie to declare her love and to let her know that she wants to live with her. To Idgie's parents she makes a pledge that also has resonances with the biblical Ruth's oath: 'I'll never leave again. I should never have left her four years ago, I know that now. But I'm going to try and make it up to her and never hurt her again. You have my word on that.' Idgie's mother tells her, '...we couldn't be happier for our little girl to have such a sweet companion as you'. It is a lifelong relationship.

Other examples of lesbian appropriation of the book of Ruth, both in the search for role models in general and in ceremonies of commitment in particular, are given by Rebecca Alpert in a sensitive essay devoted primarily to writing lesbian midrash. While affirming that commitment, family, friendship, and cross-cultural and intergenerational relationships are important issues in the book, Alpert stresses that 'without romantic love and sexuality, the story of Ruth and Naomi loses much of its power as a model for Jewish lesbian relationships'. She therefore advocates reading Ruth 'through the lens of lesbian feminist experience'.[29]

> When other scholars and commentators look at the Book of Ruth, they fail to see what we see. They are sure that Ruth means only to dedicate herself to Naomi's God. They are convinced that the important love relationship is the one between Ruth and Boaz. They can't imagine that there is a theme of love between women written between the lines.[30]

Her concluding comments illustrate forcefully the point I want to make: that readers can and will claim the right to interpretation of their cultural heritage as they see fit.

> We must insist on our right to find hints of the existence of women like ourselves in the past where we can. Reading Ruth this way should be considered an obligation to our nameless ancestors, to give them, too, an opportunity to speak. It is our hope that our midrash will find an honored place in Jewish tradition.[31]

This brings us back to Calderon's painting. It, too, by virtue of the intensity and tenderness of the embrace, the look of rapture on Ruth's face, and the erotic pose struck by the couple, suggests a sexual dimension to the relationship between the two women. They appear oblivious to the presence of another woman, who looks on approvingly. Only she holds a bundle under her arm. Is she holding everyone's possessions? Have Ruth and Naomi forgotten theirs, so wrapped up are they in each other? Orpah, with her pack, is ready to start the journey home, where her future lies; does their lack of accoutrements signify that Ruth and Naomi have found their destination in each other? Alternatively, these are all of Naomi's worldly possessions, which Orpah is holding for her.[32] Ruth will make the journey with

29. Alpert, 'Finding Our Past', p. 93.
30. Alpert, 'Finding Our Past', p. 95.
31. Alpert, 'Finding Our Past', p. 96; cf. in the same volume, Apfel and Grondahl, 'Feminine Plurals', p. 60: 'Though Naomi and Ruth were mother-in-law and daughter-in-law, we see similarities to some other relationships between women that go beyond the usual limitations to a true, lifelong love relationship'.
32. There is a textual gap involving the women's preparations for the return to Judah. All three women set out on the road to return to Judah. Have Ruth and Orpah been planning to go with Naomi to Judah; if not, why does she have to urge them to 'return'?

Naomi with nothing but the clothes on her back and her unswerving devotion—an indication of her total commitment. The couple's faces are close together, and Ruth's head is cast back dramatically, as though she were poised to be kissed on the neck or to swoon. The position of Ruth's hands indicates that she is holding on fervently. Her right hand, with fingers splayed, grasps Naomi just below her neck and pulls her toward her. With her other hand she seems to be clutching Naomi's arm or holding it firmly in place around her waist. Sharing the foreground with them is a large green cactus—uncultivated, untamed, prickly and dangerous in appearance, but sweet and fleshy inside.[33] Might we take it, merging as it does on canvas behind the women in the general area of their genitals, as somehow suggestive of female sexuality? Like the cactus, there may be more to this embrace than meets the eye.

Enter Boaz, or How a Man Changes the Picture

Readers cannot ignore the strength of the bond between women to which the book of Ruth testifies and, indeed, commentators praise it. But it is a bond made in the absence of men. What happens when a man comes along? Inevitably, he becomes a center of interest. The book of Ruth is not a story about how two women make a life together in a man's world (though it is that in part), but a story about the continuity of a family,[34] and this requires the presence of a man.

33.   There was some debate in the local press, especially at the time the picture was exhibited, over the presence of the prickly pear, which is not native to Palestine. The following remark from the *Art Journal* of 1886, p. 185, is typical: 'The figures of the mother and daughter [*sic*] are beautiful and impressive, but it is safe to say no such Ruth and Naomi ever dwelt in Moab or Bethlehem; but then, again, neither Moab nor Bethlehem is like the country depicted by Mr. Calderon'. In a letter to Edward Morris, Keeper of Foreign Art at the Walker Art Gallery in Liverpool, dated 30th October, 1985, Richard A. Foster, Director of Museums, seeks to identify all the flora in the painting and confirms the objection of a Colonel Yule (*The Athenaeum*, June 12, 1886, p. 788) that the prickly pear in the painting is anachronistic. I have one clipping, from *The Field, The Country Gentleman's Newspaper* of March 24, 1927, in which an H.S. Thompson claims to have shown that the doubt about the prickly pear's existence in Palestine in ancient times was needless. This material was kindly provided to me by the Volunteer Services at the Walker Art Gallery. The setting may not be 'authentic', but it seems to me to be a representation of what Europeans of the time might have imagined the countryside would look like.

34.   Cf. Adele Berlin, 'Ruth and the Continuity of Israel', in Kates and Reimer

Naomi and Ruth need a redeemer (*go'el*); this is the narrative lack that sets the story in motion. The Gattung of the book is romance, where the perilous journey, struggle, and exaltation of the hero are set in an idyllic and idealized world of the past,[35] the period of the judges (Ruth 1.1), devoid of the violence and socio-political upheaval we read about in the book of Judges. Ruth is a variation on the fabula in which a poor maiden finds her rich prince. Girl meets boy, girl gets boy, with two climactic moments: (1) girl resorts to a risky ploy and boy agrees to marry (or redeem) girl, and (2) the question, Will the nearer next-of-kin relinquish his right to redeem?, is resolved with a resounding 'yes'. Presumably Ruth and Boaz live happily ever after; at any rate, a line of kings descends from them. The family, and the nation, perpetuates itself.

When Ruth marries Boaz, her symbolic marriage to Naomi, in which she left her mother and her father and 'clung' (*dbq*) to her mother-in-law is not negated, but must share the stage with this new, legally recognized bond. Interestingly, in their important commentaries on Ruth neither Campbell nor Sasson mentions the connections between Gen. 2.24 and Ruth 1.14 that lend the women's relationship its marriage-like quality. Is this an insignificant oversight or an unconscious heterosexist bias? Whereas he speaks of *dbq* as a key word, and thus key concept, Campbell merely lists its other occurrences in Ruth (2.8, 21, 23).[36] Sasson alludes to the Genesis text when he observes

(eds.), *Reading Ruth: Contemporary Women Reclaim a Sacred Story*, p. 259: 'The theme of family continuity becomes the theme of national continuity'. Berlin points out how 'references to land in the Book of Ruth not only provide the setting for a pastoral romance, they link the story to the biblical theme of land, both private land and the land of Israel', and adds that 'More prominent than the theme of land in the book of Ruth is the theme of family and people' (p. 257). Ruth is, as Mieke Bal (*Lethal Love*, p. 87) observes, a *mise en abyme* of the Torah, a story about '"the continuity of history, or how to admit love." In other words: the building of the house of Israel, against all odds...'

35. See Northrop Frye, *Anatomy of Criticism* (New York: Atheneum, 1966), pp. 186-206.

36. Campbell, *Ruth*, pp. 72, 81. Campbell points out that in Ruth 1.14 the Septuagint uses *ēkolouthēsen*, 'she followed after', rather than *ekollēthē* from *kollaō*, 'to adhere', though the Septuagint regularly uses forms of *kollaō* to translate *dbq* (as in 2.8, 21, 23). He speculates that this is due to a hearing error on the part of the scribe. He goes on to note that both the Old Latin and the Septuagint use a different verb for *dbq* in 1.14 than in ch. 2, and asks, 'Does this mean that both versions sensed that there should be a special meaning in 1.14?' (p. 72). Could it be that the Septuagint

that *dbq* 'expresses the ideal closeness experienced by a married couple'. He notes that it is most often paralleled with forms of *'ahav*, 'to love', but the example he cites, Prov. 18.24, is of brotherly love.[37] Hubbard, in contrast, acknowledges that the expression *dbq b* 'implies firm loyalty and deep (even erotic) affection', and gives Gen. 2.24 as his first example.[38] His placement of 'even erotic' in parentheses, however, indicates that he does not see erotic affection in the case of Ruth, and his treatment of the concept of 'clinging' concludes with the observation that Ruth 'sacrificed her destiny to "cling to" an *aged*, hopeless mother-in-law'.[39]

This remark raises the question of age, not just Naomi's age but the ages of Ruth and Boaz as well. What effect do readers' assumptions about the ages of the main characters have on they way they visualize the characters' relationships? The older readers think Naomi is in relation to Ruth, the less likely they are even to imagine a sexual relationship. Conversely, the younger she is, the more conceivable is the prospect. Campbell's calculations for Naomi's and Ruth's ages seem reasonable:

> If usual ancient Near Eastern procedure was followed, Naomi was probably married in her early to mid-teens, and had had her two sons by the time she was twenty. They in turn would have married by the time they were fifteen or so, to girls a bit younger. Ten years of childless marriage for them would bring us to the mid-forties for Naomi. Given the rigors of life in ancient Palestine, that would be years enough, almost certainly, for her to have reached the menopause. The story-teller will establish that Boaz and Naomi are of the same generation, and we can assume that Ruth was between 25 and 30 when the events in the story took place.[40]

Apart from some serious questions about fertility (At what age would girls have begun to menstruate? Given dietary factors and the 'rigorous life' of the times, how likely is it that women would have menstruated regularly?), according to Campbell's reckoning we could have a Ruth of nearly thirty and a Naomi of forty-two. (The rigors of life would be the same for both women, so one would presumably not

---

translator sensed the erotic implications of translating *dbq* with a form of *kollaō* here and wanted therefore to avoid using the term?

37. Sasson, *Ruth*, p. 28.
38. Hubbard, *The Book of Ruth*, p. 115.
39. Hubbard, *The Book of Ruth*, p. 116; italics mine.
40. Campbell, *Ruth*, p. 67.

have aged more quickly than the other.) Is this, then, the 'old Naomi',[41] 'gray-haired Naomi',[42] 'aged widow',[43] and 'old and wise mother-in-law'[44] that commentators speak of?

Boaz's age is also in question, but does not pose a serious problem for imagining his sexual union with Ruth. He is frequently taken to be an older man (the Midrash makes him eighty!),[45] an assumption that involves romanticizing. This is the male fantasy in which an old man finds new life and fulfillment in a younger woman. That Boaz can easily be older than Ruth for a sexual relationship, but Naomi not, reflects both a heterosexist double standard according to which older men are sexually attractive but older women are not and a related cultural tendency to deny the sexual desire of older women. Is Boaz an older man? In his calculations cited above, Campbell places Boaz in Naomi's generation, which would make him in his mid-forties. Elsewhere he speaks of them as 'senior citizens'[46] and representatives of the 'older generation'.[47] Whatever happened to 'middle-age'? My point here has to do with modern readers in Western culture, and not what people in an ancient culture (and some today) would have considered 'old' with regard to a woman, since what I am questioning is the difference between Ruth's and Naomi's ages. By insisting 'senior citizens they are, and the audience should appreciate them as such',[48] Campbell encourages his readers to imagine Naomi and Boaz

41.   Zenger, *Das Buch Ruth*, p. 73; p. 96, where the contrast is with the 'young mother', Ruth. Sasson, too, speaks of Naomi's 'old age' (pp. 42, 62), though he considers speculations on Naomi's age 'irrelevant' (p. 24). In discussing Ruth 1.12, he says Naomi's point 'is not that she is too old to be married, but, having passed menopause, too old to have sexual relations that would result in pregnancy' (p. 25).

42.   Hubbard, *The Book of Ruth*, p. 274.

43.   Trible, *God and the Rhetoric of Sexuality*, p. 174; 'aged Naomi', p. 166.

44.   Edith Deen, *All of the Women of the Bible* (New York: Harper & Row, 1955), p. 83, where the contrast is to her 'young and beautiful daughter-in-law'.

45.   Ruth Rabbah 6.2; Ruth was forty according to Ruth Rabbah 4.4; 6.2, but looked like a girl of fourteen.

46.   Campbell, *Ruth*, pp. 110, 111.

47.   Campbell, *Ruth*, p. 110; Trible, *God and the Rhetoric of Sexuality*, p. 180. Trible simply assumes Boaz is an 'older man', 'a senior adult, a male counterpart to Naomi' (p. 176).

48.   Campbell, *Ruth*, p. 111. It may well be that Campbell is trying to give his readers a sense of the way an ancient culture would define the older generation, but by not making this clear, he gives the impression that Naomi and Boaz are considerably older than his numerical reckoning makes them. Moshe J. Bernstein ('Two

as considerably older than Ruth, and this has serious implications for
their assumptions about sex and sexuality. Sasson, rightly I believe,
sees 'puritanical issues at stake' in the age issue: '...it would be much
easier to accept the possibility that the threshing-floor involved no
sexual activity, if the protagonist were sketched as a wise old man'.[49]
If this is true for Boaz, how much more so for Naomi.

On this point, the treatment of the respective ages of the characters
in the 1960 film, *The Story of Ruth*, directed by Henry Koster, is
illuminating.[50] Boaz (Stuart Whitman) is older than Ruth (Elana
Eden), but probably not more than ten years or so. Naomi (Peggy
Wood) is old enough to be Boaz's mother, and Ruth's grandmother.
In the scene where Naomi bids farewell to her daughters-in-law,
Ruth is the bitter one (Mahlon has just died, having married Ruth
moments before) and Naomi is mawkishly philosophical: 'Pain on
entering the world, anguish on leaving it. But the interval between is
worth it all.' When Ruth asks, 'Where is Mahlon's invisible God of
mercy? Where are his blessings?', a look of recognition mingled with
great tenderness comes over Naomi's face as she walks toward Ruth
and says, 'You are one of them...' She presses her cheek against
Ruth's and says she will remember her with tenderness and love.
When Ruth makes her famous oath of loyalty, looks of fond devotion pass between them. This is only one moment of tender affection
between the two women in the film; at other times they embrace to
console each other in adversity or to share their joy. Naomi's
advanced age and motherly attitude toward Ruth and Ruth's defer-
ential and protective treatment of Naomi rule out even the slightest
suggestion of erotic feelings on the part of either woman. If Naomi
had been played by a woman in her forties, their intimacy would
make a different impression on theater viewers (fig. 5.3).

Multivalent Readings in the Ruth Narrative', *Journal for the Study of the Old Testament*
50 [1991], p. 21) notes the incongruity of applying the term *na'arah* to Ruth in
the blessing of 4.12 'since Ruth is apparently no youngster by ancient standards',
and thus concludes that the blessing was used traditionally to celebrate betrothals
(see pp. 21-23).

49.   Sasson, *Ruth*, pp. 85-86; the citations appear on p. 86.

50.   Twentieth Century Fox; produced by Samuel G. Engel; directed by Henry
Koster; screenplay by Norman Corwin; and starring Stuart Whitman as Boaz, Tom
Tryon as Mahlon, Peggy Wood as Naomi, Jeff Morrow as Tov, and Elana Eden as
Ruth.

Figure 5.3. Peggy Wood and Elana Eden, in *The Story of Ruth*

Calderon gives us a Naomi who does not look like a candidate for a senior citizen's retirement village. The cinematic version of the story of Ruth finds its point of contact in the works of other painters, those who portray Naomi as noticeably older than Ruth. In William Blake's 'Naomi and Her Two Daughters-in-Law', for example, a young Ruth clings to a wrinkled, aged Naomi. Although her head rests against Naomi's breasts and her arms encircle her lower body, the difference in ages, coupled with the solemn expressions and the fact that Naomi does not embrace Ruth in return (her hands are outstretched to each side), render the painting asexual. Similarly, in a triptych by the nineteenth-century English painter Thomas Matthew Rooks, a sweet, young Ruth grasps the arm and hand of a haggard and care-worn Naomi.[51] In Pieter Lastman's painting 'Ruth Swears Loyalty to Naomi' (dated 1614) Naomi is an old crone sitting on a donkey, pushing away a young, appealing Ruth. Naomi is also an

51.   Blake's painting is in the Victoria and Albert Museum; Rooks's, in the Tate Gallery. Reproductions of these two paintings can be found in Sölle *et al.*, *Great Women of the Bible in Art and Literature*, pp. 148, 157.

old woman in 'Ruth and Naomi' by the seventeenth-century Dutch painter Willem Drost.[52] These more common artistic representations have none of the erotic energy of Calderon's painting.

Ruth and Boaz

Why do so many viewers whose opinions I have solicited say the couple in Calderon's painting is Ruth and Boaz? Does it have something to do with this erotic energy, or with the ideational difficulty posed by two women embracing passionately? The desire (or need) to see the figures as Ruth and Boaz is so strong that some viewers insist on maintaining this identification in spite of the fact that there is no scene in the biblical story to which it corresponds. This cannot be simply the result of heterosexist bias. Rather, for these viewers the erotic power of the Ruth–Boaz relationship is so self-evident that they assume the painting represents the artist's vision of their relationship—a vision that finds its basis in the source text, but does not attempt to capture on canvas a particular scene from the source text. What is this basis? What features of the book of Ruth, apparent or latent, are such readers relying on to produce affirmations of opposite-sex relationships by constructing a romantic bond between Ruth and Boaz?

Just as in the discussion of same-sex relationships I considered readings that ranged from intense friendship to lesbianism, so under romantic readings I want to consider randomly a range of responses to the Ruth–Boaz relationship from occasional slippages into melodramatic or impressionistic language in scholarly commentary to the full-fledged transformation of the text into a love story in its cinematic version. The heterosexual bond is already considered 'natural'. What concerns me here is the further naturalizing of the heterosexual relationship by romanticizing it, by which I mean adding a love interest. Romanticizing readings find more in Ruth and Boaz's relationship than a kinsman's willingness to take responsibility for the welfare of two needy female relatives, or the juridical issue of redemption, or the obligation of a kinsman to perpetuate his relative's family and 'the name of the dead in his inheritance' (4.10),[53] or even a

---

52.   Lastman's painting is in the Niedersächsische Landesgalerie, Hannover; Drost's, in the Ashmolean Museum, Oxford.

53.   Cf. the emphasis on these themes in Sasson, *Ruth*; Hubbard, *The Book of Ruth*.

model for living according to the dictates of *ḥesed*.[54] They find *feelings*. They probe into characters' emotions that the text only hints at. The love interest between Ruth and Boaz does not have to be consciously developed, as it is, for example, in Dana Fewell and David Gunn's reading of Ruth, where Ruth and Boaz are sexually attracted to each other when they first meet in his field.[55] I am also interested in the implicit romanticizing that takes place in even the most reserved scholarly prose. Here, too, as was the case with readings that affirmed same-sex relationships, it should come as no surprise that the strongest romantic readings are to be found outside the scholarly literature, in the cinematic and in literary metatexts.

The character of Boaz becomes a likely site for romanticizing. As a third party in the equation, Boaz will now vie with Naomi for Ruth's loyalty, if not her affection. If Ruth and Naomi are motivated by *ḥesed*, Boaz must exemplify it, too. In other words, he cannot be less worthy of Ruth's devotion than Naomi. Emphasizing that both Ruth and Boaz are people of substance (*'eshet* and *ish ḥayil* respectively), Campbell concludes, 'How effectively the story-teller hints that these two people should marry...'[56] His remark is mildly romanticizing in that it seems to suggest that Ruth and Boaz were made for each other, and, since Campbell views God as working behind the scenes, this must be a match made in heaven. Trible espouses the same kind of romanticizing theology: 'Intercourse between Ruth and Boaz is itself divine activity'.[57] Such remarks indicate more at stake than the redemption of land and familial responsibility under the levirate law.

Although the text does not speak of Boaz's affection for Ruth, here, as was the case with Naomi, readers infer it—and, indeed, his

54. A major theme of the book according to Campbell, *Ruth*; Hubbard, *The Book of Ruth*; and Sakenfeld, *Faithfulness in Action*; among others. The interpretation is ancient; Rabbi Ze'ira said, 'This scroll tells us nothing either of cleanliness or of uncleanliness, either of prohibition or permission. For what purpose then was it written? To teach how great is the reward of those who do deeds of kindness' (Ruth Rabbah 2.14).

55. Fewell and Gunn, *Compromising Redemption*.

56. Campbell, *Ruth*, p. 125. Zenger (*Das Buch Ruth*, p. 73) observes that the narrator wants us to see Ruth and Boaz as an 'ideales Paar'.

57. Trible, *God and the Rhetoric of Sexuality*, p. 193; cf. p. 195. She is speaking of 4.13, not of ch. 3, which she wants to leave private, a move I am also inclined to label romanticizing; see below.

desire—from his actions. He notices Ruth in his field and is particularly solicitous, advising her not to leave his field for another one and
charging his reapers not to molest her (2.8-9). He tells her to drink
from the young men's vessels when she is thirsty (v. 8), and at meal-
time invites her to join them (v. 14). He even instructs the reapers to
let her glean among the sheaves and to pull out some from the
bundles to leave behind for her (2.5-16). 'What lay behind the
unusual interest in this foreigner?' asks Hubbard. 'Had Boaz fallen in
love with Ruth?'[58] The mention of molesting in v. 9 explicitly raises
the issue of sex, whether it is a real issue ('The field is a place of some
menace for an unattached young foreign woman', say Fewell and
Gunn[59]) or only an issue in Boaz's mind ('Even if one were to adopt
the most innocuous meaning for the verb "to molest", it would
certainly have been an infraction against the most elemental forms of
courtesy and custom, should a widow be "molested" as she gleaned',
argues Sasson).[60]

Readers also infer Ruth's desire. Gerry Brenner speculates whether
it really is premature at this point, as Campbell and Sasson maintain,
for Ruth to use the language of courtship in acknowledging Boaz's
attentions ('you have spoken to the heart of your maidservant',
2.13).[61] And Ronald Hyman finds clues of Ruth and Boaz's mutual
attraction in the dialogue that takes place between them in the field:
'The contrast between Boaz's questions to Ruth and Boaz's commands to his young men serves to highlight the emerging relationship
between Boaz and Ruth: he is attracted to her and uses the question
form as a way of sending a positive, emotional message; she is attracted

58.   Hubbard, *The Book of Ruth*, p. 178; see his discussion of the suggestiveness
of the language in the scene, pp. 146-78. Already Hermann Gunkel ('Ruth', in
Reden und Aufsätze [Göttingen: Vandenhoeck & Ruprecht, 1913]) saw this scene as
preparing the way for the marriage, although he cautioned 'die Erzählung ist keine
Liebesgeschichte' (p. 72) and Ruth and Boaz 'sind kein Liebespaar' (p. 78).

59.   Fewell and Gunn, *Compromising Redemption*, p. 76. Fewell and Gunn make
much of Naomi's not warning Ruth about the dangers in the field; see pp. 44-45,
76-77, 98. But if they are so well-known, would Ruth not know anyway? Would
Moabite gleaners have behaved differently from Israelite gleaners?

60.   Sasson, *Ruth*, p. 50. Naomi, however, knows of this possibility in 2.22.

61.   Brenner, 'Readers Responding', p. 254 n. 28; contra Campbell, *Ruth*,
pp. 100-101; and Sasson, *Ruth*, p. 53. Fewell and Gunn (*Compromising Redemption*,
pp. 84, 101-102, 126 n. 29) also note the sexual overtones in Boaz's speeches to
Ruth and her reply to him in ch. 2.

to him and responds nonverbally, in a positive manner, to the messages sent by his questions'.[62]

The vital scene for romantic interpretation, for literary and critical metatexts alike, is the encounter between Ruth and Boaz, at night, on the threshing floor (3.6-13). Campbell declares, 'At no other point does dramatic tension and suspense reach such a pitch'.[63] Paul Humbert calls it 'l'heure pathétique par excellence',[64] and for Francis Landy, 'the story is constructed in order to enable the central scene to take place, for the sake of romance',[65] which recalls Edith Deen's description of the scene as 'the culmination of a beautiful romance'.[66] Singling this scene out as momentous and as the climactic point in the book is one way of privileging it over the emotional scene between the two women that inspires same-sex readings; in other words, of romanticizing it.

Of any scene in Ruth, the threshing floor scene has the greatest potential for development of the heterosexual love interest, and I suspect it is the one in the back of the minds of viewers who identify Calderon's embracing couple as Ruth and Boaz. In preparation for going to the threshing floor, Ruth bathes, anoints herself, and dresses in her finest clothes—all preparatory, in Kirsten Nielsen's view, to 'un rendez-vous d'amour'.[67] She waits until Boaz has eaten and drunk and, in a mellow mood,[68] gone to lie down. She comes to him so softly that he does not notice her or the fact that she lies down at 'the

62.   Ronald T. Hyman, 'Questions and Changing Identity in the Book of Ruth', *Union Seminary Quarterly Review* 39 (1984), p. 195.

63.   Campbell, *Ruth*, p. 130. This view is echoed by Hubbard (*The Book of Ruth*, p. 195), 'Indeed, there is no higher level of dramatic tension and suspense than here'.

64.   Paul Humbert, 'Art et leçon l'histoire de Ruth', in *Opuscules d'un Hébraïsant* (Neuchatel: University of Neuchatel, 1958), p. 101.

65.   Landy, 'Ruth and the Romance of Realism', p. 292. Landy uses 'romance' in the dual sense of an emotional attraction and a class of literature.

66.   Deen, *All of the Women of the Bible*, p. 85.

67.   Nielsen, 'La choix contre de droit dans le livre de Ruth', p. 205. These details are not repeated in the threshing floor scene of 3.6-13, but are part of Naomi's instructions to Ruth in 3.3-4, which the text tells us Ruth followed (3.5-6). Some versions add, 'and rub yourself with myrrh', which Campbell (*Ruth*, p. 120) says would 'make much clearer the implication that Ruth was to make herself enticing'; such clarification, however, hardly seems necessary.

68.   Commentators discuss whether or not the text means to suggest he is drunk; it is generally assumed he is simply in a good mood, more open to suggestion.

place of his feet', for it is midnight before he wakes up with a start to discover a woman at his side.[69] 'The place of his feet' (*margelotav*) that Ruth lies beside (3.8, 14) is almost certainly a euphemism for the lower part of Boaz's body, if not specifically his genitals; and the word for 'lie down' (*shakav*, 3.4, 7, 13, 14) is frequently used of sexual intercourse. Whether 'the place of his feet' is also what Ruth uncovers or whether she uncovers herself[70]—and if she is naked, her request that Boaz 'spread your skirt over your maidservant' makes better sense—is a tantalizing question, and another place for speculation. In either case, the entire scene is rife with sexual innuendo, as biblical commentators explain, and as readers without benefit of the Hebrew are aware anyway. When Landy says that 'Ruth becomes a symbol of sexual culture; as such, she conforms with the cultural stereotype of the seductive woman', he is accurately describing the impression she makes; when he continues, 'for example through the intoxication of her perfume, while also blending with the coolness and fragrance of the night from which she emerges', he adds his own romantic vision to the picture.[71]

Is any of this—Ruth's action, her speech, or both—an invitation to marriage? Is it an invitation to sex? Erich Zenger lapses into romanticizing language when he observes that Ruth asks for Boaz's love.[72] The Targum clearly saw the possibility of an interpretation in terms of sexual intimacy here and thus took steps to rule it out by

69.   Berlin (*Poetics and Interpretation of Biblical Narrative*, pp. 90-91) thinks that Naomi meant for Ruth to lie beside Boaz when he had just lain down and was still in a receptive mood, before he went to sleep, but that Ruth misunderstood that 'her mission was a romantic one' (p. 91) and waited too long. According to Berlin, Ruth turned her 'romantic mission' into a 'quest for a redeemer' (p. 90). If Naomi had intended to ask Boaz to be a redeemer, Berlin argues, the middle of the night is not an appropriate time to do so. The argument makes Ruth rather obtuse. She thinks she is going on 'secret legal business' (p. 91) and does not find it odd to do it in the middle of the night in a compromising situation.

70.   Nielsen, 'La choix contre de droit dans le livre de Ruth', pp. 205-207.

71.   Landy, 'Ruth and the Romance of Realism', p. 290. Hertzberg (*Die Bücher Josua, Richter, Ruth*, p. 274) speaks of Boaz as an old man, who most likely is or has been married, who needs encouragement to fulfill his role; thus the scheme to catch him in a good mood when he will likely be swayed by Ruth's 'Jugend und Schönheit'.

72.   Zenger, *Das Buch Ruth*, p. 71: 'So bittet sie nicht um das Brot des reichen Grundbesitzers [as in ch. 2], sondern um die Liebe des Mannes Boas'.

having Boaz control his desire.[73] Boaz stammers an awkward reply in which he (1) blesses Ruth, (2) praises her for making 'this last kindness better than the first' by not going 'after young men, whether poor or rich', and (3) promises to do what Ruth asks—whatever that is—but then (4) speaks of a nearer kinsman, one who might be willing to do the part of the next of kin for her, but then again might not, in which case, (5) he, Boaz, will do it (3.10-13). Both for its syntax— 'Speaking too much is a sign of unease, in which the urgency of desire and the fear of frustration mingle', remarks Landy[74]—and for what it allows readers to infer about Boaz's self image, Boaz's speech offers a remarkable occasion for romanticizing. 'Kindness' is hardly the best translation for *ḥesed*, especially here in v. 10, but it is notoriously difficult to find a suitable English equivalent.[75] It encompasses both attitude and action,[76] and so something like 'act of devotion' might fit well in this context. Most readers take the former kindness to which Boaz refers to be Ruth's devotion to Naomi, and the latter, her seeking out of Boaz.[77] If this is the case, then a character in the story (not surprisingly, the man in this story of two women and one man) elevates the opposite-sex relationship above the

73.   'And he controlled his inclination, and refrained from approaching her, just like Joseph the Righteous who had refused to approach the Egyptian wife of his master; just like Paltiel bar La'ish who had planted a sword between his body and Michal daughter of Saul, the wife of David, for he refused to approach her' (Étan Levine, *The Aramaic Version of Ruth* [Analecta Biblica, 58; Rome: Biblical Institute Press, 1973], p. 32).

74.   Landy, 'Ruth and the Romance of Realism', p. 302. Landy offers an excellent discussion of this speech.

75.   For frustratingly detailed discussion, see Gordon A. Clark, *The Word* Hesed *in the Hebrew Bible* (Journal for the Study of the Old Testament Supplement Series, 157; Sheffield: JSOT Press, 1993).

76.   Sakenfeld, *Faithfulness in Action*, p. 3. Sakenfeld chooses the translation 'loyalty', asking readers to 'break open the horizons of the English term "loyalty"' and keep in mind the biblical sense of 'faithfulness in action'.

77.   An important exception is Sasson, *Ruth*, who argues that marriage and redemption are separate issues; he sees the former *ḥesed* as Ruth's proposing marriage to Boaz and the latter, better one, her seeking a redeemer for Naomi. Campbell (*Ruth*, p. 137) expresses a widely held view that suppresses the obvious (i.e. the reason Boaz actually gives) when he says the latter *ḥesed* is 'her determination to play her part in keeping Elimelek's inheritance in the family and in making provision for two widows, not only for herself but for Naomi also'.

same-sex one, and thereby invites readers to follow suit.[78] Prompted by the reference to not going after 'young men (*baḥurim*) whether poor or rich' most readers also find here evidence that Boaz is an older man, who is surprised and delighted that Ruth might desire him.[79]

Victor Hugo's poem, 'Booz endormi', is built around this theme. Hugo imagines Boaz as a childless widower of eighty, who sees himself 'half dead', and who perhaps fears impotence.[80]

> His beard was silver like an April brook.
> His sheaf was neither miserly nor hateful...

Dreaming of an oak rising from his belly bearing a chain of descendants, he finds the possibility of engendering offspring inconceivable.

> A race would be born from me! How can I believe it?
> How could it be that I should have children?
> When one is young, one has triumphant mornings;
> Day comes from night as from a victory;
>
> But old, one trembles as a birch in winter;
> I am widowed, I am alone, and on me falls the evening...

Feeling hopeless and alone, he dreams of something more, and as the perfume of flowers and the night air mingle with the sweetness of nature, his dreams of potency and progeny are realized when Ruth, 'her breast naked', comes to lie at his feet in the nuptial shade. As Bal points out, this poem 'stresses feelings that [Ruth 3.10] only touches upon'.[81] In the metatextual world of biblical commentary, even so cautious a reader as Hubbard slips here into the language of romanticizing when he proposes that Boaz is 'flattered and inwardly pleased'.[82]

78.   As I said above about the women of Bethlehem, his point of view may not be reliable; that is, it may not reflect the narrator's or other characters' points of view, all of which could be different. And readers will bring their own views into the equation.

79.   Against this view, Sasson (*Ruth*, pp. 85-86) argues that *baḥurim* does not indicate that these men are necessarily younger or more attractive than Boaz but rather refers to men of means.

80.   See Bal's analysis of this feature of the poem, *Lethal Love*, pp. 68-88; see also Landy's reading of the threshing floor scene ('Ruth and the Romance of Realism'), in which he emphasizes Boaz's psychological state.

81.   Bal, *Lethal Love*, p. 71.

82.   Hubbard, *The Book of Ruth*, pp. 213-14; also, his description of Ruth 'watching nervously in the darkness' and her 'excited heartbeat' (p. 209).

Is a marriage actually contracted or does Boaz simply promise to pursue the matter on Ruth's and Naomi's behalf? Why does Boaz tell Ruth to lie with him until the morning? Did they or did they not have sexual intercourse on the threshing floor? My purpose here is not to enter the debate; it is rather the very existence of the debate and its nature that holds significance for my thesis about the romanticizing of the bond between Ruth and Boaz at the expense of the bond between Ruth and Naomi.

Speculation about a man and woman who spend the night together of their own free will inevitably involves a certain amount of romanticizing. Readers respond to the question whether or not Ruth and Boaz engaged in sexual intercourse on the threshing floor in various ways. Campbell believes Ruth and Boaz would not have had sex because they 'are worthy, and will do things in righteous fashion'.[83] Moshe Bernstein also appeals to the 'nobility of character shared by Ruth and Boaz' which would preclude sexual activity on the threshing floor, and argues, moreover, from a narratological point of view that 'the book of Ruth has a fourth chapter whose impact would be vitiated and whose very existence would be threatened if the third chapter ended with Boaz and Ruth consummating their relationship'.[84] Landy finds strong suggestions of sexual intimacy in the encounter, but observes coyly, 'Nothing need transpire under the bedclothes, if one of the parties so wishes...'[85] Fewell and Gunn imagine a Boaz who is not sure whether or not he might have had sex with Ruth while he was drunk.[86] Anthony Phillips thinks this is the point: Boaz believes that Ruth, following the example of her ancestor, Lot's daughter, had intercourse with him while he was

---

83.   Campbell, *Ruth*, pp. 130-38; the citation is from p. 138. In an illuminating structural analysis, Harold Fisch ('Ruth and the Structure of Covenant History', *Vetus Testamentum* 32 [1982], pp. 425-37) sees the Ruth–Boaz story as 'redeeming' its structural predecessors, Gen. 13, 19, and 38, in a movement from what is morally objectionable to what is morally questionable to what is morally sanctioned.

84.   Bernstein, 'Two Multivalent Readings in the Ruth Narrative', p. 17. He proposes that the function of the *double entendre* in the threshing floor scene is to convey to the reader a sense of the sexual and emotional tension felt by the characters (p. 19). Yair Zakovitch (*Ruth: Introduction and Commentary* [Tel Aviv: Am Oved, 1990], pp. 91, 96) also thinks nothing would have happened.

85.   Landy, 'Ruth and the Romance of Realism', p. 298.

86.   Fewell and Gunn, *Compromising Redemption*, p. 87.

drunk.[87] D.R. Beattie speaks of the 'folly of assuming that "nothing happened"'.[88] Campbell and, in particular, Trible would have us not invade the couple's privacy; in other words, not to ask.[89]

In a way, it is irrelevant when Ruth and Boaz have sex, since they do have sex. But 'Boaz took Ruth and she became his wife, and he went in to her and the Lord gave her conception and she bore a son' is not romantic. Bathing and anointing oneself, seeking out a man secretly, uncovering either part of his body or one's own, and spending the night with him is. Most commentators agree that the narrator intends to be provocative in ch. 3—clearly, with success. The gaps and the innuendo in this scene are too significant and tantalizing to be ignored. Indeed, not to speculate about what happened on the threshing floor is simply an evasive tactic that attracts attention to the question. To say, as Campbell does, 'It is not prudery which compels the conclusion that there was no sexual intercourse at the threshing floor; it is the utter irrelevance of such a speculation',[90] having spent eight pages reaching the conclusion that nothing happened, is rather ingenious. Trible, in a footnote, wishes Campbell 'had left intact the ambiguity of this episode in the dark of night'.[91] Reacting against such moral delicacy, the fictitious Ruth in Gerry Brenner's 'Readers Responding: An Interview with Biblical Ruth' has Campbell's words particularly in mind when she complains: 'Disdaining the issue as one of utter irrelevance (a response common to prudes), the stuffy may be as bad as the salacious...'[92]

What I am calling 'romanticizing', filling gaps by supplying feelings, whether of solicitude, respect, disquiet, or desire, is not simply irresistible, it is a way of valuing the characters in the story. Readers in general do not like to think that people have sex without mutual feeling, especially in a tale where everything is so 'idyllic'.[93] Whereas

---

87.   Anthony Phillips, 'The Book of Ruth—Deception and Shame', *Journal of Jewish Studies* 37 (1986), p. 14. But Phillips knows better than Boaz that 'she has not in fact had sexual intercourse with him'.

88.   D.R. Beattie, 'Ruth III', *Journal for the Study of the Old Testament* 5 (1978), p. 41.

89.   Campbell, *Ruth*, p. 138; Trible, *God and the Rhetoric of Sexuality*, p. 198 n. 23.

90.   Campbell, *Ruth*, p. 138.

91.   Trible, *God and the Rhetoric of Sexuality*, p. 198 n. 23.

92.   Brenner, 'Readers Responding', p. 234.

93.   Cf. my remarks in Chapter 1 about Bathsheba, that what a character felt or

traditional biblical commentators like Campbell, Sasson, and Hubbard might prefer to keep modern sentiments out of it, others, like Fewell and Gunn and Landy, speak more freely of the character's emotions in terms familiar to a contemporary reading public. Reading from the point of view of Boaz, Landy offers a kind of scholarly version of Hugo's poem, 'Booz endormi', whereas Fewell and Gunn, whose creative retelling is actually something of a combination of popular and scholarly metatext, supply the mutual desire of Boaz for Ruth and Ruth for Boaz.

The mutual desire of Ruth and Boaz is beautifully captured by Else Lasker-Schüler in two poems from her *Hebräische Balladen*. One represents Boaz's perspective; the other, Ruth's. Written in the poet's distinctive evocative style, with fantastic imagery and invented words whose sensuousness is difficult to capture in translation, they play off each other like a lover's duet. The poem, 'Boas', which appears first, tells of the effect Ruth has on Boaz. Ruth arouses Boaz's heart, which Lasker-Schüler describes as growing high like the stalks of grain in his field and waving to Ruth in a surge of feeling.[94]

> Ruth sucht überall
> Nach goldenen Kornblumen
> An den Hütten der Brothüter vorbei—
>
> Bringt süßen Sturm
> Und glitzernde Spielerei
> Über Boas Herz;
>
> Das wogt ganz hoch
> In seinen Korngärten
> Der fremden Schnitterin zu.
>
> [Ruth seeks everywhere
> For golden cornflowers
> Beyond the huts of the guardians of bread—

did not feel is not the issue. But we want to supply mutual feeling, as the films do. I use the term 'idyllic' in reference to Goethe's famous description of Ruth as 'das lieblichste kleine Ganze…das uns episch und idyllisch überliefert worden ist', in his 'Noten und Abhandlungen zu besserem Verständnis des West-östlischen Divans' (cited in Hertzberg, *Die Bücher Josua, Richter, Ruth*, p. 17), which Gunkel ('Ruth', p. 65) and many others cite with approval; cf. Ilana Pardes's discussion of Ruth in terms of 'idyllic revisionism' (*Countertraditions in the Bible*, pp. 98-117).

94.   'Wogen' can refer to the waving to and fro of grain in a field and also to a surge or welling up of feeling.

Brings sweet stirring
And glittering play
Over Boaz's heart;

Which waves high
In his corn garden
To the alien gleaner.]

In the poem entitled 'Ruth', Ruth describes how Boaz's desire finds its counterpart in her own, and, in the clearest possible terms, declares her love.

Und du suchst mich vor den Hecken.
Ich höre deine Schritte seufzen
Und meine Augen sind schwere dunkle Tropfen.

In meiner Seele blühen süß deine Blicke
Und füllen sich,
Wenn meine Augen in den Schlaf wandeln.

Am Brunnen meiner Heimat
Steht ein Engel,
Der singt das Lied meiner Liebe,
Der singt das Lied Ruths.

[And you seek me in front of the hedges.
I hear your steps sigh
And my eyes are heavy dark drops.

In my soul your glances bloom sweetly
And well up,
As my eyes wander off to sleep.

At the well of my native land
Waits an angel,
Who sings the song of my love,
Who sings the song of Ruth.]

Ruth has one more poetic line than Boaz, in which she identifies her song, and synecdochically the book of Ruth, with her song of love.

'Did you ever find out, miss, who you are going to marry by means of the Bible and key?' This appropriation of the book of Ruth for heterosexual love and marriage comes from Thomas Hardy's *Far from the Madding Crowd*. At her friend Liddy's urging, Bathsheba tries it. She opens her well-worn Bible to 'the special verse in the Book of Ruth', with its 'sublime words' that 'slightly thrilled and abashed her'. She places the door key on the page, where 'a rusty patch immediately upon the verse, caused by previous pressure of an iron substance thereon, told that this was not the first time the old volume had been used for the purpose'. The verse is repeated and the book turned around (Bathsheba keeps to herself the name of the man she is thinking about). Though he does not cite the biblical verse, Hardy does not need to. Readers of *Far from the Madding Crowd* will recognize that the sublime words can hardly be any others than Ruth 1.16-17, 'whither thou goest I will go', etc. The book of Ruth, the valentine as a symbol of (heterosexual) love, and (heterosexual) marriage are linked when Bathsheba sends a valentine to Mr. Boldwood with a large red wax seal bearing the words, 'Marry Me'. In addition to illustrating the romantic appeal of the book of Ruth, this example from Hardy also shows how readers' responses can diverge widely from authors' intentions. Bathsheba sends the valentine as a joke, but this is not the way Boldwood, the recipient, takes it.

The Story of Ruth: *Transforming Text into Love Story*

I turn now to my final and, after Calderon's painting, most important metatext, the 1960 Hollywood film *The Story of Ruth,* written for the screen by Norman Corwin. That in its cinematic version the story of Ruth becomes a love story reflects, on the one hand, a popular belief that it is one. At the same time, it reinforces in popular culture the perception of the biblical book as a love story. Film is particularly valuable and instructive as a metatext because it combines the visual, the narrative, and the interpretive. As a visual medium, *The Story of Ruth*, like Calderon's painting, shows us what the characters look like rather than leaving it to our imagination. Peggy Wood's Naomi is old and gray, a sweet grandmotherly type. Elana Eden as Ruth is young, dark, and beautiful, and speaks with a dulcet accent, which serves to remind audiences of her status as a foreigner in Judah. In Moab (where she is a Moabite priestess!), Ruth wears clothes that emphasize her erotic appeal (Mulvey's 'to-be-looked-at-ness'),[95] but in Judah, she, like Naomi, dresses demurely, but always becomingly. Her long dresses have sleeves, and she wears a veil to cover her hair, though it is never allowed to hide her face. Stuart Whitman is a strong, handsome, and hot-headed (= hot-blooded) Boaz with thick

95. Mulvey, *Visual and Other Pleasures*, p. 19; see the discussion of Bathsheba and the female star as object of the gaze in Chapter 1 above; see also below, Chapter 6.

dark, curly hair, who wears sleeveless, short tunics to show off his muscular physique (only Mahlon wears shorter skirts than Boaz in this film).[96] I have already mentioned the effect that viewers' perceptions of the characters' ages are likely to have on their perceptions of the characters' relationships, both in the painting, where the embracing figures do not appear to be of different generations, and in the film, where Naomi is significantly older than both Ruth and Boaz. By making Naomi old, while Ruth and Boaz are young and attractive, the film effectively defines the one relationship as parental, and the other as romantic.

As a narrative medium, like the biblical book, the film can show the development of character; significantly, it uses this opportunity for extensive development of the love interest. The love interest begins in Moab, with Mahlon, though it is not a very significant love interest. Mahlon loves Ruth, while Ruth is attracted mainly to his beliefs. They are not married for ten years, as appears to be the case in the biblical story;[97] in fact, Mahlon dies the instant they are married, thus making it possible for Ruth to be a virgin when she marries her true love, our hero Boaz.[98] Whereas the biblical story introduces a complication in the plot by suddenly and unexpectedly revealing the existence of a nearer next-of-kin, the film uses the next-of-kin to introduce a complication of its own, one designed to make the love angle more interesting. Boaz is given a rival. Tov, the nearest kinsman, is attracted to Ruth, and while Boaz gets off to a number of false starts, Tov seems to be scoring points. But Tov is not an appealing character and we, like Naomi, see through him. More important, Ruth is falling in love with Boaz. However—and here lies the real obstacle to true love's realization—Tov wants Ruth for his wife and he, in a rather neat touch, is the one who remembers

96.   In contrast, Jeff Morrow as Tov, the next of kin, and all the other men in Judah wear robes that reach at least to mid-calf, and that have sleeves of some sort.

97.   Whether Mahlon and Chilion lived in Moab for ten years or were married for ten years is not entirely clear; see the discussion in Sasson, *Ruth*, p. 21.

98.   The film does not emphasize this fact. It is an interesting variation on the rabbinic tradition that Boaz died on or shortly after their wedding night (Ruth Zuta on 4.13). This is in keeping with the notion that virtuous women do not have sex, at least not any more than is necessary; the story of Judith, the heroine who puts aside her widow's garb to 'seduce' Holofernes and after assassinating him returns to a life of seclusion, is another variation on this theme.

the levirate law. When he claims his right to marry Ruth, Ruth and Naomi are despondent. 'I should have remembered the levirate law before we ever reached the banks of the Jordan', bemoans Naomi.

As both a visual and a narrative interpretation, the film is constantly having to fill gaps, from the mundane (What clothes did they wear? What kind of houses did they live in? Where did Ruth and Naomi find their house, anyway?[99]), to the personal interest (What was Ruth's background? Why did she marry a foreigner?), to the crucial questions that inform the same-sex and opposite-sex readings we have been considering: Why did Ruth choose to go with Naomi? What did happen on the threshing floor? Although the film takes liberties with the plot and makes conspicuous changes, it has, in my view, done a brilliant job. Much of its gap filling is based on midrashic sources,[100] and its changes are not only dramatically effective, they make sense[101] (which is more than can be said for parts of the biblical story).[102] The most incredible cinematic contribution involves Ruth's origins: the film makes her a Moabite priestess.[103] This is perhaps no more far-fetched than the midrashic tradition that she was the

---

99.   In the film, Naomi and Elimelek's old house is still standing, though practically in ruins, and Ruth and Naomi move in. Boaz and, in particular, Tov help them rebuild it and bring them provisions (Ruth goes gleaning only twice, once in each of their fields).

100.   For example, the name Tov for *ploni 'almoni*; Elimelek blames himself for the evil that befalls the family in Moab [he and Chilion are about to be killed, and Mahlon will die soon] because he was well off but left his people in Bethlehem in time of trouble; a messenger appears to Naomi to prophesy the birth of a future king from Ruth's line.

101.   In contrast, for example, to the film *King David*, discussed above in Chapter 1, where the story is so altered that sense is sacrificed.

102.   Though Ruth is often admired as a story, it has some problematic gaps (blanks) that call into question its reputation as a finely crafted tale. Where do Ruth and Naomi live when they return to Bethlehem? Has Elimelek's old house really stood empty all that time, or is there some sort of public housing for the poor? Has Naomi forgotten she owns a field? Has everyone forgotten the levirate law? Why don't Boaz, who is evidently well off, and the next-of-kin help their poor, widowed relatives instead of leaving Ruth to glean in the fields?

103.   The Moabites are caricatured. The king and his priests are fat and bald; Moabite priestesses live in a kind of convent; the salient feature of Moabite religion is child sacrifice, about which the Moabites are, understandably, 'very sensitive'. Ruth as a child is *sold* by her needy father to the temple of Chemosh.

daughter of the king of Moab.[104] The effect is to make her
'conversion' all the more spectacular. Mahlon starts her thinking
about an invisible god of mercy and justice, who abhors child sacrifice and whose laws forbid the striking of slaves. When Mahlon dies
and Ruth determines to return to Judah with Naomi, it is for theological reasons: 'Because I saw a new light in her beliefs, in her god',
she tells Boaz later.[105] Some might argue that this change makes
explicit Ruth's implicit theological motivation in the biblical story;
however, in the biblical book Ruth does not say that Naomi's god is
the true god but only that Naomi's god will be her god.[106] Be that as
it may, the change has serious implications for the audience's
understanding of the *personal* bond between the two women. Unlike
the biblical account, it is not possible here to see Ruth as in any way
motivated by love for Naomi. Indeed, she hardly knows Naomi,
having met her only the night before. To be sure, a devoted relationship develops between the two women, but by subordinating Ruth's
personal attachment to Naomi to her religious conviction, the film
makes plain that the bond between the women, while strong, is not
primary.

Clearly the primary bond as far as the film is concerned is the
opposite-sex bond. *The Story of Ruth* resolves the question about
events on the threshing floor in a way that succeeds in being
romantic, while at the same time being moralistic and removing the
ambiguity of the biblical story. Though there are hints throughout
the film of a developing romantic interest, Ruth and Boaz have their
big love scene, not surprisingly, on the threshing floor. Up to this
point, they have not spoken of their love (though Ruth has asked
Naomi if what she feels for Boaz is only gratitude).[107]

Wearing a fine dress given to her by Tov to mark their betrothal,
Ruth follows Naomi's instructions and waits for Boaz to go to sleep
at the conclusion of the harvest festival. In a clever touch, she nearly

104. Ruth Rabbah 2.9. Whereas the midrash emphasizes Ruth's nationalistic
change of allegiance, the film foregrounds her religious conversion.

105. Boaz asks, 'Why did you come here, Ruth? Because you love Naomi?' She
nods and replies, 'And because I saw a new light in her beliefs, in her god'.

106. Duffy picks up on this in her poem, 'Mother and the Girl', when she has
Ruth say to herself, 'Now what was he called?'

107. Naomi's response is 'No, Ruth, it's not that. How can you mistake what
it is?'

stumbles over Tov (who has passed out from drunkenness) as she makes her way to the secluded place where Boaz has settled down for the night. She does not lie down beside him, however, as in the biblical story. He wakes up with a start to see her standing there, and says, 'I was dreaming of you. And you are here.' This cinematic addition provides a nice intertextual link with Hugo's poem about Boaz's dream of posterity and, through it, with Jacob's famous dream in Genesis 28. When Boaz declares his love for her ('I love you, Ruth. I've loved you from the day we met in my field'), Ruth replies, 'It must have been God's goodness that brought me to your field that day. Perhaps he's been directing me to you all my life.' The audience knows this is the case, for the film began with an important event from Ruth's childhood: she was chosen to be sacrificed to Chemosh but a blemish appeared suddenly on her arm. No sooner was another child chosen in her place than the blemish vanished. Later on in the film, in one of their theological discussions, Ruth tells this story to Mahlon as an example of how Chemosh has been good to her, concluding, 'Chemosh spared me'. When Mahlon proposes that perhaps it was a higher god and, anyway, he thought that to be sacrificed to Chemosh was a 'coveted honor', Ruth becomes confused, a sign that her theological awakening is beginning. Her observation to Boaz about God's directing her to him 'all my life' connects all these events under the rubric of divine providence.

The moment viewers have been waiting for comes when Ruth and Boaz kiss, and Boaz tells Ruth he wants her for his wife. Ruth is concerned about Tov and the levirate law, but Boaz assures her that he can get Tov to renounce his claim ('...he will come to terms. He likes property'). Unlike the biblical account, Boaz does not ask Ruth to stay the night; on the contrary, he remarks that it is getting light and she should therefore leave before people will have reason to talk. In spite of the departure from the text, Boaz's admonition does echo 3.14: 'He thought, "Let it not be known that the woman came to the threshing floor"'. With this climactic scene between the lovers, the film gives us an inclusio as aesthetically satisfying as any in the biblical tale:[108] at the scene's end, before she leaves, Ruth touchingly

---

108.   See the stylistic analyses of D.F. Rauber, 'Literary Values in the Bible: the Book of Ruth', *Journal of Biblical Literature* 89 (1979), pp. 27-37; Stephen Bertman, 'Symmetrical Design in the Book of Ruth', *Journal of Biblical Literature* 84 (1965), pp. 165-68; Trible, *God and the Rhetoric of Sexuality*, pp. 166-99.

utters the magic words Boaz had spoken to her at the scene's beginning—'I love you'. She runs home, without the burden of all that biblical grain (3.15), to tell Naomi the joyous news.

The obstacle to the lovers' happiness is not so easily removed, however, and the romantic interest is thereby heightened. As in the biblical book, the threshing floor scene does not provide the film's final resolution. *The Story of Ruth* introduces a new twist in the plot by having Tov refuse to renounce his claim to Ruth even though Boaz 'offered him everything I own'. When it appears that there is no way out for Ruth and she is about to be married to Tov, she tells him that, although she honors his claim, she does not love him. She goes on to say that, on the night of the harvest festival, she sought out Boaz on the threshing floor. Everyone looks on suitably aghast, and Tov, his anger rising, refuses to enter a marriage with a woman of dubious repute.[109] At this point, Boaz steps in to marry Ruth.

What is particularly interesting about this climactic resolution scene is the way the film removes uncertainty about what happened on the threshing floor for the audience only to introduce it for Tov.[110] Tov is tricked into giving up his claim to Ruth because he believes that something sexual did happen on the threshing floor. Lest there be any doubt among the people of Judah, as well as in audiences' minds, Boaz and Ruth swear a 'holy oath' before the elders that 'nothing passed between us on that night or any other time except spoken vows of love'.[111] With the question about what transpired between Ruth and Boaz on the threshing floor settled once and for all, the film draws to a close with the happy couple's marriage (fig. 5.4). 'Love'—that is, heterosexual love—'triumphs over all' could be considered the film's message. In addition, by virtue of its framework, in which a holy man introduces the story and brings about the happy ending, the film also suggests that God has been guiding events to this

109. No doubt the film is here offering a nod of recognition to the biblical ambiguity.

110. Another important contribution of this ending is that it makes Ruth, and not Boaz as in the biblical account, dissemble in a clever way that gets the next-of-kin to renounce his claim. Giving her a voice at the end makes the film Ruth's in a way the book is not; on the question whether Ruth is erased or affirmed by the biblical book, see Amy-Jill Levine, 'Ruth', in Newsom and Ringe (eds.), *The Women's Bible Commentary*, pp. 79, 84.

111. Note the 'at any other time', just to be sure.

romantic conclusion.[112] It is a marriage made in heaven. (This is also the outcome Naomi had expected on the basis of a prophecy the same holy man had made to her that a famous line would descend from Ruth. 'Who but Boaz could father such a family?', she reasons.)[113]

Figure 5.4. Elana Eden and Stuart Whitman, in *The Story of Ruth*

In Hollywood's version of the story of Ruth, when the romantic relationship between Ruth and Boaz is foregrounded, it is at the expense of the bond between the women. Not only is Naomi too old and non-sexual to be a serious romantic interest for anyone, but also Ruth goes with her to Bethlehem for theological, and not personal, reasons. When it comes to affirming the heterosexual bond over the

112. This ties in with Ruth's statement to Boaz in the threshing floor scene, 'Perhaps he [God]'s been directing me to you all my life'. The hidden activity of God is thought by many to be the theme of the book of Ruth; see, *inter alia*, Ronald M. Hals, *The Theology of the Book of Ruth* (Philadelphia: Fortress Press, 1969); Campbell, *Ruth*, pp. 28-29, 112-113, 138 and *passim*; Hubbard, *The Book of Ruth*, pp. 63-74, 212, 217-218; for a more critical evaluation, see Sasson, *Ruth*, pp. 44-45, 220-21, 249 and *passim*.

113. She says this when Ruth tells her that Boaz has asked her to be his wife, but before she and Ruth learn from Boaz that Tov has refused to give up his claim to Ruth. Naomi recounts to Ruth a visit she had from a holy man who prophesied that a famous house would descend from Ruth, that would include a great king and a prophet many would worship as the messiah.

bond between the women, the film's crowning touch is achieved through the use of the musical score, composed by Franz Waxman, to signal the shift in Ruth's devotion. Early in the film, just after Ruth makes her famous entreat-me-not-to-leave-you speech, we hear her words set to music and sung by a female voice while we watch the two women journeying across the wilderness to Judah. The same musical theme is played again the moment Ruth says to Boaz, 'I love you'. As she leaves the threshing floor, it is to the tune of 'Where You Go I Will Go'. The music is repeated at the film's end, when Ruth and Boaz leave the screen as man and wife. By transferring the moving musical setting of Ruth's oath of loyalty from Naomi to Boaz, the film has managed not only to foreground the heterosexual bond but dramatically and effectively to replace the bond between the women with the romantic bond between a heterosexual couple.[114]

The Ruth–Naomi–Boaz Triangle

I have deliberately not mentioned the title of Calderon's painting, 'Ruth and Naomi'. Three people, however, are represented, not just the two, Ruth and Naomi. Although the title reflects the importance of the central figures and the key event in the story the painting is meant to represent, the decision to call a painting of three people by the names of two of them inevitably draws attention to the third figure. Once we recognize the central figures as Ruth and Naomi, we are not troubled by the extra person. Just as Orpah is a marginal character in the biblical story, so she is marginal in the painting. But if we take seriously the sexual ambivalence of the figure in black and allow for the possibility of seeing the two central figures as Ruth and Boaz, as did many viewers to whom I did not reveal the title in advance, then we are left with the problem of identifying the third person. I mentioned at the beginning of this chapter that I find the identification of the figure in blue as Naomi especially suggestive. Whereas Orpah is a minor character, who like *ploni almoni* serves as a

---

114. There is one other time this music is played, after Naomi has told Ruth of Tov's intention to invoke the levirate law in order to marry Ruth. There it signals that Ruth's devotion to Naomi has led to consequences she is willing to accept though it breaks her heart, while also pointing forward to a heterosexual bond, albeit marriage to the wrong man. Though the music is repeated, we hear the lyrics only in the scene where the women cross the wilderness to return to Judah.

foil to highlight the qualities of a main character, Naomi is a, if not the, book's main character. The three central characters in the story—Naomi, Ruth, and Boaz—correspond to the three figures that our alternative (mis)reading of Calderon's painting presents us with. Misreading Calderon's painting draws attention to the biblical Naomi's refusal to be written out of the story once the goal—Ruth's marriage to Boaz and the birth of Obed—is achieved.

This brings me to the problem of the third person and the triangular nature of interpersonal relationships in the biblical tale. The third person is a surplus in any romantic equation and is difficult to account for in terms of bonding. In what follows I want to suggest that the figure of Naomi in the Bible is as sexually ambivalent as the figure in black in Calderon's painting and that this ambivalence, in both the metatext and its source text, challenges our notions of gender by destabilizing our gender categories. We have already examined the bond between Ruth and Naomi and that between Ruth and Boaz as presented in the biblical text and as transformed in various metatexts. But relationships in the book of Ruth are more complex than analysis in terms of patterns of bonding reveals. There is a striking blurring of gender roles, indeed of sexually determined roles—husband, wife, mother, father—in this tale, with Naomi symbolically holding all four of these roles.

In Ruth 4.17, the women of Bethlehem say, 'A son is born to Naomi'. The expression, 'a son is born to...', is normally used of fathers, never simply of mothers.[115] Naomi is thus symbolically in the position of a father to Obed, and, as Obed's father, she is also symbolically a husband to Ruth, who has borne him (4.15). In 4.16, we learn that Naomi 'set the child on her breast', as a mother would do,[116] and became his nurse (*'omenet*). How could Naomi, who claimed in 1.12 to be too old to have a husband, possibly nurse the child? Commentators usually answer this question by referring to the wider sense of *'omenet* as foster-parent or guardian.[117] But the fact that

115. See, e.g., Gen. 17.17; 21.5; 44.20; 2 Sam. 3.2, 5; 12.14; Jer. 20.15; Isa. 39.7; Job 1.2; 1 Chron. 3.1; 22.9; 2 Chron. 6.9.

116. Cf. Hubbard, *The Book of Ruth*, p. 274: 'The language ("breast") suggests that Naomi did so as a warm, tender mother'.

117. E.g., the term is used to refer to the guardians of Ahab's children in 2 Kgs 10, and to kings (in parallelism with nursing mothers) in Isa. 49.23; Mordecai is Esther's foster parent, Est. 2.7. See also the discussion in Hubbard, *The Book of Ruth*,

it is used elsewhere to refer to a wet-nurse (Num. 11.12; and possibly
2 Sam. 4.4?), in combination with Naomi's act of placing the child
on her breast, reinforces the symbolism of Naomi as a mother to
Obed. As Obed's 'mother', Naomi is also symbolically Boaz's wife.

Both Naomi and Boaz call Ruth 'my daughter' (2.2, 8, 22; 3.1, 10,
16, 18). In addition to making Naomi symbolically a mother to
Ruth, this epithet also puts Naomi and Boaz in the position of Ruth's
parents—and thus reinforces the symbolic husband–wife relationship
of Naomi and Boaz from another angle.

Although Naomi and Boaz never actually meet in the story, if we
pursue certain implications of a curious textual feature, we can find
the three major characters somehow all involved in the intimacy of
the threshing floor scene. A fascinating instance of the blurring of
roles is created by a *ketiv-qere* problem, fascinating precisely because
the problem occurs twice. In Naomi's instructions to Ruth in 3.3-4,
where the vocalized text (the *qere*) reads,

> …wash and anoint yourself, put on your finest dress, and go down to the
> threshing floor. Do not make yourself known to the man until he has
> finished eating and drinking. When he lies down, mark the place where he
> lies down and go and uncover the place of his feet and lie down—and he
> will tell you what to do,

the consonantal text (*ketiv*) reads,

> …wash and anoint yourself, put on your finest dress, and I will go down
> to the threshing floor. Do not make yourself known to the man until he
> has finished eating and drinking. When he lies down, mark the place
> where he lies down and go and uncover the place of his feet and I will lie
> down—and he will tell you what to do.

By having Naomi put herself into the scene twice, in a sort of pre-
Freudian slip, the consonantal text conflates Naomi with Ruth as the
'seducer' of Boaz on the threshing floor.[118]

pp. 274-75. Sasson (*Ruth*, pp. 170-72, 235-37), who disputes the interpretation of
Naomi's action as adoptive or legitimating, 'wonder[s] whether a translation such as
"wet-nurse" might yet be relevant, despite the fact that Naomi was an elderly widow'
(p. 233). He finds similarities to ancient Near Eastern examples, where a royal child
is said to be placed on the lap of a deity and be suckled by her (pp. 236-37).

118.   Campbell (*Ruth*, p. 120) thinks the form is not first person singular but
rather an archaic second person feminine ending. Sasson (*Ruth*, pp. 68-69) mentions
the first person consonantal form and the 'allegedly "archaic" second person feminine
singular', but decides that the context 'requires us to opt for the "archaic"

Finally, Naomi is also represented on a symbolic level as a wife to Ruth, for Ruth leaves her father and mother and cleaves to Naomi as a man leaves his father and mother and cleaves to his wife (Gen. 2.24). In sum, Naomi holds the following symbolic positions: husband to Ruth, wife to Ruth, mother to Ruth, wife to Boaz, father to Obed, and mother to Obed. It would be difficult to imagine a more radical blurring of sexually defined roles.[119]

Ruth is literally Boaz's wife and Obed's mother: she marries Boaz, conceives and gives birth to a son (4.13). She also stands in the position of both husband and wife, daughter and son, vis-à-vis Naomi. As Naomi's 'husband' she leaves her parents and cleaves to her 'wife', and as the mother of the son 'born to Naomi', she stands in as

sufformative'. Pardes (*Countertraditions in the Bible*, pp. 104-105), in contrast, recognizes the potential that reading with the *ketiv* has for Naomi's 'sympathetic identification with her daughter-in-law' (p. 105). On the *ketiv-qere* relationship and 'double writings' indicating both interpretive possibilities, see James Barr, 'A New Look at Kethibh-Qere', in *Remembering All the Way* (ed. A.S. van der Woude; Oudtestamentische Studiën, 21; Leiden: Brill, 1981), pp. 19-37.

119. The significant role Naomi does not hold is husband to Boaz, nor will Ruth hold this symbolic role. Unlike the women, who take a man's symbolic position, the man never symbolically takes a woman's position, though he does take on a woman's point of view (see below). The roles and positions shared by Ruth with Naomi led Brenner to posit two sources behind the present book, a Naomi story and a Ruth story ('Naomi and Ruth', *Vetus Testamentum* 23 [1983], pp. 385-97); for her later refinement, but not dismissal, of this position, see Brenner, 'Naomi and Ruth: Further Reflections', in Brenner (ed.), *A Feminist Companion to Ruth*, pp. 140-44. A number of the shared gender (as well as other) roles I discuss here are treated by Jon L. Berquist ('Role Dedifferentiation in the Book of Ruth', *Journal for the Study of the Old Testament* 57 [1993], pp. 23-37) as examples of the sociological process of role dedifferentiation, where a person takes on additional roles, including roles that would ordinarily be socially inappropriate, in a time of crisis. Through sociological analysis, he anticipates my conclusion by suggesting that in Ruth 'women deconstruct their gender by dedifferentiating their roles' (p. 35). Others who observe the complex gender symbolism, but do not develop its implications for gender blurring, include Pardes, *Countertraditions in the Bible*, and Fewell and Gunn, *Compromising Redemption*. Fewell and Gunn speak of Boaz as Naomi's surrogate husband (p. 82) and of Ruth as 'husband' to Naomi (p. 97), and they describe Ruth's mediating role, when after the threshing floor encounter she brings the grain from Boaz to Naomi, in terms of her playing 'wife' to Boaz and 'husband' to Naomi (p. 103). Pardes (pp. 102-17) offers a particularly perceptive discussion of what she terms 'the doubling of the female subject'. She concludes that, 'In a strange way Ruth and Naomi manage to share not only a husband and a son, but also textual subjectivity' (p. 108).

Naomi's 'wife'. Referred to by Naomi as 'my daughter', Ruth also fills the role of son in at least two respects: by providing for Naomi after the death of her natural sons, when no *go'el* was in sight (ch. 2), and by being 'more than *seven* sons' (4.15) by virtue of her role in perpetuating the family line—a line traced through sons (4.18-22).[120]

The book's third main character, Boaz, is, on the literal level, the father of Obed, so much so in fact that the genealogy of 4.18-22 ignores the levirate law that would require that Mahlon be Obed's father. He is also in the position of a father to Ruth, whom he addresses as 'my daughter'. In addition to his role as father, Boaz is a husband to *both* women: literally Ruth's husband, he is symbolically husband to Naomi, who sets his child on her breast and nurses him as if she were his mother. Although Boaz does not hold a woman's symbolic position in the story, he nonetheless 'accepts being reflected... in a female role', as Bal has shown. Boaz takes on a woman's point of view, argues Bal, by acknowledging his dependence on the other, Ruth, in order to establish his subject position, allowing himself to be fulfilled through her.[121]

If all three main characters in the book of Ruth participate in the symbolic transgression of gender and sexual boundaries, it would seem that the book poses an important challenge to traditional gender categories, what Judith Butler refers to as our 'binary frame for thinking about gender'.[122] Indeed, if sexuality is a modern construct, as Michel Foucault maintains,[123] the recognition of it as such might give us a different way of approaching relationships in the book of Ruth, a way that destabilizes our familiar gender categories. Can we refuse to choose between the Ruth-Naomi and the Ruth-Boaz dyad and happily live with an eternal(ly unstable) triangle? By posing this question, I am not proposing that such an intellectual position should, or could, replace the kinds of appropriation I have been describing in my earlier metatextual examples but rather that it gives us another, important interpretive option. Appropriations of the Ruth-Naomi

---

120.   Cf. Fewell and Gunn (*Compromising Redemption*, p. 97), who observe that 'Ruth replaces husband and son as Naomi's caretaker'.

121.   Bal, *Lethal Love*, p. 87.

122.   Judith Butler, *Gender Trouble: Feminism and the Subversion of Identity* (New York: Routledge, 1990), p. viii.

123.   See Michel Foucault, *The History of Sexuality: An Introduction*, I (New York: Vintage Books, 1990).

and Ruth-Boaz relationships for readers' own interests serve to remind us that we readers have a stake in our cultural heritage, and that, if the only way we can lay claim to our cultural heritage is to reinterpret or, indeed, misread it, then reinterpret and misread it we shall. For to allow notions of inviolate 'original meanings' or 'authentic contexts' to prevent us from doing so would leave us impoverished.

A noticeable difference between the popular and scholarly metatexts that I have used as my examples is the willingness of popular works to appropriate in more extreme forms the Ruth-Naomi or Ruth-Boaz relationships for their purposes, and, as a consequence, to ascribe feelings more freely to the characters. Only in the metatexts can the characters truly fulfill their desire, and thereby fulfill the reader's desire for mimesis. Whereas traditional biblical commentators, such as Campbell, Sasson, and Hubbard, would prefer to keep modern sentiments out of it, other interpreters, pursuing a more postmodern reading, might question the repression of desire such attempts entail.[124] Hubbard, for example, thinks that Ruth acts solely out of concern for Naomi. In other words, he uses Ruth's loyalty to Naomi as a means of denying any romantic feelings for Boaz on Ruth's part; in effect, denying Ruth's sexual desire altogether (since he does not entertain sexual desire on her part for Naomi). Is this realistic?[125] It

124. Biblical scholars influenced by postmodern approaches are most ready to acknowledge the characters' desire; e.g. Fewell and Gunn, *Compromising Redemption*; Landy, 'Ruth and the Romance of Realism'. Cf. Brenner, 'Naomi and Ruth: Further Reflections', p. 141: 'One can leave this important and interesting issue undecided [what happened on the threshing floor], provided the foregrounding of Ruth's sexuality *per se* is recognized'. Although some interpretations may aim more than others to discover what the original author had in mind or the original audience might have understood, no reading, whether more traditional or more postmodern, is neutral or objective or free from the interpreter's interests, as I have maintained throughout this study; see esp. Chapter 3 above. For an analysis that illustrates this point for the book of Ruth by illustrating how different scholarly readings are not only based upon different theoretical premises but also serve the different ideological objectives of their proponents, see Edward L. Greenstein, 'Reading Strategies and the Story of Ruth', Chapter 1 in his *Reader Responsibility: The Shaping of Meaning in Biblical Narrative* (Journal for the Study of the Old Testament Supplement Series; Gender Culture, Theory, 6; Sheffield: Sheffield Academic Press, forthcoming). (It was Greenstein who sent me back to Borges, where I discovered that I had long ago underlined the lines cited as my epigraph in Chapter 3.)

125. Hubbard, *The Book of Ruth*, pp. 213-15. Note, however, that Hubbard engages in what I call 'romanticizing' when he speaks of the threshing-floor scene's

seems to me that to answer that question we would need more extensive analysis of ancient views of sexuality, which has not been my
subject here, and which has hardly been investigated in the field of
biblical studies.[126]

Reading texts in terms of our own interests reflects a high regard
for those texts, and usually some kind of personal investment in them,
as the long and varied history of biblical interpretation powerfully
illustrates. I doubt very much that Alpert, for example, whose sensitive lesbian midrash I mentioned earlier, would care very much about
finding role models in the book of Ruth if it were not part of a
cultural and religious tradition in which she wants to participate. The
influence of gender and sexual orientation on reading and viewing
needs to be recognized in any kind of reader-response approach to
literature and art. At the same time, texts and their visual representations have a way of eluding our attempts to fit them into molds, of
destabilizing our interpretations. Relationships in Ruth are not rigidly
defined and gender blurring occurs on a large scale, with sexually
identified roles shared and transgressed by the book's three major
characters. Reading Ruth as an eternally unstable triangle offers a third
alternative to reading in terms of same-sex and opposite-sex relationships, yielding an interpretive triangle analogous to our Ruth-Naomi-
Boaz triangle created by the irrepressible third person. By destabilizing
our gender categories, the book of Ruth, like Calderon's painting
with which I began, invites readers to collapse the gender distinctions
with which they themselves operate. Or at least to examine, and
perhaps to reconfigure, them.

'delicate sensuality' (p. 209); see also above. This is, not surprisingly, a fairly typical
scholarly view, where the emphasis is on understanding the story in its ancient
context. See also Bos, 'Out of the Shadows', pp. 63-64, who sees the sexual allusions
in Ruth 3 as referring 'not to a romantic enterprise but rather to a business one'
(p. 63). Though remarking (*Ruth*, p. 135), 'Whether or not the two whiled away the
night at the threshing-floor in tender embrace is doubtless of psychological
significance', Sasson nonetheless does not speculate on it.

126. I have in mind approaches like those taken to classical literature in David
M. Halperin, John J. Winkler, and Froma I. Zeitlin (eds.), *Before Sexuality: The
Construction of Erotic Experience in the Ancient Greek World* (Princeton, NJ: Princeton
University Press, 1990); John J. Winkler, *The Constraints of Desire: The Anthropology
of Sex and Gender in Ancient Greece* (New York: Routledge, 1990); see also Thomas
Laqueur, *Making Sex: Body and Gender from the Greeks to Freud* (Cambridge, MA:
Harvard University Press, 1990).

6

Why, Why, Why, Delilah?

Men have never tired of fashioning
expressions for the violent force by which
man feels himself drawn to the woman, and
side by side with his longing, the dread
that through her he might die and be
undone.
    Karen Horney

The name Delilah will be an everlasting
curse on the lips of men.
    Victor Mature to Hedy Lamarr in
    Samson and Delilah

Why should I humbly sue for peace, thus scorn'd,
With infamy upon my name denounc'd?
    Delilah in Handel's *Samson*[1]

In Andrew Lloyd Webber's *Phantom of the Opera*, when Christine pulls off his mask, the Phantom exclaims, 'Damn you, you little prying Pandora, you little demon! Is this what you wanted to see? Curse you, you little lying Delilah!' Drawing on Greek and biblical mythology, this name-calling effectively conjures up a vision of female curiosity that is simultaneously a betrayal. 'Prying' and 'lying' attribute evil intention to her. In a song made popular by Tom Jones,[2] entitled simply 'Delilah', the unidentified male singer asks Delilah to forgive him for killing her in a jealous frenzy because 'I just couldn't take

---

1.   The libretto is by Newburgh Hamilton, based on Milton's *Samson Agonistes*, where Delilah's speech is somewhat different:

> Why do I humble thus myself, and, suing
> For peace, reap nothing but repulse and hate?
> Bid go with evil omen, and the brand
> Of infamy upon my name denounced?

2.   The song predates Jones; the recording I have of it, sung by the Platters, is older (Audio Archive Collectors Edition [n.d.]).

any more'. The song, from which I take the title for this chapter, is about a woman who betrays her lover with another man and then adds insult to injury by laughing at him when he confronts her. It is not about the biblical Delilah at all. Or is it? Since naming this woman 'Delilah' is neither accidental nor entirely innocent, I shall return to this song and its connection with the biblical character in the discussion below. In the 1949 Hollywood film, *Samson and Delilah*, when Samson, played by Victor Mature, is betrayed into the hands of the Philistines, he says to Delilah (Hedy Lamarr), 'The name Delilah will be an everlasting curse on the lips of men'. This judgment on the woman, which is meant to represent the biblical hero's words at the time of his betrayal, already confirms the status Delilah's name has achieved over the centuries, and of which the film is a reflection.

In the examples above, the name 'Delilah' is clearly overdetermined; in common parlance, her name is synonymous with treachery and deceit. Indeed, Delilah has become a trope for the *femme fatale*, the woman fatal to man—sexually irresistible, at once both fascinating and frightening, and ultimately deadly. As a cultural symbol, what she represents is rivaled perhaps only by two other biblical figures, whose names, like hers, have passed into popular usage: Jezebel, whose image as a shameless or abandoned woman is rather unwarranted, and that other arch-fiend whose name connotes betrayal, and who, like Delilah, does it for money—Judas. All three names, in addition to designating infamous literary figures, have dictionary definitions as common nouns. Under 'Delilah' the *Oxford English Dictionary* has 'used allusively to mean a temptress or treacherous love'. In a recent work of fiction, the two arch-betrayers are linked: 'I surrendered my seed to Delilah after she bestowed upon me the kiss of Judas', says a character in Pat Conroy's *Beach Music*.

Delilah's place as temptress *par excellence* in popular culture is so well established that it needs no documentation. In this chapter I propose to explore her bad reputation and its embellishments by looking first at its roots in the biblical account of Judges 16 and then at some of the ways selected metatexts flesh out Delilah's character. In the biblical story of Samson and Delilah, a story told from a decidedly andro-centric point of view, the woman is coded to represent the attraction and danger of female sexuality.[3] She personifies that 'violent force',

---

3.   See, especially, Bal, *Lethal Love*, pp. 37-67; Exum, *Fragmented Women*, pp. 61-93.

the male longing and dread that Karen Horney speaks about in my epigraph above, and this encoded representation paves the way for her metatextual development as temptress, vamp, and one of film's most compelling *femmes fatales*. The metatexts considered here can be seen as responses to a perceived need to know, or to show, more about this obscure but fascinating character. In the discussion below I shall seek to link this quest for knowledge with the desire to control. Particularly striking in these metatexts is the desire to supply two things lacking, or insufficiently developed, in the biblical account: motivation and closure. They supply one or both of these without, however, ever challenging the fundamental trope of the *femme fatale*. Thus even when some of them manage to portray Delilah in a better light, they nonetheless reinscribe the male attraction to and fear of female sexuality that she represents.

As in the previous chapter, I shall be dealing here primarily with metatexts, and using only a few metatextual examples through which, among many others that could be adduced, Delilah has passed into popular culture as larger than life. Since I am not undertaking to trace the development of Delilah's image nor to offer anything like a comprehensive survey of its manifestations (which would be a fascinating subject in itself), I make no claim that my observations will hold true in every case or that notable exceptions do not exist. My interest lies in the familiar stereotype, and what I offer here is a montage of Delilahs, drawn from art, music, film, literature, and, of course, the biblical account. I want to see how the 'legend' has grown, and to approach this question by allowing for a degree of free-play of and between metatexts, while at the same time drawing attention to the intransigence of the *femme fatale* trope in these various cultural appropriations of Delilah. Finally I want to suggest how we might deconstruct the *femme fatale* trope by inquiring into what motivates the view of women encoded in the source text and reinscribed in the metatexts.

If the appeal to film and my attempt in this book to describe in words what the screen shows us are ambitious, the use of musical metatexts poses a greater challenge. As this approach is rather experimental, I ask the reader, if at all possible, to pause and listen to the love duet from Camille Saint-Saëns's opera, *Samson et Dalila*, before reading further. In Chapter 5, I used Calderon's sexually ambivalent representation of Naomi to spark a series of misreadings that eventu-

ally brought us back to the sexually ambivalent role of Naomi (as well
as Ruth and Boaz) in the biblical account. Saint-Saëns gives us something of a musical equivalent to the painting, in my opinion. Like
Calderon, who identified his central figures as Ruth and Naomi, Saint-
Saëns, by locating his music in its 'proper' place, instructs his listeners
how to hear it. Delilah and Samson sing this duet just before he yields
to her sexual allure and she betrays him to his enemies. But must we
listen to it as the composer intended? What if, as sometimes happens,
we hear it out of context? The erotic power of the music, I submit,
overwhelms the libretto. Could music so beautiful be sung by someone so treacherous? It is difficult to believe that the intensity of passion
conveyed by the musical score could be anything less than sincere.
How could Delilah sing so convincingly of tenderness (*tendresse*) and
rapture (*ivresse*) if deception is on her mind? Does the music perhaps
attribute greater depth to Delilah than the libretto allows?

Just as viewers of Calderon's painting were willing to debate what
part of the book of Ruth it represents, so we might consider where
else in the story of Samson and Delilah this magnificent love duet
could be placed. Another of my metatexts, the film *Samson and Delilah*,
produced and directed by Cecil B. De Mille, offers one answer.[4] De
Mille gives us a Delilah and Samson who could well sing this duet
after the betrayal. His cinematic Delilah repents of her misdeed and,
tormented by guilt and grief, she goes to visit Samson in the granary
at night. As she enters, he is praying for God's guidance. She walks
over to him softly and places her hand on his shoulder. He asks if she
is an angel, but when she speaks, he recognizes her devil's voice.
Declaring she would give anything to undo what she has done, she
begs him to escape with her to Egypt, where she will be his eyes,
share his laughter and shed his tears. To his bitter question how she
will respond when he curses her for his darkness, she replies that she
will kneel and ask his forgiveness. He does not want to forgive her
but his love for her prevails. 'Vengeance is yours, O Lord. Strike her,
destroy her, for I cannot', he says, and takes her in his arms. Saint-
Saëns's musical score would serve very well at this point in the film to
convey the intensity of feeling between the lovers.

There is another scene in the film where it would also fit well. The

4.   Twentieth Century Fox, 1949. The screenplay by Jesse Lasky, Jr, and Fredric
Frank is based on works by Harold Lamb and Vladimir Jabotinsky, as well as on the
biblical account, and the film has a superb musical score of its own by Victor Young.

following morning, when Samson is brought into the temple for the Philistines' amusement, Delilah abandons her seat of honor beside the Saran, the supreme ruler of the Philistines (played by the ever cynical George Sanders), and goes to join Samson in the arena.[5] It is Delilah, and not a young boy as in the biblical account, who leads Samson to the two pillars that support the temple. She touches his shoulder, and he leans against her. He urges her to leave and declares his enduring love: 'Wherever you are, my love is with you. Go.' She caresses his hand against her cheek, kisses it, and pretends to take her leave. If this were an opera and not a film, one could easily imagine Samson and Delilah singing a reprise of Saint-Saëns's duet before he pulls down the temple and they die together (and, in either this scenario or the one in the granary, the tension in the strings and woodwinds would anticipate the impending doom in the temple).

My point with this musical and cinematic example is that it is not axiomatic that the story must be developed in a certain way and not another. The biblical account is not the only version of the fabula in which a woman learns the secret of a strong man's strength and betrays it to his enemies; the themes are timeless and widespread.[6] An ancient storyteller adapted the fabula to characters named Samson and Delilah, and his version has become famous and influential in Western culture because it was included in the Bible. As a cultural commodity it has subsequently been embellished and adapted in ways that can not be controlled by its ancient biblical context nor fully accounted for by recourse to it. Before considering some of these embellishments and adaptations, let us take a closer look at the biblical story with an eye to discovering what it is about it that enables and encourages development along different possible lines.

---

5.   In using the designation 'Saran' for the supreme ruler of the Philistines, the film adopts the term the Bible uses for the rulers of the Philistines, which is itself a Philistine loan word (BDB, p. 710b).

6.   Numerous parallels are provided by Gunkel, 'Simson', in *Reden und Aufsätze*, pp. 38-64; and Theodor H. Gaster, *Myth, Legend, and Custom in the Old Testament*, II (Gloucester, MA: Peter Smith, 1981), pp. 436-39. 'Demonic archetypes of woman, filling world mythology, represent the uncontrollable nearness of nature', argues Camille Paglia in her controversial study of *Sexual Personae: Art and Decadence from Nefertiti to Emily Dickinson* (New York: Vintage Books, 1990), p. 13: 'Their tradition passes nearly unbroken from prehistoric idols through literature and art to modern movies. The primary image is the femme fatale, the woman fatal to man.'

The Biblical Delilah

Could the biblical narrator have anticipated that Delilah would become so infamously famous? Delilah is a relatively minor biblical character, but one whose action has serious consequences. What we know about her as a character is minimal. The entire biblical story of Samson and Delilah consists of a mere 18 verses, and just over 300 words in the Hebrew.[7]

> After this he loved a woman in the valley of Sorek, whose name was Delilah. The rulers of the Philistines came to her and said to her, 'Entice him, and see by what means his strength is great, and by what means we may overpower him and bind him in order to humiliate him; and we will each give you eleven hundred pieces of silver'.
>
> Delilah said to Samson, 'Please tell me by what means your strength is great, and how you might be bound in order to humiliate you'. Samson said to her, 'If they bind me with seven fresh bowstrings that have not been dried, then I shall become weak and be like any other man'. Then the rulers of the Philistines brought her seven fresh bowstrings that had not been dried, and she bound him with them. Now she had men lying in wait in an inner chamber. She said to him, 'The Philistines are upon you, Samson!' But he snapped the bowstrings as a string of tow snaps when it touches the fire. So the secret of his strength was not known.
>
> Delilah said to Samson, 'You have mocked me and told me lies; please tell me how you might be bound'. He said to her, 'If they bind me with new ropes that have not been used, then I shall become weak and be like any other man'. Delilah took new ropes and bound him with them, and said to him, 'The Philistines are upon you, Samson!' And the men lying in wait were in an inner chamber. But he snapped the ropes off his arms like a thread.
>
> Delilah said to Samson, 'Until now you have mocked me and told me lies; tell me how you might be bound'. He said to her, 'If you weave the seven locks of my head with the web and make it tight with the pin, then I shall become weak and be like any other man'. So while he slept, Delilah took the seven locks of his head and wove them into the web. She made them tight with the pin, and said to him, 'The Philistines are upon you, Samson!' But he awoke from his sleep, and pulled away the pin, the loom, and the web.

7.   In the translation that follows I am restoring with the versions material that appears to have been inadvertently left out in the Hebrew text of vv. 13-14; for discussion of the problems, see Jichan Kim, *The Structure of the Samson Cycle* (Kampen: Kok Pharos, 1993), pp. 161-63.

She said to him, 'How can you say, "I love you", when your heart is not with me? These three times you have mocked me and not told me by what means your strength is great.' When she harassed him with her words day after day, and urged him, he was vexed to death. So he told her all his heart, and said to her, 'A razor has never come upon my head, for I have been a Nazirite to God from my mother's womb. If I be shaved, my strength will leave me, and I shall become weak and be like any other man.' When Delilah saw that he had told her all his heart, she sent and called the rulers of the Philistines: 'Come up this time, for he has told me all his heart'. The rulers of the Philistines came up to her and brought the money in their hands. She made him sleep upon her knees; then she called to the man, and she shaved off the seven locks of his head. Then she began to bully him, and his strength left him. She said, 'The Philistines are upon you, Samson!' He awoke from his sleep and said, 'I will go out as at other times, and shake myself free'. But he did not know that the Lord had left him. The Philistines seized him and gouged out his eyes, and brought him down to Gaza, and bound him with bronze fetters; and he ground at the mill in the prison house (Judg. 16.4-21).

Stylized repetition accounts for much of the story and helps to make it memorable. Who could forget the childishly nagging, 'you have mocked me and told me lies', or the repeated alarm, 'The Philistines are upon you, Samson!'? Like the few lines about Bathsheba bathing, this brief account has fired the imagination of its readers, producing a greater amount of commentary than would seem warranted. But what exactly do these verses tell us about Delilah? We know her name, which is more than we know about the other two women with whom Samson becomes amorously involved, the woman from Timnah in Judges 14 and the harlot at Gaza in 16.1-3. We know where she lives, in the valley of Sorek, which lies between Israelite and Philistine territory, though this does not tell us much about her, not even that she is a Philistine. The picture we get is of an independent woman, for she is not identified, as biblical women typically are, in relation to a man, usually their father or husband. She appears to have her own house, but how she came by it is not revealed. Is she a foreign woman of independent means? A wealthy widow with property, like Judith? A harlot, as is commonly supposed? We cannot be sure about Delilah's social position, or even about her house, which is not described beyond the fact that there is an inner chamber where ambushers could hide from Samson's view.

We are not told whether or not Delilah loves Samson, only that he loves her (v. 4). Should we take the textual silence about her feelings

as a hint that she does not love him in return? Is this a situation similar to that of David and Michal, discussed above in Chapter 2? In
their case, I argued, the fact that we are told that Michal loved David
but not that he loved her suggests he did not. But in assessing Michal
and David's relationship, we had a larger body of evidence from
which to draw this conclusion than we have for Delilah and Samson.
Here there is not much to go on, apart from the facts that Delilah and
Samson are probably lovers and she betrays him. Delilah obviously does
not love Samson enough to refuse to betray him at any price, but it
does not necessarily follow that she feels no affection toward him.
The textual gap concerning Delilah's feelings leaves us sufficiently in
the dark for later retellings to fill it in completely opposite ways. In
Saint-Saëns's opera Delilah secretly despises Samson and desires his
downfall, whereas in the film *Samson and Delilah* she loves him obsessively and wants to make him her prisoner. We could easily imagine a
character whose feelings lie anywhere between these extremes.

Delilah's relationship with Samson is no secret; the Philistine rulers
know about it and take advantage of it. They offer her money to
betray him and she accepts. Does this mean the narrator wants us to
think of her as inspired by greed? Not, at any rate, to the extent that
he makes capturing Samson her idea. The Philistine rulers come to
her; she does not offer her services to them.

Her actions testify to her persistence; she does not give up just
because Samson does not reveal his secret at first. Her dialogue and
the narrative comment that 'she harassed him day after day with her
words until he was vexed to death' indicate both her skillful way with
rhetoric and her recourse to nagging to break down Samson's
resistance. Does she also use feminine 'wiles', 'flattering prayers and
sighs/ And amorous reproaches',[8] as the metatexts I have selected
simply assume? Is this what the Philistine rulers have in mind when
they instruct her to 'entice' Samson (*patti*, v. 5)? Delilah cleverly
exploits Samson's affections ('How can you say, "I love you", when
your heart is not with me?', v. 15), and she knows it when, at last, he
tells her the truth ('When Delilah saw that he had told her all his
heart, she sent and called the rulers of the Philistines...', v. 18). Since
at first she had ambushers waiting in the inner chamber (vv. 9, 12),
but in the end she has to send for the Philistines (v. 18), we might
conclude that while she was gaining power over Samson, she was

8.   Milton, *Samson Agonistes*, ll. 403, 392-93.

losing credibility with the Philistines.[9]

Delilah herself carries out the different procedures Samson describes for binding him (first with fresh bowstrings and then with new ropes) and for weaving his hair into the web on her loom. But we cannot be entirely sure whether she, or someone else, cuts his hair. The verb in v. 19 is third person feminine singular, 'she cut the seven locks of his head', but just before it the Hebrew text reads, 'she caused him to sleep upon her knees and she called to the man'. Who is this man and where did he come from? Jack Sasson argues convincingly that 'the man' referred to here is none other than Samson himself: 'Bringing him to sleep on her lap, she called to the man [Samson], then began to cut the seven braids on his hair'. Why does she call to him? To make sure he is deeply asleep, answers Sasson.[10] Still, one must admit that the Hebrew is somewhat awkward. In what appears to be an attempt to make sense of it, some ancient versions make the man a barber and have him shave Samson.[11] They are followed by most commentators and modern translations, such as the New Revised Standard Version, for example, where we read: 'She let him fall asleep on her lap; and she called a man, and had him shave off the seven locks of his head'. Thus we have two important and influential textual traditions, one that has Delilah cut Samson's hair and the other that has a barber do the cutting, both of which are firmly established in the metatextual tradition, as we shall see.

After cutting Samson's hair, Delilah 'began to bully him (*le'annoto*) and his strength left him', v. 19. The term I translated 'bully' can be rendered variously as 'afflict', 'humiliate', 'torment', or 'subdue'.[12] But how should we understand it here? Earlier the Philistine rulers used the same terminology when they instructed Delilah, 'Entice him and

9.   Jack M. Sasson, 'Who Cut Samson's Hair? (And Other Trifling Issues Raised by Judges 16)', *Prooftexts* 8 (1988), p. 337.

10.   Sasson, 'Who Cut Samson's Hair?', pp. 336-38.

11.   The Septuagint[A] and the Vulgate specify a barber; the Septuagint[B] has the 'man' do the shaving.

12.   The root *'nh* in the piel has a wide range of meanings; it is used, for example, to describe the way Sarah treats Hagar that causes her to flee (Gen. 16.6), and also for the way Laban does not want Jacob to treat his daughters (Gen. 31.50); in Ps. 105.18 it describes Joseph's feet in fetters, as a slave; it is used of the Egyptians' treatment of their Israelite slaves (Exod. 1.11-12), but also of God's treatment of Israel in the wilderness to prove them (Deut. 8.2-3, 16). *'nh* in the piel also has sexual connotations; it is a term for rape (e.g., Gen. 34.2; Deut. 21.14; Judg. 20.5; 2 Sam. 13.12).

see by what means his strength is great and how we may overpower him and bind him in order to subdue/humiliate/torment/bully him' (*le'annoto*, v. 5). Does it mean that Delilah teases or pushes Samson around in some way, for example by hitting him or poking at him, in order to test whether or not he is helpless? Is she checking just to be sure he is 'weak like any other man', since Samson has fooled her before? Or is the narrator hinting at something more harsh and heartless?

The biblical story of Samson and Delilah raises more questions than it answers. To make matters worse for readers interested in the woman's point of view, as soon as she has accomplished her mission and enabled the Philistines to capture Samson, Delilah disappears from the narrative. This suggests that Delilah's importance to the story is simply to further the plot, and that her characterization is of little consequence to the narrator. After all, the story is really about Samson, his adventures and misadventures, and how he ultimately fulfills his mission to 'begin to deliver Israel from the hand of the Philistines' (Judg. 13.5). As in the story of David and Bathsheba, the woman's subjectivity is irrelevant. Its absence, however, opens the door for all manner of gap filling on the part of readers. Not content with such scanty and tantalizingly ambiguous information about the woman, we want to know more about the mysterious Delilah.

Delilah, the Philistine Prostitute?

Two of the most common assumptions about Delilah is that she is a Philistine and that she is a prostitute, neither of which is expressly stated in the biblical account. One encounters these assumptions not only in popular thinking but in the scholarly literature as well. Let us take them in turn, though, as we shall see, they are mutually influencing. A few biblical commentators raise the possibility that Delilah might be Israelite. In support of this identification are the facts that she has a Hebrew name and her home is located between Israelite and Philistine territory, neither clearly part of one or the other. So many foreigners in the Bible have Hebrew names, however, that this interesting bit of evidence does not prove anything. Even when the possibility that Delilah is an Israelite is raised, its implications are never pursued. Against it, there appear to be three main reasons for believing that Delilah is a Philistine: (1) because Samson's fatal weakness is his attraction to Philistine women, as his other liaisons show; (2) because Delilah has dealings with the Philistine rulers, and it is unlikely that the Philistines would appeal to an Israelite woman for assistance; and (3) because she betrays Samson to the Philistines, and surely an Israelite woman would not betray the hero of her people to their enemy. These are all good reasons, but they involve certain assumptions and prejudices.

If we examine closely the claim about Samson's attraction to foreign women, we discover that in actuality only one of the women with whom Samson becomes involved is specifically identified as a Philistine, the woman from Timnah who becomes his wife, with disastrous consequences for everyone involved (Judg. 14.1–15.6). The harlot (16.1-3), just because she lives in the Philistine metropolis of Gaza, is not necessarily a Philistine; she might be a foreigner, possibly even an Israelite woman for all we know. Yet, to my knowledge, no commentator identifies her as anything other than Philistine. Perhaps it is not only the harlot's place of residence but the fact that she is a harlot that disinclines biblical commentators and ordinary readers alike from thinking she might be Israelite. Such a conclusion, however, is based on an unexamined presupposition that Israelite women would not behave in such a way, or, to put it in literary-critical terms, that the Bible would not present an Israelite woman behaving in such a way. This applies especially to the second and third reasons given above. I suspect that readers find it difficult, if not downright troubling, to imagine that an Israelite woman would have any dealings with the 'uncircumcised Philistines', as the Bible disparagingly calls them, let alone betray her people's champion to their dreaded foe! Or if we *can* imagine it, we feel it must be a misreading, for we deem it highly unlikely that a biblical narrator would portray one of his own countrywomen so negatively, especially without further comment or explanation.

And what about the identification of Delilah as a harlot? This identification, too, seems to be based on three reasons: (1) she and Samson appear to be lovers, but there is no indication that they are married; (2) she seems to be a woman of independent means and she is not identified in terms of her familial relationship to a man; (3) we know of Samson's involvement with one harlot, so why not view this as another? Again, all good reasons, but none definitive. The woman and man in the Song of Songs, for example, are lovers and not married, yet we do not rush to label this woman a harlot. Would we be so quick to jump to this conclusion about Delilah if it were not for the harlot at Gaza? We are not told that Delilah has other lovers besides Samson. Why identify *Delilah* as a harlot because of *Samson's* profligacy?

Although nothing in the biblical text specifically confirms the identification of Delilah as a Philistine or a prostitute, nothing in the text discourages readers from drawing such conclusions either. Indeed, like Bathsheba, Delilah is betrayed by a kind of conspiracy against the woman, not necessarily conscious or deliberate, between the narrator and his implied androcentric audience. As I argued in Bathsheba's case, our response to the suppression of information about the woman's subjectivity is a combination of reading preconceptions and familiar stereotypes back into the text and of picking up on latent messages within the text. In particular, the process that results in typecasting Delilah as a Philistine prostitute can be understood as what happens when readers automatically adopt the view of women encoded in this story.

The story of Samson in Judges 13–16 recognizes basically two kinds of women, good and bad. This is simply a variation on the age-old division of women into two types, the woman on the pedestal who is venerated (the virgin, the mother) and the whore, the fallen woman, the woman to be scorned and looked down on. The story offers one example of a good woman, Samson's mother (Judg. 13). She is a wife and mother, the two valued roles for a woman in ancient Israelite society, and she knows her place. She may be cleverer than her husband, sensing something of the true identity of the mysterious 'man of God' who appears to her to announce Samson's birth and showing superior understanding of the divine intention, but she does not challenge his authority. The other women in the story are 'bad women', for whom we have three examples, women whose sexual attraction leads Samson astray.[13] Delilah is a bad woman.

Another opposition as important to the story as the good woman–bad woman dichotomy, and one that, unlike the good woman–bad woman opposition, is readily apparent in its surface structure, is the

13. To say that their attraction leads Samson astray is to use the patriarchal perspective reflected in the story, in which women are blamed for male desire and are held responsible for male sexual behavior. We saw this same kind of logic at work in the Bathsheba story.

opposition between the Israelites, who are privileged as the 'us', the 'right side', the heroes of the story (personified in their hero, Samson), and the Philistines as the villains.[14] Hatred of the Philistines has deep biblical roots. The Philistines are the arch-enemy against whom Israel is engaged in a fierce struggle for possession of the land, and the animosity toward them in the Samson story is but a reflection of this. No self-respecting Israelite man should become involved with one of their women, as Samson's parents' incredulous response to his marriage plans makes clear: 'Is there not a woman among the daughters of your brothers and among all your[15] people, that you are going to take a woman from the uncircumcised Philistines?' The only good woman is an Israelite woman.[16] And with this assumption, an(other) important stereotype comes into play, the foreign woman as an evil snare.

Foreign women are a threat, both to Israel's ethnic and religious identity in general and to the well-being of the Israelite man in particular. Deuteronomic legislation counsels against intermarriage with foreigners: 'You shall not make marriages with them, giving your daughters to their sons or taking their daughters for your sons. For they would turn away your sons from following me, to serve other gods; then the anger of the Lord would be kindled against you, and he would destroy you quickly' (7.3-4). Even though daughters are not to be given in marriage to foreigners, the concern here is for the sons who the biblical narrator fears will be led astray. The allure and danger of the foreign woman or 'strange woman' is particularly emphasized in the book of Proverbs, where the impressionable young man is repeatedly warned against her charms and against the danger she poses to life itself: 'for her house sinks down to death...none who go to her come back nor do they regain the paths of life' (2.18-19).[17]

14. For a fuller treatment of oppositions in the story and its inability to maintain them, see Exum, *Fragmented Women*, pp. 72-77, 90-92.

15. Reading with the Lucianic recension and the Syriac; the Masoretic text has 'my people', but both parents are represented as speaking. From a text-critical perspective, I view the Masoretic text as the preferred reading (with the singular possessive pronoun suggesting that only his father's point of view is important). In v. 3 Samson's response is addressed to his father.

16. Matters are not quite so simple, for women are by nature suspect. The text is uneasy about the Israelite woman, who undermines from within its neat system of hierarchies; see the discussion in Exum, *Fragmented Women*, pp. 76-77, 86-93.

17. Saint-Saëns's *Samson et Dalila* repeats this ideology. At her first appearance

   The narrator of the Samson story does not need to establish any of
these negative characterizations; he can simply assume and build on
the prejudices against Philistines and foreign women that he expects
his audience to hold. The fact that these stereotypes are interrelated
makes them all the more effective. Within this ideology, it seems only
'natural' to conclude that if Philistines are trouble, surely Delilah must
be one.[18] As a foreign woman who entices the unwitting Israelite
man Samson, she can be easily identified with the seductive, deadly
foreign woman of Proverbs. In addition, the juxtaposition of the
story of Delilah (16.4-22) to that of the harlot (16.1-3) with only the
clause 'and it happened after that' to separate them exerts a consider-
able influence on our reading. It is difficult not to naturalize this
encounter in the light of that one, and as a result to assume that
Samson has embarked on another 'illicit' union—this in spite of the
fact that the text does not specify that Samson and Delilah have sexual
relations, as it does for Samson and the harlot. All it says is that
Samson loved Delilah. Naturalizing, however, happens so automatically that, encouraged by the context as well as by numerous sexual
innuendoes in the story,[19] readers readily supply the sexual dimension
to Samson and Delilah's relationship. An early reader who draws on
the text's latent message to identify Delilah as a harlot is Josephus (*Ant.*
5.8.11). And the moral he draws from the story will be repeated over
the centuries: 'But as for his being ensnared by a woman, that is to be
ascribed to human nature, which is too weak to resist the temptations
to that sin; but we ought to bear him witness, that in all other
respects, he was one of extraordinary virtue' (*Ant.* 5.8.12). The moral
that describes yielding to feminine temptation as the result of human
nature is, of course, a moral about *male* nature, taken as the norm.
The moral of this story does not address women at all, except to
define their role as temptation and snare.

(Act 1 Scene 6) Delilah is presented as alluring and threatening. Samson recognizes
her as a dangerous attraction and prays to God to close his heart to her. An old
Hebrew warns him, 'Turn aside, my son, from her path! Shun and fear this alien girl.
Close your ears to her lying tongue, and avoid the serpent's venom.'

   18. See the remarks about naturalization and the control convention exercises
over the reading process in Chapter 2 above. For the influence of convention in the
Samson story in particular, see Exum, *Fragmented Women*, pp. 68-72.

   19. See Exum, *Fragmented Women*, pp. 77-80.

Delilah Painted as Prostitute

Western art has played a role in perpetuating the contemporary image of Delilah as a prostitute. For the purposes of this chapter, I want to consider closely only four rather typical examples: one, because it shows Delilah alone; two by the same artist, but representing the variant textual traditions discussed above, in which a barber cuts Samson's hair or Delilah does the cutting; and the fourth, because it shows Delilah's response to Samson's capture in a way that dramatically links it to the first example and to the *femme fatale* trope. Since the *femme fatale* as we now imagine her owes much to the nineteenth-century styles of Decadence, Symbolism, and Art Nouveau, it is perhaps appropriate to begin with a painting by Gustave Moreau (fig. 6.1), whose paintings helped shape her image (Salome, Semele, and the Sphinx were some of his favorite subjects). As in some of the paintings of Bathsheba we looked at, where David could barely be seen or was not even present, the woman's body here, in the absence of Samson, serves as a signifier of male desire. Displayed for the pleasure of the male spectator, her voluptuousness accounts for Samson's inability to resist. Unlike Bathsheba, however, whose privacy is invaded by the voyeuristic look, Delilah the courtesan invites and plays to the gaze (and in this, she is more like the movie star Bathshebas). She is aware of her erotic power and knows how to use it. Moreau's Delilah captures on the canvas the attributes we expect of the *femme fatale*: sensuality, excessiveness, temptation, shamelessness, and excitement tinged with danger.[20] Moreau originally exhibited this painting under the title *Biblical Courtesan*, implicitly judging the woman for her display of sexuality which he chose, on more than one occasion, to paint. The painting thus functions in much the same way as the paintings of Bathsheba we looked at in which the woman is held morally accountable for the way painters depicted her body for both their pleasure and that of (male) spectators.[21]

Delilah's left breast is bared. Jewelry is the only adornment on the otherwise exposed flesh of her shoulders, left arm, hands, and legs. Her left arm and fingers are extravagantly bejeweled and she wears

20. It should be obvious that I am speaking about the impression she makes on men. Women know the stereotype as well as men do, for we are all socialized into it.

21. Like the nudes John Berger discusses in *Ways of Seeing*; see above, Chapter 1.

Figure 6.1. Gustave Moreau, *Delilah*, Museo de Arte de Ponce,
The Luis A. Ferré Foundation Inc., Ponce, Puerto Rico

jewels around her ankle and even on her toes, a particularly decadent touch. Her opulent clothing and headdress are heavily ornamented. One is struck by the fact that she is dressed almost wholly in white, as if flagrantly defying its conventional association with virginity. There is, however, a dramatic strand of scarlet in her robe to signal her true status as a harlot, as well as touches of red among the ornaments in her hair and in what appears to be a jewel provocatively located at her lap. The artificiality of the bright red birds flying about in the background signals her artifice. She seems to be awaiting a suitor (Samson?) in a kind of temple of love that calls to mind the temple Samson will destroy—both forbidden temples of infidels. Her rich clothing, countless jewels, and the flowers strewn at her feet suggest she has conquered many hearts in addition to Samson's.

Since Samson is not portrayed in the painting, we might ask, Is this before or after the betrayal? Perhaps it is before, and we should imagine that Delilah is waiting for him, possibly even plotting how to discover his secret. If so, does Moreau want to underscore her greed (for she appears well enough provided for by her admirers not to *need* the money she will receive for betraying Samson)? In another painting by Moreau, located in the Louvre, Delilah is similarly portrayed in an opulent setting, this time with a languorous Samson draped across her lap in an intoxicated slumber. In this painting, too, the temptation to condemn the *femme fatale* as avaricious is great, for she is already wealthy enough. On the other hand, could it be that greed plays no role whatsoever? Does the painting in figure 6.1 suggest that betraying a man is simply something this kind of woman would do, that it is simply in her nature as *femme fatale*? If we take the painting to represent a time after the betrayal rather than before, then perhaps Delilah's opulent apparel is a sign of her ill-gained wealth. If she is contemplating the foul deed she has done, it is without the slightest trace of remorse, much like some of Moreau's paintings of Salome contemplating the head of John the Baptist. Regardless of whether the betrayal has already taken place or soon will, the depiction of the *femme fatale* in isolation conveys her availability to the male spectator in a more direct way than if Samson were with her, and, along with it, the allure and danger of female sexuality that could destroy him.

Two paintings by Rubens also perpetuate the image of Delilah as prostitute. In neither of them is she surrounded by the decadent opulence of Moreau's Delilahs, but rather she looks as if she could use the money the Philistines offer her. In *Samson and Delilah* in the National Gallery in London (fig. 6.2), Delilah appears as a young prostitute in a rather tawdry brothel, whose dim lighting barely camouflages the dingy brown walls. Among the rather stock furnishings (a flaming brazier, heavy curtains, and a patterned Oriental carpet), a statue of Venus and Cupid in an alcove provides a bordello atmosphere. An old madam looks over Delilah's shoulder and holds a candle for the barber, who deftly snips off Samson's hair while he sleeps, apparently exhausted after spending his passion in arduous love-making. Amid the warm, rich hues that lend to the painting a feeling of sensuality, the stark whiteness of Delilah's face, shoulders, and large breasts catches the viewer's attention. The exposure of her breasts, 'some of the fleshiest [flesh] ever painted' according to the

Figure 6.2. Peter Paul Rubens, *Samson and Delilah*,
reproduced by courtesy of the Trustees, The National Gallery, London

National Gallery Companion Guide[22] strikes me as rather gratuitous—a bid for the male gaze—but it does serve, along with the red dress she wears, to mark her as a harlot.

In addition to the presence of the madam and the barber, Philistine soldiers stand ready, if somewhat apprehensively, at the door. It is as if all these people have been waiting for this moment to rush onto the scene. Delilah, however, seems not to mind—or not really to notice—all the activity going on about her. Her attention is focused on Samson, at whom she looks down languidly, with something of an expression of tenderness on her face. Her hand rests almost affectionately upon his back. The painting thus suggests a reading of the story according to which, although she is 'doing her job', Delilah is actually rather fond of Samson. There seems to be, as in Rembrandt's Bathsheba, a humanizing of the woman that competes with the blaming of her. The intensity of their love-making is suggested by the position of Samson's body, the disheveled carpet and bedclothes, and Delilah's state of undress. Samson still lies partially upon Delilah, with his head in her lap and his hand resting on her lower abdomen. A modern example of reader response to the painting plays up suggestions both of a shared passionate intensity and of Delilah's affectionate disposition. In Paul Durcan's 'Samson and Delilah II',[23] one of a series of poems inspired by paintings in the National Gallery in London, the barber recounts what Delilah has whispered to him:

> He make the big love…
> He do the whole intercourse—
> Not just middle
> But beginning end middle.
> He jump up, he jump down.
> He carry me around room.
> He put me down.
> He caress me…
> He wait for me until I am so far out
> I think I am going to vanish my throat.

Another painting of Samson and Delilah by Rubens (fig. 6.3) represents a moment slightly later in the story, when Samson, his hair

22. Erika Langmuir, *The National Gallery Companion Guide* (London: National Gallery Publications, 1994), p. 240.

23. 'Talking Pictures', *The Independent Magazine*, 12 March 1994, p. 25 (the collection, *Give Me Your Hand* by Paul Durcan is published by Macmillan).

shorn, is set upon by the Philistine soldiers. Delilah is again depicted as a prostitute; the red bedclothes and curtains signify her profession. The old madam stands over her shoulder, and a dog and slippers, conventional symbols for sex, are in the foreground. It seems apparent from their positions on the bed and their state of undress that the couple has recently made love. Samson attempts to get up and 'shake [himself] free' from his captors, as in Judg. 16.20. Here even more of Delilah's fleshy flesh is exposed, though her left hand covers her genitals. Once again the woman's nakedness accuses her as 'loose' and as the activator of desire, and her ample white flesh, which as in fig. 6.2 sets her apart from the other figures in the painting, suggests perhaps a pampered life style. This Delilah is less sympathetic than the other. In this painting, she, and not a barber, has cut Samson's hair. She still holds the scissors in her hand. This makes it easier for viewers to hold her more accountable than the Delilah Rubens painted as watching passively and perhaps with regret.[24]

The British artist Solomon Joseph Solomon, in a painting dating from around 1886 or 1887, also gives us a Samson and Delilah in a bordello setting, where, once again, the evidence indicates that the couple has made love (fig. 6.4). There is a great deal of erotic energy in this painting, not just in the *femme fatale*'s pose and the muscular torso of Samson but also in the taut bodies of the men who are straining to restrain him. Why they too are so scantily clad is not

---

24. Accountability is not automatically decided by who does the cutting, but depends on other factors of the pose. Two paintings of this subject by Anthony van Dyck (1599-1641) also follow the double tradition regarding who cut Samson's hair, but with Delilah's attitude seemingly the reverse of that in the Rubens paintings. In one, in the Dulwich Picture Gallery, Delilah, with her hand raised in front of her bare breasts as if cautioning quietness, looks on as a barber cuts Samson's hair. The procuress and another figure look over her shoulder, while the soldiers wait in the background. In the other painting, in the Kunsthistorisches Museum, Vienna, Samson's hair has just been cut and the soldiers are seizing him, wrenching him as it were out of Delilah's arms. She holds out her arm as if reaching for him and their mutual looks of anguish suggest their attachment. But the scissors lie on the floor by the bed, where they appear to have fallen out of her hand—or perhaps she threw them aside. These variations show something of the wide range of feelings artists attributed to Delilah even when they depicted the same elements of the story. Reproductions of both paintings can be found in Sölle *et al.*, *Great Women of the Bible in Art and Literature*, pp. 144, 146-47.

Figure 6.3. Peter Paul Rubens, *Gefangennahme Simsons*, Alte Pinakothek, Munich

clear (except, perhaps, to give the artist the opportunity to demonstrate his skill in representing anatomy). Should we take them as bordello patrons as well, or as the ambushers of Judg. 16.9 and 12 who are *posing* as bordello patrons in order to respond swiftly to Delilah's call? The number of men it takes to subdue Samson and their apparent difficulty convey a sense of his enormous strength. One can almost see the motion in the painting: Samson struggles against the men, who are actively gripping and pulling, other soldiers are bursting in at the door, a table is about to crash to the floor, and delicate brush strokes give a blurring effect that makes us feel we are watching Delilah waving Samson's shorn locks.

Just by looking at her we know she is a prostitute and a *femme fatale*. Her bare breasts are provocatively exposed and accented both by her dark, disheveled hair and by the gaudy necklace she wears; her jewelry and gold-trimmed garment are vulgarly showy. She exudes sensuality. The furnishings are a mixture of the extravagant and

Figure 6.4. Solomon Joseph Solomon, *Samson*, The Board of Trustees of the
National Museums & Galleries on Merseyside, Walker Art Gallery, Liverpool

tawdry; who but a *femme fatale* would have a tiger-skin rug in her
boudoir? Samson looks at her with what strikes me as fear, and
possibly even disbelief, more than accusation in his eyes, as if he only
now realizes the *femme fatale*'s deadly danger, and she gazes back with
a look of absolute wild frenzy in her wide eyes. Waving his hair
proudly before him like a trophy, a gesture that will be copied by the
cinematic Delilah, she taunts him with his weakness. This Delilah has
no affection for Samson, only contempt. This makes her an even
more formidable *femme fatale*. She resembles Moreau's courtesan (fig.
6.1) both in physical appearance and in the impression she gives of
being vain and unscrupulous—only she is more animated.[25] This is
what we might imagine Moreau's Delilah to look like at her moment
of victory over Samson.

From Prostitute to Wife to Cinematic Courtesan

Having considered the suggestiveness of the biblical account and the
more explicit representation of Delilah as a prostitute in art, we might

25. She also looks a bit like pictures of Oscar Wilde in the title role of his play,
Salome.

ask at this point, What is achieved by making Delilah a prostitute? If she is a prostitute, we have less respect for her; and if we have less respect for her, we can more easily put all the blame for Samson's downfall on her. More important, casting Delilah as a prostitute is a way of controlling the danger she poses, for a prostitute has a clearly defined role within society and a circumscribed place within the patriarchal symbolic order. A prostitute poses less of a threat to a man than a woman from whom sex cannot be bought for money because the whole point of sex with a prostitute is sex without commitment and obligations, love without strings. A man can love them and leave them, as, interestingly, the biblical story of Samson illustrates rather well. There is only one time in the biblical story that Samson is clearly involved with a harlot. When the Philistines learn that Samson has gone to visit a harlot, they set an ambush for him ('let us wait until the light of the morning, then we will kill him', Judg. 16.2). Samson, however, leaves her in the middle of the night, taking his would-be ambushers by surprise, and escapes, carrying the city gates with him.

The text does not say who told the Philistines that Samson was in Gaza with a harlot.[26] Readers often assume that the woman informed them, on the grounds that the other two women, the Timnite and Delilah, both betray him to the Philistines.[27] The important difference, however, is that in this case Samson escapes unscathed from a Philistine trap. The Philistines succeed in getting the better of Samson only when they manage, by hook or by crook, to enlist a woman's help. Since the incident with the harlot does not end in a Philistine victory over Samson, we might conclude that it is precisely because the woman was *not* involved. In other words, the biblical account does not consider the harlot to be a threat. Only in the two cases where commitment is involved does Samson suffer defeat. Samson gave in to the other two women and disclosed his secrets to them out of love. The story provides an object lesson in the danger of love.

In terms of their tacit recognition of the danger of committed love, two of my metatexts, Milton's *Samson Agonistes* and Handel's oratorio

26. Even the verb, 'told', is lacking in the Masoretic text of 16.2, which reads defectively, 'To the Gazites, "Samson has come here"'.

27. Even so astute a reader as Bal, who warns against confusing the women, succumbs to the temptation to naturalize here, when speculating about the identity of the person who informed the Philistines of Samson's presence in Gaza: 'It is plausible to assume that it is the prostitute' (*Lethal Love*, p. 49).

based on it, are more akin to the biblical story than are the artistic representations of Delilah as a prostitute. They portray Delilah as Samson's wife. There is, of course, no more evidence in the biblical story that she is his wife than that she is a harlot; metatexts are simply filling a perceived gap when they clarify the relationship for their audiences. I am not suggesting that these metatexts represent a conscious reflection on the implications of love with commitment versus sex for sex's sake. They have a different agenda altogether.[28] Casting Delilah as Samson's wife is more an attempt to rehabilitate Samson than Delilah, for Samson the profligate has disappeared from the poem and the oratorio. The question then arises, What does becoming a 'respectable woman' do for Delilah? It can not render her any more dangerous, for in these versions of the story the damage has already been done, but it does underscore her ever-present danger. These metatexts begin almost at the point where the biblical story ends, with Samson in prison. If Delilah is to have a role in them at all, one has to be provided, since the seduction and betrayal scene has been eliminated and is referred to only in the dialogue. Making Delilah Samson's wife helps explain her (re)appearance to seek a reconciliation. More important, her appearance with another offer of temptation ('though sight be lost,/ Life yet hath many solaces, enjoyed/ Where other senses want not their delights,/ At home, in leisure and domestic ease')[29] provides the opportunity to show that Samson has learned his lesson: he is able to resist her this time. The temptation scene is thus replayed, with the dangerous woman still plying all her deceptive charms, but this time without the duping of the hero.

In the cinematic version, Delilah is neither Samson's wife, as in the poem and the oratorio, nor a prostitute, as the paintings suggest. By the time she sets out to seduce him, in her lavish tent in the valley of Sorek, she is clearly the Saran's woman, and Samson knows it. His description of her as 'the great courtesan of Gaza' and 'the woman

---

28. John Guillory ('Dalila's House: *Samson Agonistes* and the Sexual Division of Labor', in *Rewriting the Renaissance: The Discourses of Sexual Difference in Early Modern Europe* [ed. Margaret Ferguson, Maureen Quilligan and Nancy Vickers; Chicago: University of Chicago Press, 1986], p. 108), who sees the conflict between Samson and Delilah in *Samson Agonistes* as a conflict between vocation and marriage, observes, 'For Milton, the cutting off of Samson's hair, not simply by a woman but by his *wife*, is the precise point of impact on the narrative of its historical conditions'.

29. Milton, *Samson Agonistes*, ll. 916-17.

that rules the ruler of the five cities' makes her sound infamous already, but since the Saran is the only man besides Samson with whom Delilah is involved, she hardly qualifies as a prostitute. Indeed, De Mille is subtle rather than explicit about her sexual relationship with the Saran. There are no sex scenes between Hedy Lamarr and George Sanders in the film; they never even kiss. At the same time, there is never a moment in the film when Delilah is not clearly aware of her sexual appeal. She is an independent woman, in control of her sexuality ('I have no husband', 'I have no master', she tells Samson). She decides when and to whom to grant her sexual favors. But her sexual freedom is something of an illusion, for she is really a one-man woman. 'You are all I want', she tells Samson. So why does she betray him?

The Problem of Motivation

The biblical Delilah betrays Samson for money. The simple acceptance of a bribe, which is all the biblical account gives us, has proved insufficient to clarify her motives to the satisfaction of readers. Over the centuries numerous reasons have been put forward to explain her deed, among them, avarice, patriotism, jealousy, and revenge. In some versions of the story, Delilah has been cast as the unknowing pawn of the Philistines, or even removed from blame altogether by having her sister betray Samson.[30] The popular identification of Delilah as a prostitute partially satisfies the need for motivation. A harlot can be bought for betrayal as well as for sex. No one expects fidelity from her. Already considered morally reprehensible, her nature is to dissemble. Both the outrageously decadent and confidently poised Delilah of Moreau's painting and the jeering vamp of Solomon's look like women devoid of moral scruples. In the paintings by Rubens, in contrast, there is nothing to suggest unambiguously that Delilah is either unfeeling or mercenary. In these paintings, the Philistine rulers who offer Delilah one thousand pieces of silver each are not represented. Does the presence of the old madam encourage viewers to replace them with her as the one who puts pressure on Delilah to betray Samson? Delilah seems to be working for her as much as for the Philistines. Might we not therefore imagine that she, and not Delilah, has made the deal to hand over Samson to them?

30. For a sketchy but interesting survey of some versions, see Sölle *et al.*, *Great Women of the Bible in Art and Literature*, pp. 142-45.

If prostitution can be said to provide Delilah with a motive for betraying Samson, the commonly assumed identification of Delilah as a Philistine suggests another, even stronger one. If Delilah is Philistine, we could conclude that she is patriotic. Why should she betray her own people by protecting Samson when offered the opportunity to perform a great national service? On the other hand, if she is patriotic, why is a bribe necessary? Perhaps she cares for Samson, or is interested in him sexually. Perhaps her loyalty to her people comes first and the payment is incidental, as Saint-Saëns would have us believe (see below).

In a long dialogue between Delilah and Samson in *Samson Agonistes*, Milton explores and rejects several explanations for the betrayal. The fact that he considers a variety of motives, if only to reject them, demonstrates the need to find compelling reasons for Delilah's behavior. The reader of the poem is given various possibilities to consider, through which Delilah becomes a fuller and, in many ways, more believable character. Some readers, especially resisting ones, may even find her sympathetic.[31]

The first explanation Milton has Delilah offer for her conduct is an appeal to the nature of woman. It is the same kind of argument that is often applied to the prostitute: if dissimulation is in her nature, her behavior is self-explanatory. Curiosity and not being able to keep a secret are 'both common female faults', Milton's Delilah maintains, and Samson should therefore have known better than to trust a woman. The stereotype thus becomes the 'truth' about Delilah. She proceeds to justify what she has done by attributing it to jealousy, or possessive love. She believed that knowledge of Samson's secret would place him in her power, and that, if he were a captive of the Philistines, she would have no cause to fear that he might leave her for another woman (a theme the cinematic version exploits with verve). More important, she did not know that any real harm would come to him: 'I was assured by those/ Who tempted me that nothing was designed/ Against thee but safe custody and hold...' All this is, of course, her version of events. Though Milton gives Delilah a plausible case, he refutes it by privileging Samson's point of view, which

31. See the attention given to gender issues in John Guillory, 'Dalila's House', pp. 106–22; Virginia Mollenkott, 'Relativism in *Samson Agonistes*', *Studies in Philosophy* 67 (1970), pp. 89–102; John C. Ulreich, Jr, '"Incident to All Our Sex": the Tragedy of Dalila', in *Milton and the Idea of Woman* (ed. Julia M. Walker; Urbana: University of Illinois Press, 1988), pp. 185–210.

his audience is also expected to privilege. Samson does not believe any of her excuses. He does not accept weakness as a motive, except insofar as it was 'weakness to resist Philistine gold'. He objects to her describing her possessive jealousy as 'love', insisting it was only 'furious rage to satisfy thy lust'.

The simple explanation that Delilah betrays Samson for money proves, for Milton as for most readers, unsatisfactory by itself. He thus furnishes her the rather convincing argument that, urged on by the Philistine leaders, she acted out of a sense of civil and religious loyalty. Delilah becomes all too human as she describes herself as torn between the rival claims of love versus patriotic and religious duty.

> Only my love of thee held long debate,
> And combated in silence all these reasons
> With hard contest. At length, that grounded maxim,
> So rife and celebrated in the mouths
> Of wisest men, that to the public good
> Private respects must yield, with grave authority
> Took full possession of me and prevailed;
> Virtue, as I thought, truth, duty, so enjoining (ll. 863-70).

Religion supplies a very believable motive (Delilah calls Samson an 'irreligious Dishonorer of Dagon'), but it rarely receives serious attention because, like Milton, most readers privilege Samson's god as the true god and reject Delilah's god as false. Discrediting Delilah's religion as 'superstition' is a way of discrediting her religious motivation; the betrayal of a follower of the true god by someone in the service of an idol hardly merits our admiration, only our scorn. Samson, who knows that her god is only an idol, remains unconvinced and rejects her suit.

Patriotism is also a believable motive. In her parting speech, Delilah entertains a vision of herself as a national hero—a Philistine Jael, remembered for delivering her people from a tyrant:

> My name, perhaps, among the circumcised
> In Dan, in Judah, and the bordering tribes,
> To all posterity may stand defamed,
> With malediction mentioned, and the blot
> Of falsehood most unconjugal traduced.
> But in my country, where I most desire,
> In Ecron, Gaza, Asdod, and in Gath,
> I shall be named among the famousest
> Of women, sung at solemn festivals,

Living and dead recorded, who, to save
Her country from a fierce destroyer, chose
Above the faith of wedlock-bands, my tomb
With odours visited and annual flowers.
Not less renowned than in Mount Ephraim
Jael, who, with inhospitable guile,
Smote Sisera sleeping, through the temples nailed.
Nor shall I count it heinous to enjoy
The public marks of honour and reward
Conferred upon me for the piety
Which to my country I was judged to have shown (ll. 975-94).

Her speech is so passionate that some readers might find her behavior laudable if it were not in the service of the wrong people and a false god.[32] The honors Delilah speaks of are honors she never receives, but perhaps only because the story is never told from the Philistines' point of view. Even the brief glimpse of their point of view given to us in the Bible leaves her out: the Philistines celebrate their victory by singing, 'Our god has given Samson our enemy into our hand' (16.23) and 'Our god has given our enemy into our hand' (16.24). It is important to keep in mind, however, that this is the Israelite story-teller's version of the Philistine point of view. That the biblical narrator does not let her compatriots praise Delilah is not without significance. Is she really not of interest, or does she need to be ignored in order to underplay her importance?

The comparison that Milton's Delilah draws between herself and Jael, which could lead to an alternative, more laudatory version of Delilah's story, is, interestingly, omitted from Newburgh Hamilton's libretto for Handel's *Samson*, which is based on *Samson Agonistes*. For an audience acquainted with Handel's *Deborah*, in which Jael's praises are roundly sung, the comparison to Jael could easily be seen as favorable to Delilah.[33] In general, Handel and Hamilton's Delilah is a flatter

---

32. *Samson*, Milton's spokesperson, does not. According to Barbara K. Lewalski ('Milton on Women—Yet Again', in *Problems for Feminist Criticism* [ed. Sally Minogue; London: Routledge, 1990], p. 64), his response, in which he denies ultimate authority to civil and religious leaders, has 'all the polemic of the English civil war echoing in the background'. On the political significance of *Samson Agonistes*, see Mary Ann Radzinowicz, *Toward Samson Agonistes: The Growth of Milton's Mind* (Princeton, NJ: Princeton University Press, 1978), pp. 167-79.

33. *Deborah* was first performed in 1733, and *Samson* in 1741; the order in which one listens to the oratorios, however, does not affect my point.

character than Milton's, and her motivation receives less elaboration.[34] Curiosity and the inability to keep secrets are collapsed into one female fault, curiosity 'greedy of secrets but to publish them', and Delilah's jealous love becomes her primary motive: 'Fearless at home of partners in my love,/ 'T was jealousy did prompt to keep you there/ Both day and night, Love's pris'ner, wholly mine'. What in Milton was a clear protest on her part that she was ignorant of what the Philistines would do to Samson becomes in *Samson* a mere suggestion ('Alas! th' event was worse than I foresaw') that could be lost on anyone who does not know its basis in *Samson Agonistes*. Religion and patriotism are not specifically invoked, which leaves the impression that what most motivates women is emotional attachment to a man.[35]

Motivation lacks all complexity in Saint-Saëns's opera, *Samson et Dalila*, which features a single-minded Delilah whose sheer hatred of Samson and desire for vengeance are never too well explained. We can only assume that Samson's victories over the Philistines drove her to avenge 'her god, her people, and her hatred'. Here too, significantly, the simple motive of betrayal for money is rejected in favor of something else. It is as if librettist Ferdinand Lemaire felt that Delilah needed strong emotions to make her a powerful stage presence, and so he made her vengeful. Greed is too weak a motive for this Delilah, who does not care about the money at all:

> Qu'importe à Dalila ton or!
> Et que pourrait tout un trésor
> Si je ne rêvais de vengeance!
>
> [What matters your gold to Delilah?
> And what would avail an entire treasure
> were I not dreaming of vengeance?]

34. The scene between Samson and Delilah is not short, but greater musical attention is given to a rather charming duet between Delilah and one of her virgins, with a reprise by a chorus of virgins, on the theme, 'Her faith and truth, O Samson, prove, But hear her, hear the voice of love!', and a memorable duet between Delilah and Samson, 'Traitor to love! I'll sue no more/ Traitress to love! I'll hear no more'.

35. Handel's *Samson*, like Milton's *Samson Agonistes*, nonetheless has a political message. On some of the differences between Hamilton's libretto and Milton's *Samson Agonistes* and their political significance, see Ruth Smith, *Handel's Oratorios and Eighteenth-Century Thought* (Cambridge: Cambridge University Press, 1995), pp. 292-99.

Why does Delilah hate Samson so much? At best, her statement about 'aveng[ing] her god, her people, and her hatred' points to religion and nationalism as having a role, and the fact that she is cast as a Philistine priestess lends further support to a religious motive. But in the end, as happens in opera, it is the music that conveys the emotion, and, as I suggested above, Saint-Saëns's music gives Delilah greater depth than she has in the libretto.

Delilah's motive is similarly single-minded yet anything but clear-cut in Cecil B. De Mille's Oscar-winning epic, *Samson and Delilah*. Hedy Lamarr as Delilah has top billing over Victor Mature. Lamarr's character is clearly the more interesting and complex of the pair, with Victor Mature seeming almost as simplistic as the biblical character he plays. Promoting his star gave De Mille the opportunity for developing and exploring Delilah's character. He shows us a woman acting out of a complex, volatile mix of love, desire for revenge, hate, and jealousy. Not one to leave the audience guessing, however, he offers enough guidance throughout the film to establish that it all comes down to one thing. Delilah is motivated by love—but a love so obsessive it must destroy and be destroyed by the object of its desire in order to obtain it. Because De Mille's Delilah is such an impressive creation, outrageous but still convincing, and because his film is so brilliant, not just as cinema but as interpretation, I want to consider motivation in *Samson and Delilah* at length. For the benefit of readers who may not be that familiar with the film, I shall try to provide enough description for my remarks to have a meaningful context.

Film's Femme Fatale *and Her Motivation*

Who is Delilah? How does Samson meet her? *Samson and Delilah* begins by answering questions that held no interest for the biblical narrator. But this background is essential for establishing her motivation in the cinematic version. As in Vladimir Jabotinsky's *Samson*, one of its primary source texts, the screenplay by Jesse Lasky, Jr, and Fredric Frank makes Delilah the younger sister of Samson's Timnite bride. She is thus identified with the 'little sister' of the biblical account who is offered to Samson by his father-in-law in place of his bride, who has been given to another ('Is not her little sister fairer than she? Take her instead', Judg. 15.2). When Samson comes to visit Semadar, the Philistine woman he wants to marry (played by a golden-haired, youthful Angela Lansbury), we get our first glimpse of Delilah. She is perched provocatively on the garden wall, nibbling plums and tossing plum pits at Samson (as with Gregory Peck's grapes in *David and Bathsheba*, there is an implicit connection between sex and food as gratification). Already Delilah has her hungry eye on Samson, and from the outset she plots and schemes to get him, regardless of who gets hurt in the process. Having Samson kill the lion is her idea ('If *you* killed the lion, they'd call you great'), and she steals the family chariot to enable Samson to reach the lion ahead of the Saran and his entourage (Samson's biblical chance fight with the lion has been turned into a lion hunt). To her surprise, Samson chooses her sister Semadar rather than her as his prize for killing the lion. But Delilah does not accept rejection. Ever.

What, in the biblical story, is a series of chance occurrences, reprisals, and counter-reprisals that Samson gets caught up in before he ever meets Delilah becomes, in the film, a plot driven by Delilah's cunning, single-minded determination to obtain the object of her desire. She proposes inviting thirty Philistine warriors as wedding guests, knowing that it will cause trouble. She advises them that the way to find out the answer to Samson's riddle is through his bride. When Samson rushes off in a fury to get the thirty garments to pay off his debt, Delilah gives her father the idea to marry off Semadar to the best man—all to prevent Samson's marriage to Semadar so that Samson can be hers. When Samson returns to pay his debt and claim his bride, Delilah is more than willing to take her sister's place. But Samson does not want a 'thorn bush'. Oblivious not only to the fact that he does not want her but also to any other feelings he might have, such as shame at being dishonored and heartache at losing Semadar, Delilah bursts into a declaration of her obsessive love that hides nothing of the lengths to which it has driven her:

> Did a thorn bush steal the chariot that took you to the lion? Did a thorn bush tell the Saran how you killed it with your bare hands? No, I did. And he believed me. Then you chose Semadar...I made Artour steal the secret of the riddle from Semadar. I lied to stop you from marrying her. I'd kill to keep you. You're the only thing in the world I want.[36]

---

36. Samson interrupts her where I have ellipses in the citation to exclaim, 'Take your claws out of me'. 'You'll never get them out of you', she announces before continuing her tirade, and the audience knows what these words portend.

This is clearly a dangerous kind of love and a dangerous woman, and even the otherwise rather obtuse Samson seems to sense it when he says to her father, 'And you want me to marry this wildcat?!' Undaunted, she clutches at him: 'If you crushed the life out of me, I'd kiss you with my dying breath.' This is not the last we will hear of this theme.

When Samson repays the Philistines with 'fire for fire and death for death' and she watches all she has go up in flames, Delilah vows revenge. Shaking her clenched fist at the heavens, she swears, 'If it takes all my life, I'll make him curse the day he was born'. Has her love for Samson turned to hatred? When we next see her, she has conquered the heart of another man, the Saran, chief ruler of the Philistines. When she learns of Samson's capture at Lehi, she proposes to the Saran that Samson be made to turn the gristmill, 'whipped and driven like an animal, where all Gaza can mock him and laugh at him', a foreshadowing of what will happen to him later. The very mention of Samson's name arouses in her such strong emotion that the Saran can see his powerful hold over her, and this is not lost on the audience either. Later, when news arrives of Samson's victory over their army at Lehi, with only the jawbone of an ass as a weapon, the Philistine rulers are at a loss. Upon hearing them bemoan the impossibility of capturing a man with such superhuman strength, Delilah volunteers to discover its secret source. In the cinematic version, unlike the biblical account, the betrayal is her idea, and revenge her stated motive: 'When my father and sister lay dead in the ashes of our home, because of Samson, he laughed at my tears.[37] You cannot refuse me, my lord', she tells the Saran. For some reason, however, perhaps the fact that she protests too much, we cannot quite believe her when she tells the Saran 'I go to destroy your enemy and mine' and 'my love is only for you'. Nor can he. He voices our doubts: 'A man who could stop the heart of a lion might stir the heart of a woman'.

Love? Hate? Revenge? Only when we see Samson and Delilah together again can we begin to appreciate how complex a web of motivation De Mille has provided for his Delilah. The seduction scene is set in a splendid oriental tent by a pool, beside the ruins of a

---

37. Since the film does not show this (and Samson is off burning Philistine fields while Delilah watches everything go up in smoke), we might wonder if Delilah is making it up.

temple. Delilah has camped with her caravan in the valley of Sorek, waiting for Samson, the renegade, to plunder her tent. Tall palm trees cast their shadows against a star-studded dark blue sky as the soft strains of music fill the (what one imagines as scented) air. Not knowing whose tent it is, Samson sneaks in to steal. Seeing the form of a woman behind a diaphanous curtain, he tells her not to cry out. 'I won't', she answers, 'are you afraid?' 'Of a woman', he pauses, 'yes'. And well he should be, as Delilah puts her seductive arts into action. Samson is almost, but not quite, the fool he is in the biblical version. Although he recognizes what is going on—'The oldest trick in the world, a silk trap baited with a woman'—he falls for it. The *femme fatale* is irresistible. Moreover, she knows it: 'Do you know a better bait, Samson? Men always respond.' Her forward speech is part. of her seductive trap. When he asks why the Saran has used her as bait, she admits she asked to come because 'I knew you would yield to any other woman'. Has she therefore come to save him from a trap?, he wants to know. 'No, I came to betray you.'

At the beginning of the seduction and betrayal scene, Delilah is behind a curtain and holds a veil over her face. Both curtain and veil signify the woman's dissimulation,[38] yet there is both dissembling and forthrightness in this scene. As in the biblical account, Delilah does not hide her intention to betray Samson. Having told him she came to betray him, she is not afraid. 'You could crush me between these two hands, why don't you? I told you once I'd kiss you with my dying breath', she says, referring to the time her father offered her to him and he rejected her. On the other hand, we have reason to doubt that betrayal is really her intention. Everything she says and does testifies to her intense desire to possess Samson, to have him for herself, not to turn him over to the Philistine rulers. As he prepares to leave, she blocks his way and proclaims, 'You're all I want'—again an echo of what she said on that earlier occasion ('you're the only thing in the world I want')—and she looks at him with such adoration and longing and speaks with such fervor that we, the audience, feel sure we must be back in the presence of the obsessively-in-love Delilah, and, in fact, have been there all along.

They spend some happy days together, during which she tries to discover his secret, but his secret does not seem to be her primary

38. See Mary Ann Doane, 'Veiling over Desire: Close-ups of the Woman', Chapter 3 in her *Femmes Fatales*, pp. 44-75.

interest. She seems to be enjoying her assignment too much. De Mille uses her interest in the source of Samson's strength to highlight the possessive nature of Delilah's love. 'What would you do if you— knew the secret of my strength?', Samson asks. 'Bind you', she replies. 'Why?' 'So you could never leave me.' Here she resembles Milton's and Handel's Delilah, who wants to make Samson the prisoner of her love. She is not jealous of any specific rival, but rather jealously possessive of Samson in general. A rival will arrive soon enough, in the form of Miriam, the wholesome girl-next-door, who provides a safe but uninteresting alternative to the *femme fatale*.[39]

In the meantime, however, Delilah decides to break off the relation- ship because Samson does not love her enough to trust her with his secret. The question arises whether this is simply a ploy or an expression of her true feelings. Having earlier passed up two oppor- tunities to have Delilah as his bride (first when he chose Semadar as his prize for killing the lion, and then when he refused to accept Delilah in Semadar's place), Samson now asks her to marry him. He is about to reveal his secret to her, when she puts her hands over his mouth and declares, 'No, Samson, no. I don't want to be armed with a weapon to destroy you.' Should we believe her? Like Delilah in Saint-Saëns's opera, she sounds so convincing that it is hard to see her as insincere. Why would she call it a weapon otherwise? Samson wonders, too. 'It wouldn't be a weapon if you really loved me', he protests. But that remains to be seen.

After he tells her that his strength comes from his hair, there is a moment when Delilah's mood seems to take a sudden, cruel turn. 'Shall I pull it out and steal your power?', she chides as she wraps his dark, curly hair around her fingers and tugs at it. To a certain extent, her remarks about being armed with a weapon to destroy him and stealing his strength keep the audience guessing about Delilah's true motive, thus building on the mystery of the *femme fatale*. When

---

39. DeMille also uses the 'good woman versus temptress' motif in *The Ten Commandments*, where Moses finds inner beauty in his wife Sephora (actually the rather beautiful Yvonne de Carlo) to match the charms of the seductive siren Nefretiri (played by the gorgeous Anne Baxter). It is difficult not to compare De Mille's biblical temptresses. Each of them openly desires the hero, Moses or Samson, and offers herself to him. Neither too good nor too bad, each is driven by obsession (Nefretiri even kills to protect Moses). Like Nefretiri, Delilah has an opposite in the 'hometown girl'. Like Nefretiri, she loses him not to this other woman, of whom she is so jealous, but to his higher mission, his calling, his people, and his god.

Samson answers that 'You can't steal what's yours already', her mood again rapidly changes, this time to one of wistfulness. She asks him to come away with her to Egypt, away from the conflict between their peoples, to a place where they will no longer be Danite and Philistine but simply Samson and Delilah. Her love is everlasting: 'For all eternity nothing can ever take you out of my arms'. At that moment, Miriam, the hometown girl, shows up, with the young boy Saul (who is destined to become Israel's first king). They have come to bring Samson back to his people, who need him to deliver them from Philistine persecution. Now Delilah's jealousy has a specific object: 'I cannot fight against his god', she tells Miriam, 'but no woman will take him from me'. She invites Samson to drink with her a farewell cup of wine, which she has drugged. As a *femme fatale* whose desire is all-consuming, she would rather destroy him than risk losing him. Miriam will give her one more opportunity to express this jealousy later, in the temple scene, when she comes to beg for Samson's life and Delilah refuses: 'I'd rather see him dead than in your arms'.

De Mille keeps the focus on Delilah's excessive, obsessive jealousy as the betrayal scene reaches its conclusion. Waving Samson's hair in his face as Delilah does in Solomon's painting, she mocks her helpless captive: 'I've taken away your strength, Samson. Your little Danite sparrow will nest alone.' When Samson hears about the money and curses the name 'Delilah', she pronounces the film's definitive revelation about her feelings and her motive:

> I could have loved you with a fire to make all other loves seem like ice. I would have gone with you to Egypt, left everything behind, lived only for you. But one call from that milk-faced Danite lily and you run whining at her heels.

Once before, when Samson turned down the chance to marry her, Delilah confessed her love of Samson and described the ends to which it drove her. Then she spoke, as she does here, out of anger at being rejected and she told him she would kill to have him. Now, when at last he *wants* to marry her, she perceives his leaving with Miriam as a rejection, and her response is to destroy him. Both confessions of love reveal how dangerous her obsession is. Ironically, even though this time he does not reject her—on the contrary, he says he will come to her in Egypt—she cannot see it as anything else. She concludes this second confession with a finishing touch worthy of the *femme fatale*: 'No man leaves Delilah'.

As the above discussion indicates, De Mille uses every possible explanation to lend complexity to Delilah's motivation. He takes her through the gamut of motives: love, revenge, hate, jealousy. The only motive he underplays is greed. Delilah volunteers to discover the secret source of Samson's strength, but the idea to do it for payment appears to be an afterthought, for the first reward she asks for is simply the Saran's favor.[40] She comes up with her outrageous price when the Philistine leaders patronize her by asking if she wants some bauble as a reward. The other motives—hatred, revenge, and jealousy—are but manifestations of her obsessive love. De Mille emphasizes obsession as her overriding motive in two ways. One is by means of the you-could-kill-me-and-I-would-still-love-you motif ('If you crushed the life out of me, I'd kiss you with my dying breath'; 'I told you once I'd kiss you with my dying breath'). The motif appears a third time at the end of the film, when, unable to bear the thought of his suffering any longer, Delilah goes to Samson in the granary. When he threatens to kill her if she comes close to him (as in Milton's poem and Handel's oratorio), and she offers herself willingly—'I am here; I will not cry out'—we see that she meant what she said.

De Mille's other strategy for conveying his message about the nature of Delilah's love is using the unflappable George Sanders, as the Saran, to provide a kind of reliable narratorial commentary on events. It is Sanders, for example, who observes wryly, 'one tax collector is worth a thousand soldiers', 'the weak always band together to pull down the strong', and, of Samson, 'he'll not kneel to any god but his own'.[41] But his most important lines are about Delilah's attachment to Samson. 'I'm jealous of your hatred. Don't share even that with anyone else', he tells her when she speaks of wanting to see Samson humbled. What is intimated here is spelled out clearly when, after the betrayal, Delilah says that her greatest reward was in serving her king. The Saran's reply is a clichéd but vital insight into her motive: 'Men have been betrayed by love. Love and hate are but two

40. 'Such devotion is touching but what will you gain from his capture?', asks the Saran after Delilah volunteers to discover Samson's secret. 'My lord's favor', replies Delilah. 'But you have that. Is that all you want?', he asks again. She pauses for a moment, as if thinking (and perhaps intuiting that her first answer was too transparent), says 'No', and then lights upon the idea of silver.

41. Also, 'Like all soldiers, when you fail by the sword, you ask for more swords', 'No man with eyes could resist you, Delilah, but only a fool would trust you'.

sides of the same coin.' Finally, in the film's closing scene in the temple, the Saran lets Delilah decide whether or not to hand over the blinded Samson to Miriam. When she refuses, the Saran's response captures perfectly the film's ultimate verdict on the *femme fatale*: 'Your mercy is like your love, Delilah—ruthless'.

De Mille uses the Saran not just as a commentator but also as a counterpart to Delilah, a kind of rational male alternative to her irrational female passion.[42] Whereas her jealousy burns hot, his is cool and dispassionate. He is realistic, and even open-minded; his jealousy of Samson does not lead him to curtail her freedom. The Saran agrees to let Delilah serve as bait to discover Samson's secret because, he philosophizes, 'As a king, I have no choice. As a man, I am letting you leave because you want to.' Delilah, in contrast, does not respect Samson's freedom, and because she will not let him go, she destroys him. The Saran allows Delilah the right to choose, even when it means he will lose her. In the temple scene, unable to bear Samson's humiliation any longer, Delilah says she will go to him in the arena. 'If you go to him, you cannot return to me', the Saran warns her, and then sits by and watches her walk away.

In weaving a complex web of motivation for Delilah, De Mille also exploits the 'she is duped by the Philistines' theme. Before she goes to entice Samson into revealing his secret, Delilah extracts from the Saran a promise that 'no drop of his blood shall be shed; no blade shall touch his skin'. She does not know about the blinding, and discovers it only later, when she reluctantly accompanies the Saran to the granary, where Samson slaves at the mill. Her initial response is, 'He's magnificent, even in chains', but then, when she sees that he is blind, she is devastated. Not even trying to conceal her distress, she accuses the Saran of deceiving her by playing with words, to which he replies, 'It was you who betrayed him, not I'. When she complains that he showed no mercy to a helpless captive, he also has a ready answer: 'Did you show him mercy, Delilah? You wanted vengeance. You have it.'

42. But does the effete, non-athletic George Sanders not really qualify as a man's man? He is certainly not macho like Victor Mature's Samson, but actually he is a wise ruler and not really such a bad fellow at all, in spite of being a Philistine.

Lack of Closure

Just as readers are not satisfied with the Bible's simple report of a bribe offered and accepted, so also we perceive the lack of closure in the biblical story of Samson and Delilah as unsatisfactory. We want to know not only why she did it but also what happened to her afterwards. Did Delilah suffer remorse? Most people would like to think so. Did she live a long and happy life as a Philistine national hero? Why are we less likely to be drawn to this possibility? Does it have something to do with accepting the ideology of the text that privileges Israelite over Philistine? Is it a reluctance to make the woman the subject of the story? Is it simply our aversion to betrayal?[43] Our desire to see the bad woman pay for her perfidy? Metatexts satisfy our desire to hear more about Delilah by bringing her back. The desire to know what happened to Delilah is often a desire to see her punished, by, for example, dying in the destruction of the temple, although the biblical account does not mention her being there. The temptation to see her among the thousands of spectators who are killed when Samson pulls down the temple (Judg. 16.27) is so great that even some biblical commentators entertain it.

In Saint-Saëns's opera Delilah is brought back on the scene after the betrayal in order to have her die in the temple. She and the chief priest ridicule Samson for falling into her trap, urging him to entertain them by repeating to her his tender avowals of love. They revile his god and give thanks and glory to Dagon. As they stand before the sacrificial offer, awaiting an epiphany, they get one vastly different from what they anticipate: Samson, empowered by his god, pulls down the temple upon them all. In the operatic version of the story, in which Delilah appears so calculating and callous, we somehow feel

---

43. I suspect the answer has more to do with readers' political and gender ideology than with betrayal per se. At least this is the case with biblical commentators. Samson is also betrayed by *his own people*, the Judahites, in this story (Judg. 15.9-13), but they are not usually censured, probably because they do it under duress (but the same could be said of Samson's Timnite wife, yet she is blamed). In the book of Judges, Ehud is usually praised by commentators for his clever deception and murder of Eglon, the enemy king. Jael too receives acclaim (Judg. 4-5), but in the woman's case, commentators have reservations about the way she carries out the deed against the unsuspecting enemy.

she gets what she deserves. Not so when the temple comes crashing down in the cinematic version, where Delilah is Samson's accomplice, not his unwitting victim.

Delilah is not brought back to be part of the temple massacre (which takes place offstage) in either Milton's *Samson Agonistes* or Handel's *Samson*; as in the biblical version, the silence of these metatexts leaves us in the dark about her fate. Nevertheless, bringing her back after the betrayal achieves a kind of closure, though the question still haunts us, Does she regret her deed? She says as much, but Samson rejects her version of events. *Samson Agonistes* and *Samson*, as we have seen, bring Delilah back to sue her blinded, embittered husband for forgiveness and reconciliation. When Samson rejects her various self-justifications, she does not abandon her suit, but presses on, offering to take him home with her and care for him, and promising him insofar as possible to atone for her wrongful deed. This is Milton's version:

> Afford me place to show what recompense
> Towards thee I intend for what I have misdone,
> ...though sight be lost,
> Life yet hath many solaces, enjoyed
> Where other senses want not their delights,
> At home, in leisure and domestic ease ...
> I to the lords will intercede, not doubting
> Their favourable ear, that I may fetch thee
> From forth this loathsome prison-house, to abide
> With me, where my redoubled love and care,
> With nursing diligence, to me glad office,
> May ever tend about thee to old age
> With all things grateful cheered, and so supplied
> That what by me thou hast lost thou least shalt miss
> (*Samson Agonistes*, ll. 910-11, 914-17, 920-27).

In Handel's oratorio this speech becomes a charming duet, evoking the cooing of turtledoves,[44] sung by Delilah and the virgins who attend her. Delilah urges Samson to adopt a *carpe diem* attitude and savor what pleasures he can from life.

44. She begins her plea by comparing herself to a turtledove left alone, who burns with doubled raptures when her absent mate returns.

Dalila
My faith and truth, O Samson, prove,
But hear me, hear the voice of love!
With love no mortal can be cloy'd
All happiness is love enjoy'd.
Virgin
Her faith and truth, O Samson, prove,
But hear her, hear the voice of love!
Chorus *of Virgins*
Her faith and truth, O Samson, prove,
But hear her, hear the voice of love!
Dalila
To fleeting pleasures make your court,
No moment lose, for life is short!
The present now's our only time
The missing that our only crime.
Chorus *of Virgins*
Her faith and truth, O Samson, prove,
But hear her, hear the voice of love!
Dalila
How charming is domestic ease!
A thousand ways I'll strive to please
Life is not lost, though lost your sight;
Let other senses taste delight.
Chorus *of Virgins*
Her faith and truth, O Samson, prove,
But hear her, hear the voice of love!

In both *Samson Agonistes* and *Samson*, Samson rejects her appeal as insincere. In *Samson Agonistes*, but not in *Samson*, he claims that she would only mistreat him if he were helpless in her power.

> How wouldst thou use me now, blind, and thereby
> Deceivable, in most things as a child
> Helpless, thence easily contemned and scorned,
> And last neglected? How wouldst thou insult,
> When I must live uxorious to thy will
> In perfect thraldom, how again betray me,
> Bearing my words and doings to the lords
> To gloss upon, and, censuring, frown or smile?
> This jail I count the house of liberty
> To thine, whose doors my feet shall never enter
> (*Samson Agonistes*, ll. 941-50).

In both poem and oratorio, he will not even let her approach to touch his hand, fearing his anger might lead him to tear her limb from limb.

He forgives her at a distance, while shunning reconciliation.

The closure offered by Milton and, following him, Handel is a closure to the relationship for Samson. On the one hand, he does not go to his death bearing a grievance (and this makes him, as Christian tradition sometimes portrayed him, more Christ-like). On the other hand, we can see that he has come to understand the folly of his ways and his failure to live up to his calling. He has learned his lesson, something sinners do well to do, and, having paid dearly for the folly of trusting a woman's deceptive ways, he does not make the same mistake again. As for the woman, Delilah leaves the story when her plea for reconciliation is rejected. Her side of the story and her vision of a possible future together vie with Samson's, but since Samson's is the privileged version, it is the one readers and listeners are most likely to accept.[45] We tend to think he is right not to trust her again. Indeed, it might strike us as unreasonable for her to think he could forgive her, not just for the betrayal but also and especially for the darkness he must forever endure (it bears recalling, however, that she claims not to have known in advance about the blinding). But is it any more unreasonable for Samson to forgive Delilah than for an abused wife to agree to reconciliation to her abusive husband? Such was God's expectation in the examples of prophetic pornography we examined in Chapter 4. Commentators on that relationship did not find the idea of reconciliation unreasonable or unrealistic. Why, then, should it be unimaginable here? The double standard works effectively to privilege the divine and the male point of view. If we were to privilege Delilah's point of view instead, we would need to read Milton and hear Handel differently.

The chorus in *Samson Agonistes* provides us with the authorial judgment (in the oratorio, this is done by Micah, a character who does not appear in the poem): 'She's gone, a manifest serpent by her sting/ Discovered in the end, till now concealed'. Closure for these metatexts involves punishing Delilah by exposing her as a hypocrite, whose deceptive wiles Samson is able to resist this time. Moreover, the closure they offer moves beyond a concern with Samson and Delilah to draw a moral about all womankind. The chorus offers a

45. In the oratorio their competing versions are well captured in the duet, 'Traitor to love!/Traitress to love!', where they seem to be vying for the moral high ground. But this is followed by Micah's definitive evaluative judgment, 'She's gone! a serpent manifest; her sting/ Discover'd in the end.'

long commentary (shorter in the oratorio) on the enigma of woman and the treacherous mixture in women of physical beauty, lack of judgment, self-love, and mischief. It is the lucky man indeed 'who finds One virtuous'. Just as Milton had Delilah begin her defense with an appeal to the natural frailty of women, he achieves a closure of sorts (followed by Handel–Hamilton) by having the chorus end with a description of woman's fickle nature. Women are seductive and dangerous, and it is therefore in the interest of society that women be subordinate to men and their behavior controlled. Indeed, justification for this state of affairs is inscribed in the very order of creation itself:

> Therefore God's universal law
> Gave to the man despotic power
> Over his female in due awe…

The closure we seek for the story of Delilah and Samson can be discovered in the paintings we looked at as well. In Rubens's painting of Samson and Delilah (fig. 6.2), for example, the old madam's face is just above Delilah's and there is a noticeable similarity between the profiles. The conclusion drawn by the author of the *National Gallery Companion Guide*, that the juxtaposition 'reveals [the procuress's] own past and suggests Delilah's future',[46] is a form of closure. It suggests that the large sum of money the Philistines are supposed to have paid for Samson's secret plays no role; at least it makes no difference in Delilah's life. It also envisions a 'suitable punishment' in store for Delilah: she will spend all her days working in a brothel, with no option but to become a procuress herself when her youth and beauty are gone (a cruel punishment that could be compared to the one intended for Samson: spending the rest of his life grinding at the mill).

A different but significant kind of closure is provided by the popular song to which I referred at the beginning of this chapter. As I noted above, the song is not about the biblical Samson and Delilah. It does, however, deal with the same subject as the biblical story, a woman's betrayal of a man who loves her. The themes of love, jealousy, betrayal and death, together with the use of the name 'Delilah' for the treacherous woman, provide enough of a connection for us to regard the song 'Delilah' as a popular commentary on

---

46. Erika Langmuir, *The National Gallery Companion Guide* (London: National Gallery Publications, 1994), p. 240.

the biblical story and to ask what happens if we pursue its logic in the light of the biblical story. From outside the woman's house at night, the singer sees the shadows of Delilah and another man on the shade. A jealous rage comes over him ('She was my woman. As she deceived me I watched and went out of my mind'). He waits until the man leaves at daybreak. When Delilah opens the door and sees him, she makes a fatal mistake: she laughs. 'I felt the knife in my hand and she laughed no more', he tells us. The refrain, 'My, my, my Delilah; why, why, why, Delilah?', suggests that the song is about her motivation, and, indeed, he does want to know why, in a rhetorical sort of way. In reality, however, the song is about his motivation, being laughed at in addition to being deceived: 'I just couldn't take any more', he repeats in the refrain, as he asks her to forgive him before they come to take him away.

I take this song as a variation on the Samson–Delilah fabula and propose seeing it as Samson's revenge. It satisfies our need to have Delilah punished. The woman betrays the man, but he does not die as a result. Instead he kills her. The betrayer dies and not the betrayed, as in the biblical story, and this is more satisfying. (We are left with the impression that he will be punished, but the song itself is about her death, not his punishment. Perhaps he will get off with a light sentence, as men who kill women for sexual infidelity have throughout history.) Another telling variation on the biblical version is that the crime here is not the woman's betrayal of a secret, but rather a sexual betrayal with another man. This reflects the popular notion that Delilah's betrayal in the Bible has to do with sex. Unlike what we (do not) know in the case of the biblical Delilah, the singer who stands in for Samson is sorry for what he has done—in any event, he asks for forgiveness. In spite of significant differences from the biblical account, the fatal attraction of woman still lurks in the background of the song. It is the woman's fault that the man got into trouble over her in the first place: 'I could see that girl was no good for me, but I was lost like a slave that no man could free'. The irresistible attraction of the *femme fatale* and the feelings of intense jealousy she arouses in him are the man's undoing in this song—not to mention hers.

Closure in the film *Samson and Delilah* is handled in much the same way as motivation. De Mille pulls out all the stops in this biblical spectacle; there is forgiveness, reconciliation, and he even has Delilah die in the temple too. What more could an audience wish for? A love story, perhaps? We have it, and what a love story!

Classical Hollywood cinema of the forties and fifties typically dealt with the 'bad woman' in one of two ways: she was investigated and punished (usually she died in the end) or she was investigated and saved (she became a 'good girl').[47] De Mille does both for Delilah. Her death serves as punishment for her crime; she does not, as she proposed to do in the granary scene, go off with Samson to Egypt to live happily ever after. It is a punishment she accepts; 'I will not be afraid', she tells Samson when he warns her that death will enter the temple. De Mille's 'redemption' of Delilah is a *tour de force* that makes the story of Samson and Delilah into a love story for all time. Delilah, in effect, converts. She prays to Samson's god, and ends up being that god's instrument in Samson's final victory over the Philistines.

When Delilah discovers that, in keeping with the letter but not the spirit of her agreement with the Saran, Samson has been blinded, her love for Samson is evident. De Mille's mouthpiece, the Saran, tells her, 'There can be only one master in a kingdom or a woman's heart. Until you saw him like this, you could not forget him.' The audience, along with the Saran, has sensed all along that Samson is the master of Delilah's heart. 'Forget him', she says plaintively, as if she could, and we know only too well she cannot. When she insists that the guilt is not wholly hers ('No, I did not blind him'), the Saran replies, 'You cannot undo what has been done'. In the following scene, however, Delilah wakes up from her recurrent nightmare in which Samson endlessly turns the millstone, the phrase 'you cannot undo what has been done' echoing in her head, and cries out, 'I can, I can'. Distraught ('I'm being crushed like the grain beneath the stone') and weeping, she prays: 'O God of Samson, help me! He said you are everywhere, that you are almighty. Hear me! Give back the light of his eyes and take my sight for his. O God of Samson, help me!' De Mille encourages us to feel sympathy for Delilah. She is genuinely repentant and would gladly undo what she has done. She goes to the granary to seek Samson's forgiveness and to beg him to go away with her to the valley of the Nile, where they can be together.

When she enters, Samson is praying, and as the scene proceeds we realize that Delilah is the answer to his prayer. That she truly loves him, and he her, is borne out by their (under the circumstances)

---

47. Mulvey, *Visual and Other Pleasures*, pp. 21-26; and see the discussion of film's *femme fatale* below.

romantic exchange, and by her third confession of love, vastly different from her earlier angry outbursts: 'All I want is to comfort
you...Won't you believe I would give my life to undo what I have
done.' When he accuses her of selling his sight, she pleads, 'I would
endure your hatred, Samson, if it would bring back your sight. Let
me be your eyes.' When he says that 'through all the long darkness I
prayed that you'd be delivered into my hands', she answers simply, 'I
am here. I will not cry out.' He lifts her over his head to dash her to
the ground, breaking his chains in the process. This sign of his
strength's return shows him that his god has heard his prayer. Still, it
is not clear to him what he, a blind man, can do, since he even needs
someone to put food and drink to his mouth. Delilah promises to
care for him, they embrace and affirm their love, and she tells him
that she has arranged their escape. As she is leading him out of the
prison house, she mentions the plans to bring him to the temple in
the morning. He realizes now what he must do, and, choosing to
remain in prison, warns Delilah not to come to the temple.

In the climactic temple scene, all the Philistines gather to watch
Samson be humbled before their god, Dagon. Delilah joins Samson
in the arena in spite of the Saran's warning that she can never return
to him. Whereas the Philistine crowd thinks she enters the arena to
join in the tormenting of Samson, the audience, like the Saran,
knows differently. She leads Samson by the end of a whip to the two
columns that support the temple. When he tells her to go, she only
pretends to leave. He pulls down the temple and they die together in a
brilliant cinematic resolution. Delilah enables Samson to achieve his
destiny. She and he are redeemed together: he, through his new-
found faithfulness to his god, and she, through him.

Seduction and Betrayal: The Femme Fatale *and the Samson Complex*

The film *Samson and Delilah* ends with a theological message. Derek
Elley observes that 'De Mille never resolved the struggle in his films
between sexual and devout content'.[48] But must it be one or the
other, sexual or devout? Readers interested in the theological message
of the biblical story, for instance, may debate whether its purpose is to
show the consequences of not living up to one's divine calling or to

---

48. Elley, *The Epic Film*, p. 36.

illustrate God's power to use even an unworthy servant[49] but, along-side its theological agenda, a message about gender relations lies close to the story's surface, as the moral Josephus drew from it illustrates. In terms of its gender code, the biblical story serves as a warning to men about the danger posed by women and the difficulty, but importance, of resisting their allure.[50]

Twice in the biblical version Samson reveals his secret to a woman in order to prove his love. 'You only hate me, you do not love me!', the Timnite chides. 'How can you say, "I love you", when your heart is not with me?', reproves Delilah. Samson tells his Timnite bride the answer to his riddle and, in the ultimate, fatal self-revelation, he discloses the secret of his strength to Delilah. He proves his love by making himself vulnerable, by furnishing the woman with knowl-edge that gives her power over him; in other words, by surrendering himself to the woman. She uses this knowledge against him. The story thus illustrates how surrender in love is both attractive—even an apparently invincible strong man like Samson cannot resist a woman's charms—and dangerous—it costs him his freedom, his sight, and his life.[51] Women, the Samson story teaches us, are deceitful, treacherous, and lethal. A man should never yield to them, for, given the opportunity, women will use their power over him against him. A man who surrenders himself to the temptation a woman offers loses his potency, his manhood,[52] and does so, as the book of

49. I have argued against the common view that the theological point of the story has to do with Samson's failure to live up to his Nazirite calling; other theological themes, such as prayer and its answer, are more central; see J. Cheryl Exum, 'The Theological Dimension of the Samson Saga', *Vetus Testamentum* 33 (1983), pp. 30-45. I would not, however, rule out the importance of the Nazirite vow. For other ways of looking at the biblical story, see Exum, *Tragedy and Biblical Narrative*, pp. 18-44.

50. On the disciplinary tendency to read through one particular code (e.g., historical, literary, theological, anthropological, gender codes, etc.) and the call for an approach that combines several codes, see Mieke Bal, *Murder and Difference: Gender, Genre, and Scholarship on Sisera's Death* (Bloomington: Indiana University Press, 1988).

51. The rabbinic explanation that Samson sinned with his eyes and therefore lost his sight has its analogue in De Mille's film when, upon hearing about the woman he has seen in Timnah, Samson's mother tells him, 'your eyes always find what they shouldn't', 'a man's heart can be blind, son', and, lastly, 'O Samson, Samson, you're blind!'

52. Samson is symbolically placed in the position of a woman as a result of surrender; see Susan Niditch, 'Samson As Culture Hero, Trickster, and Bandit: The

Proverbs likewise warns, at the risk of his life.

This view of women encoded in the biblical story is a man's view of women, not a woman's, and as such it tells us more about the men responsible for it than it does about women. Women are not alluring and menacing *in themselves* but *to men*. Since masculinity, like femininity, is a construct, one way to dismantle the *femme fatale*, the trope of the woman fatal to man, is to ask what this image of women seeks to disavow or suppress about men. If instead of focusing on the woman as constructed by the biblical text, we focus on the man as constructed by the text, we confront not the *femme fatale*, but what I call the Samson complex.

By the Samson complex I refer to the man's desire to surrender to the woman and his fear that he will be destroyed by her, for, psychologically speaking, this is what the story of Samson and Delilah is about. With Delilah, Samson has three chances to learn his lesson about the danger of women, for three times she does to him exactly what he confided to her would rob him of his strength. It is clear the fourth time that she will use what he tells her against him, but he tells her anyway. Why? For sex? Yes, but something else seems to be involved as well, for, as we have seen, he could satisfy his sexual urges with a harlot without risking so much. From a psychoanalytic perspective, we may conclude that if Samson tells Delilah how to subdue him, knowing what the consequences will be, it can only be because he must, because he has a deep need to do so. The risk holds a certain attraction. The attraction of losing himself in love, transcending the self through the intimate knowing of the other, is overwhelming. Such is the longing that draws him inexorably to the woman. It may possibly be connected to what Freud called the 'death instinct', so that 'side by side with his desire to conquer, [the man feels] a secret longing for extinction in the act of reunion with the woman (mother)'.[53]

Empowerment of the Weak', *Catholic Biblical Quarterly* 52 (1990), pp. 616-17; Exum, *Fragmented Women*, pp. 84-85.

53. Karen Horney, *Feminine Psychology* (London: Routledge and Kegan Paul, 1967), pp. 138-39. If surrender in love is attractive and exhilarating, the oblivion/extinction of the self is also threatening, and thus the desire to yield vies with the instinct for self-preservation. In an essay on 'The Distrust between the Sexes', Horney attributes the fear of losing the self in love to our instinct for self-preservation (*Feminine Psychology*, p. 108). I am speaking in this context of male desire for the woman, but the attraction of losing the self in the other and desire for self-preservation applies to women as well, though there are cultural as well as psychological

Samson yielded, and look what happened to him, says our story. If even an apparently invincible man like Samson can be undone by a woman, how much more so should the ordinary man be on his guard. Such is the fear the woman inspires.

Karen Horney discusses the feelings of longing and anxiety that women arouse in men in her famous essay on 'The Dread of Women'. Like Freud, she finds its origins in infantile sexuality, but, unlike Freud, for whom castration anxiety was primary, for Horney, castration anxiety is rather a secondary development from the fear of the vagina, the sinister female genital. The boy desires his mother's body but, sensing that his penis is too small for her vagina, is frustrated by feelings of inadequacy, Horney argues, and he carries a deeply hidden anxiety about his potency with him into adulthood. What he fears most is being rejected and derided by the woman. The crucial issue for Horney is the subconscious threat the woman poses to the man's self-respect, a threat that men deny even to themselves by externalizing their desires and fears and projecting them onto women. Among the examples Horney gives of objectifications of men's dread of women are the sirens, the Lorelei, the Sphinx, Kali, Judith, Salome, and, not insignificantly, Delilah. She writes,

> 'It is not', he says, 'that I dread her; it is that she herself is malignant, capable of any crime, a beast of prey, a vampire, a witch, insatiable in her desires. She is the very personification of what is sinister.' May not this be one of the principal roots of the whole masculine impulse to creative work—the never ending conflict between the man's longing for the woman and his dread of her?[54]

Horney's emphasis on the 'objectifying' of this dread in artistic and scientific creative work[55] is suggestive, and, if she is correct, it should come as no surprise that we find this psychic conflict played out again and again in literary, musical, and visual versions of the story of Delilah and Samson.

What interests me here is not the validity or deficiencies of Horney's psychoanalytic theory but rather its heuristic value for illuminating the (subconscious) narrative dynamic of the story of Samson and Delilah, which I see as partly responsible for its cultural impact and

---

differences (e.g. women are supposed to surrender to men and not the other way round, as I note below) beyond my scope here.

54. Horney, *Feminine Psychology*, p. 135.
55. Horney, *Feminine Psychology*, p. 136.

lasting appeal. The fact that a psychoanalytic reading makes sense of so many elements of the story alone invites its adoption.[56] More important, psychoanalytic criticism is an important tool for the feminist critic because it allows analysis of the text to move beyond mere description to interrogation: in this case, beyond reiterating the text's view of women as deceptive and menacing to a questioning of the interests and drives that motivate that view. The division of women that I mentioned above into either good or bad (virgin/ mother or whore), for example, corresponds to Horney's observation that men seek to handle their dread of women through adoration (there is no need to fear someone so good, lovely, and, indeed, saintly) or disparagement (there is no need to fear such an unworthy creature). Debasing the love object mitigates her threat to the male ego. 'From the prostitute or the woman of easy virtue one need fear no rejection, and no demands in the sexual, ethical, or intellectual spheres', Horney writes. 'One can feel oneself the superior.'[57] Samson, we recall, had nothing to fear from the prostitute he visited in Gaza.

In giving his most secret part of himself to Delilah, in contrast, in allowing the object of his love (16.4) to have power over him, he becomes vulnerable, and as a result he becomes weak, emasculated. The fear of losing potency because of the woman is but a thinly veiled allusion to castration anxiety, fear of the *vagina dentata*. 'Metaphorically, every vagina has secret teeth, for the male exits as less than when he entered', writes Camille Paglia. 'Physical and spiritual castration is the danger every man runs in intercourse with a woman. Love is the spell by which he puts his sexual fear to sleep.'[58] Since Freud, we have come to recognize the symbolism both of the cutting of hair and of blinding—precisely what happens to Samson—as expressions of castration anxiety. Scissors or a knife according to Horney is a female

---

56. I am following here a psychoanalytic literary reading that takes the text, and not simply the characters, as its subject. On the analogy, established already by Freud, between analyzing dreams and analyzing texts, we can consider all the characters in the text as split-off parts of the narrative voice. Texts, like dreams, are over-determined. I am speaking here of unconscious drives embedded within this text, of its repressions, displacements, conflicts, and desires. When I speak of Samson's fears and desires, I am not seeking so much to psychoanalyze the character as the part of the narrative psyche he represents, the libido. See, further, Brooks, 'The Idea of a Psychoanalytic Literary Criticism'.

57. Horney, *Feminine Psychology*, p. 146.

58. Paglia, *Sexual Personae*, p. 13.

symbol; Delilah, who wields the knife (either directly or through the agency of a barber), represents the castrating woman, the woman with the terrifying, sinister genital, the *femme fatale*.

In terms of its cultural consequences, Horney considers men's most important strategy for dealing with their fears to be the diminishing of women's self-respect, for example, by viewing women as infantile, emotional, and incapable of responsibility and independence. She asks, in fact, whether the type of woman who fits this picture is 'cultivated by a systematic selection on the part of men'.[59] Milton (followed by Handel–Hamilton) illustrates this tendency to lower women's self-respect when he describes Delilah in terms that suggest her vanity and emotionality (she enters 'bedecked, ornate, and gay', 'sailing like a stately ship...with all her bravery on and tackle trim' and weeping copious tears), in addition, as we have seen, to having her appeal to unflattering stereotypes of women's inferiority in her defense.[60]

Horney's work is important for exposing the *femme fatale* as a male construct, a projection of male fears of inadequacy and an expression of the man's need to protect his self-esteem by feeling superior to the woman. She thus provides us with a useful tool for deconstructing the *femme fatale* trope. What the image of woman as *femme fatale* suppresses is the fragility of the construction of masculine superiority.[61] Samson is masculinity writ large. As the episodes with the lion (14.5-6), the thirty garments in payment of his wager (14.19), the jawbone of the ass (15.14-16), and the gates of Gaza (16.1-3) make clear, he is superior in strength, not just to women but also to other men. He is

59. Horney, *Feminine Psychology*, p. 146. The implications of her argument are disturbing. It is not, she says, the arguments that have been put forth over the centuries to prove masculine superiority. 'What really counts is the fact that the ever-precarious self-respect of the "average man" causes him over and over again to choose a feminine type that is infantile, nonmaternal, and hysterical, and by so doing to expose each new generation to the influence of such women.'

60. See, however, Lewalski ('Milton on Women—Yet Again', pp. 50-51, 60-65), who argues that whereas Milton's Delilah 'has internalized both the feminine stereotypes and the cultural constraints of her society, and makes them her excuses', the text 'refuses them as excuses' (p. 64), and that Milton honors women 'by insisting on the badness of Dalila' (p. 65). See also, Diane K. McColley, 'Milton and the Sexes', in *The Cambridge Companion to Milton* (ed. D. Danielson; Cambridge: Cambridge University Press, 1989), pp. 147-66.

61. See Jennifer A. Glancy, 'Unveiling Masculinity: The Construction of Gender in Mark 6.17-29', *Biblical Interpretation* 2 (1994), pp. 34-50.

also superior in wit, as his poetic and occasionally bawdy bon mots
reveal (14.14, 18; 15.16). He is in control, unconquerable; he has a
unique, secret potency that women want to possess and that other
men (the Philistines) envy and want to deprive him of because his
prowess exposes their weakness. Even with Delilah, Samson is in
control on the three occasions that he teases her with the wrong
answer to the secret of his strength. By toying with Delilah he is
courting disaster; he uses the game to prove to himself his manhood
by tempting fate, showing how close he can come to calamity and
still escape, like men for whom daredevil stunts are a macho pursuit.
His interactions with her represent the subconscious desire to meet
the calamity head on, and the fear that this might happen.

It does happen. Samson's yielding to a woman's lure exposes the
fissures in the edifice of masculinity. By surrendering, he reveals his
superiority over the woman as an illusion, for women are supposed
to surrender to men, and not the other way around. The text works
hard to repair the damage to the masculine image by showing
Samson's final victory in the end (where in toppling the temple he
symbolically destroys woman, his gesture of pulling together the two
pillars that support it signifying a refusal of sex or sexual difference).[62]
In an attempt to have it both ways, the text not only uses Samson as a
moral lesson, it redeems him too. Samson's god, who is *de facto* male-
identified, rescues him from his emasculated state brought about by a
woman. Moreover, the story implies that everything that has transpired has been controlled by this god for his purposes ('for he was
seeking an occasion against the Philistines', Judg. 14.4).

To some extent, putting God in control lessens both Samson's
responsibility and Delilah's power, but it does not negate either one.
The illusion of masculine superiority is maintained at the cost of the
hero's life, which is a big price to pay. And in any case, the resort to
a *deus ex machina* to vindicate the hero does not alleviate the deep-
rooted textual anxiety about the allure and danger of women, as
readers throughout the centuries have instinctively recognized.

---

62. Exum, *Fragmented Women*, pp. 84-85. Mieke Bal offers a different interpretation of his symbolic destruction of woman in this scene as a 'solution to the birth
trauma...He outdoes woman, making the gap acceptably large' and the woman
superfluous (*Lethal Love*, p. 62).

> 'Are you afraid?'
> 'Of a woman? —yes.'

This snippet of dialogue from the film *Samson and Delilah* is astonishingly revealing. The man, momentarily at least, openly admits his fear. Why is he afraid? If we follow Horney, his fear, on a subconscious level, is of being rejected and derided by the woman. Rather than risk this, to protect his male ego he projects his fear onto the woman, thus producing the *femme fatale*, the menacing woman. And this is precisely what the cinematic Delilah, like all the others, turns out to be, in spite of the fact that in some ways, as we have seen, De Mille seeks to redeem her image.

Investigating the Woman: Knowledge that Leads to Mastery

Knowledge of the other is a way of gaining mastery or control; this is a lesson the story of Samson and Delilah teaches us. Knowledge of the secret of Samson's potency gives Delilah (and, through her, the Philistines) power over Samson. What is unknown is much more frightening than what is known. This is why the *femme fatale* is so scary. Her unknowableness, her mystery and the mysterious secret of female sexuality she signifies, is the *femme fatale*'s most salient trait. Deceit is an important ingredient of her mystery; she is risky; the man cannot know for sure. The *femme fatale* seems to have no useful function in society.[63] She is neither a nurturing mother nor a dutiful wife, the principal female roles patriarchal society assigns to women, roles that men find familiar and comforting. As the woman whose sexuality appears uncontrolled, beyond the strictures of patriarchal authority, she disrupts the social order, and so she gives rise to a certain discomfort, a feeling of apprehension, in the man. And she presents him with the challenge to tame her. Her passion is fierce—'a fire to make all other loves seem like ice'—and her desire, insatiable; indeed, she seems to have no other purpose than to desire and be desired. The shadowy suggestion of the illicit and risqué that surrounds her figure provides a thrill; as the cinematic Samson tells his mother, 'Forbidden figs are sweeter'.

The *femme fatale* represents for the man both a fantasy of female sexual desire, whose nature he does not really understand, and the

---

63. Doane, *Femmes Fatales*, p. 2.

mystery of female sexuality, the secret he cannot divine. As a reminder of sexual difference and activator of castration anxiety through her possession of the castrating genital, she is frightening. According to filmmaker and critic Laura Mulvey, the male unconscious has two effective avenues of escape from the anxiety she produces. One is by investigating the woman, explaining her, which serves to demystify her mystery. Once investigated, the woman is usually either punished or saved (thus we have metatextual Delilahs whose duplicity is exposed by Samson and Delilahs who die in the destruction of the temple). The other mechanism for mitigating the threat she poses is fetishizing the woman, making her a fantasy object for the man that marks her as reassuring rather than dangerous.[64] Now the biblical text does neither of these; it neither explains Delilah nor fetishizes her. Ignoring her as the biblical text does could be viewed as yet another unconscious mechanism for mitigating her threat. But at the same time (and I do not see the two as mutually exclusive), this narrative neglect makes the biblical Delilah particularly threatening in that she cannot be accounted for.

The metatexts we have examined in this chapter respond to the need to account for her by supplying information to compensate for this narrative lack. They can all be viewed as attempts to tame the *femme fatale* by supplying knowledge about her that produces a sense of security. As we have seen, all of them endeavor in one way or another to explain what motivates her to betray Samson. Their various recipes

---

64. Mulvey, *Visual and Other Pleasures*, p. 21. Feminist film critics have taken over Freud's theory of fetishism, finding the penis in the woman in an attempt to escape from or deny the existence of the sinister female genital, to refer to the ultimate objectification of the woman in cinema. According to Freud, fetishism arises from a feeling of abhorrence due to the absence of the penis in women. Horney (*Feminine Psychology*, p. 137) locates its basis elsewhere, in anxiety, in 'dread of the vagina, [which is only] thinly disguised under the abhorrence'. Whether Freud or Horney, or either of them for that matter, is correct on this point is irrelevant for my purposes. Like the feminist film critics who have informed my thinking on this subject, I see psychoanalytic theory as a useful tool for analyzing patriarchal texts (since it pursues the same patriarchal logic) without necessarily accepting the validity of its claims. See Mulvey, *Visual and Other Pleasures*, p. 15; Doane, *Femmes Fatales*, pp. 7-9, 44-46; Kaplan, *Women and Film*, pp. 24-26; Silverman, *The Acoustic Mirror*, pp. 1-32; Teresa de Lauretis, *Alice Doesn't: Feminism, Semiotics, Cinema* (London: Macmillan, 1984), pp. 30-31.

for supplying closure are also ways of investigating her, by envisioning
how the aftermath of the betrayal affects her. The more the man
knows about the temptress, the less threatening she appears. Only one
of the metatexts discussed here, the film, goes to any length to
fetishize Delilah, and like everything else De Mille does in this film,
he carries the fetishization of the woman to impressive lengths. Since
of all my metatextual examples the film represents by far the most full-
fledged development of Delilah as *femme fatale*, it offers the best place
to examine this trope in detail.

Another Look at Looking at Film's Femme Fatale

In addition to giving me the opportunity to pay homage to his
splendid film, consideration of Cecil B. De Mille's Delilah as *femme
fatale*, the most fully developed portrayal of Delilah in popular culture
I know of, will enable me to conclude my study of cultural representations of biblical women by returning to some of the issues raised at
the beginning of this book: scopophilia or the pleasure of looking,
the positioning of the woman as object of the look, and the probable
different reactions that male and female spectators have when con-
fronted with the woman objectified by and for the male gaze. I will
limit my remarks to the film here, though, as I hope to have shown
in Chapter 1, these issues apply to texts and their readers as well.

To some extent De Mille is restrained by the biblical story. I suspect
he was not really happy with the biblical story's ending, where the
hero is betrayed and dies, and the relationship between Samson and
Delilah is not resolved. De Mille deals with the ending of biblical tale,
which he cannot change, by setting his version within the framework of the struggle between faith and superstition. At the beginning
of the film De Mille speaks to us about the growth of fear and superstition, the loss of human dignity, and the rise of tyranny ('human
dignity perished on the altar of idolatry and tyranny rose'), and about
the 'unquenchable will to freedom'. Nothing that happens in the film
after his introduction has any connection with this moral lesson,
however. (Interestingly in this respect, the film mirrors the biblical
book of Judges where the amoral Samson story is set within the
moralistic Deuteronomistic frame ['The people of Israel again did
what was evil in the eyes of the Lord, and the Lord gave them into
the hand of the Philistines for forty years...He judged Israel in the

days of the Philistines twenty years']).[65] At the film's end, Miriam serves as De Mille's mouthpiece to tell us that, to borrow the phrase from another fictive commentator, Milton's Manoah, 'Samson hath quit himself like Samson'. 'His strength will never die', Miriam assures young Saul and theater audiences everywhere. 'Men will tell his story for a thousand years.'

As we have seen, De Mille responds to the source text's unsatisfying ending by turning the relationship between the protagonists into a love story for all time. With Delilah, he does not face the same restrictions that the biblical portrayal of Samson imposed upon him. His is a sympathetic Delilah, but there is a certain tension in her presentation, for it is not possible to retell the biblical story without reinscribing its representation of woman as deceptive and dangerous. To be sure, it was not necessary to reinscribe the text's gender ideology to the extent De Mille does, but he is not merely retelling a biblical story for the edification of his audience. He is making a movie to make money, and using his film as a vehicle for insuring his star's status as erotic icon is in his interest. Furthermore, he is not just adopting the biblical ideology; his film is typical of the dominant cinema of the forties and fifties, and as such promotes and transmits conventional patriarchal values.[66] In making Delilah a consummate *femme fatale*, De Mille is simply exaggerating the gender ideology implicit in the biblical story and other versions of the fabula, pushing it to its (il)logical conclusion. 'Bring in a woman and she'll bring on trouble.'

Whereas the film focuses on Delilah and shows her point of view, Samson remains at its center, as the film's hero and the one who has, so De Mille's voice-over tells us, 'a bold dream—liberty for his nation', though we are never shown any evidence of it. Samson is the hero with whom the spectator is aligned; he is on the 'right' side, the side of truth, freedom, God, and the law of the Father. Delilah, the *femme fatale*, is on the wrong side. She is foreign, she even goes to bed with the enemy, and as activator of his desire she is a snare for the hero ('I'll never be free of you, Delilah').

65. The Deuteronomistic framework has almost totally broken down by the time we reach the Samson story; see J. Cheryl Exum, 'The Centre Cannot Hold: Thematic and Textual Instabilities in Judges', *Catholic Biblical Quarterly* 52 (1990), pp. 410-31.

66. Readers and viewers familiar with film noir and melodrama will recognize how much *Samson and Delilah* has in common with these genres.

She is also a reminder of the danger of desire ('More men have been trapped by smiles than by ropes'). She is overtly and threateningly sexual, a man-eater confident about her ability to use her sexuality to get what she wants, and she deliberately uses her body as spectacle. Mulvey argues that 'the woman as icon, displayed for the gaze and enjoyment of men, the active controllers of the look, always threatens to evoke the anxiety it originally signified';[67] that is, castration anxiety. Delilah is a castrating woman, as demonstrated by the fact that she returns the look. De Mille, who cast Victor Mature and Hedy Lamarr in the title roles because 'they embody in the public mind the essence of maleness and femininity',[68] uses the mechanisms of both investigation and fetishism for coping with the anxiety the *femme fatale* arouses. In the discussion of motivation above I described how he investigates Delilah in detail in order to show, in the end, that her conflicting emotions converge in obsessive love. I also indicated how, having investigated her, he both saves her for the man and punishes her: he redeems her by having her repent of the betrayal and by using her as the instrument of Samson's deliverance. And he punishes her, something the biblical version neglected to do, by killing her off in the end.

Hedy Lamarr's realization of Delilah on the screen as the ultimate object of the look makes her a prime illustration of the second mechanism Mulvey speaks of, fetishistic scopophilia. Fetishistic scopophilia focuses on the look; it transforms the physical beauty of the object into something satisfying in itself.[69] Besides being about the biblical Samson, and vaguely about the 'unquenchable will to freedom', *Samson and Delilah* is first and foremost a film about the woman as object of the look. The camera angles, the lighting, the close-ups of Hedy Lamarr's face (fetishization through fragmenting the female body), her lavish wardrobe of provocative outfits with color-coordinated jewelry (down to the decadent touch of anklets, as in Moreau's painting, and bejeweled sandals) all remind us that she is the object of the look for the spectators in the theater audience as well as for the characters in the film. Through the dialogue, attention is continually drawn to her beauty ('Look, look, have you ever seen eyes like that?...See the whiteness of her skin, smooth as a young dove's'), her

67. Mulvey, *Visual and Other Pleasures*, p. 21.
68. Cited in Elley, *The Epic Film*, p. 36.
69. Mulvey, *Visual and Other Pleasures*, p. 21.

sexual appeal ('Why can't I lead you like that?' 'You're not Delilah'), and her irresistibility (to men, of course: ' Do you still have the same shears, Delilah, my hair's rather long'; 'Some time you might bait a trap for me, Delilah'). Like Susan Hayward and Alice Krige in the films about David and Bathsheba, Hedy Lamarr knows we are looking, and, rehearsing her carefully cultivated screen image as siren, she plays to and holds the gaze more deliberately and more self-consciously than either of them.

As a fetish, Delilah becomes non-threatening. In every scene, she appears as a model of visual perfection—gorgeous, flawless, and most of all, sexy. Her fabulous outfits signify her fetishization, especially in the final scene where she struts around in a glamorous peacock gown, whose meaning as a symbol of her vanity is transparent.[70] An onlooker, addressing the Saran, calls her 'your peacock', an epithet that diminishes her threat and marks her as being for the man. In this scene she performs for the male spectator and not the male protagonist, for Samson, the object of her desire, cannot see her.

What about the *femme fatale*'s desire? Can the woman ever win, either in the Bible or in classical narrative cinema? De Mille's Delilah openly expresses her desire, and, as we have seen, it is all-consuming. It is not for nothing that Samson on more than one occasion calls her a 'wildcat'. But her desire is never realized; she never gets what she wants, which is Samson. When he prepares to go off with Miriam, even though he promises to return to her, she betrays him rather than lose him ('I cannot fight against his god, but no woman will take him from me'). She wants him as love's prisoner, her prisoner. She does not want him blinded, which she knows nothing about, or even harmed ('No drop of his blood shall be shed. No blade shall touch his skin'). She is caught between the good in her, her genuine love for Samson, and the bad, which is that same love carried too far, into an obsession that destroys first him and then both of them. She cannot win, which is to say, her desire, their mutual desire, is realized only in death.

The *femme fatale*'s inability to become a 'correct' or 'proper woman' and 'suitable wife' is underscored by the presence of her opposite, Miriam, the cow-eyed, sweet-natured, wholesome girl-next-door from Samson's own tribe of Dan, whose 'hands are never idle' and

70. Costumes were designed by the famous wardrober-to-the-stars, Edith Head, among others.

who would have made Samson a perfect wife. Miriam is the virginal woman, the woman on a pedestal. 'You're further above me than the moon', Samson tells her. She poses no threat to Samson, but also presents no challenge, no danger or excitement. He prefers the *femme fatale*: 'A man must marry where his heart leads him', he tells his 'little mother' (a diminutive that, like 'your peacock', shows that the woman is not to be taken seriously).[71]

Within feminist film theory, where the fetishization of woman has arguably been given most attention, Ann Kaplan observes that fetishization represses motherhood,[72] and Mary Ann Doane speaks of the *femme fatale* as the 'antithesis of the maternal'.[73] In contrast to Miriam, who would make an ideal wife and mother ('You want to bear his children', claims Delilah) there is nothing remotely suggestive of the maternal about Delilah. This is not only true for the film but for the biblical story as well, where none of the women who represent desirable sexual partners for Samson becomes a mother, and where the one woman who is a mother (Samson's mother) is desexualized.[74] The cinematic Delilah recognizes that Miriam has the 'acceptable' qualities she lacks: 'You belong to Miriam; she is the good in you. I'm the weakness, the love that would enslave you', she tells Samson. This explains in part why Delilah sees Miriam, in whom Samson has shown no romantic interest, as a rival—something that is otherwise only explicable as an irrational response on the part of an insanely jealous woman.

As I observed in Chapter 1, the gaze is male in classical Hollywood cinema, and women as well as men in the theater audience are invited to adopt the male gaze at the female image on the screen. As Mulvey observes, for women 'trans-sex identification is a *habit* that very easily becomes *second nature*'.[75] The male spectator can participate in the

---

71. He makes this statement, at the beginning of the film, about Semadar, who is also a dangerous and deadly (just not for him) liaison.

72. Kaplan, *Women and Film*, pp. 53-57.

73. Doane, *Femmes Fatales*, p. 2.

74. The story not only denies the mother's sexual pleasure, it dissociates her pregnancy from the sex act, avoiding even the typical biblical formula, 'Manoah knew his wife and she conceived'; see Exum, *Fragmented Women*, pp. 65-66.

75. Mulvey, *Visual and Other Pleasures*, p. 33; italics hers. Actors are looked at too, but in a different way: 'As the spectator identifies with the main male protagonist, he projects his look onto that of his like, his screen surrogate, so that the power of the male protagonist as he controls events coincides with the active power of the erotic

male protagonist's power and possess the woman vicariously through him. In Samson's case, the male spectator can identify with him up to the point he is duped by the woman, and then take the superior position by thinking, 'Of course, I wouldn't fall for that'. The female spectator can, as I also argued in Chapter 1, resist the identification with the male point of view. Does this mean, as I speculated there, that the resisting female spectator must forgo the pleasure of narrative cinema?[76] If so, what accounts for the attraction feminist film critics admit to, and I share, to classical Hollywood cinema of the forties, fifties, and sixties?[77]

It seems to me that the female spectator, though not necessarily approving of it, might envy Delilah's power to get what she wants, her ability to use her sexuality to manipulate the men around her.[78] There is, after all, a way that women can control men. 'Even Samson's strength must have a weakness', insists Delilah. 'There isn't a man in the world who will not share his secrets with some woman.'

Desire for the male spectator is active. For the female spectator desire is passive: the desire to be attractive like the woman, the desire to be desired.[79] For both there is likely to be something fascinating about the possibility of being loved obsessively, at least in the safe

look, both giving a satisfying sense of omnipotence. A male movie star's glamorous characteristics are thus not those of the erotic object of the gaze, but those of the more perfect, more complete, more powerful ideal ego conceived in the original moment of recognition in front of the mirror' (p. 20). The comparison is with Lacan's mirror stage.

76. It seems to me that this is Mulvey's contention, at least in her earlier article on 'Visual Pleasure and Narrative Cinema', but she puts a different spin on the question in 'Afterthoughts on "Visual Pleasure and Narrative Cinema" Inspired by King Vidor's *Duel in the Sun* (1946)', reprinted in *Visual and Other Pleasures*, pp. 29-38. Kaplan and other feminist film critics have resisted this conclusion; the influence of their work, and Mulvey's, on my discussion here will be evident to those familiar with feminist film theory.

77. Mulvey, *Visual and Other Pleasures*, p. 29; Kaplan, *Women and Film*, p. 26; Doane, *The Desire to Desire*, pp. 3-13, 178-83; and especially the survey of female spectators in Jackie Stacey, *Star Gazing: Hollywood Cinema and Female Spectatorship* (London: Routledge, 1994), pp. 126-75.

78. It is not entirely clear why Samson is able to resist Delilah at first. Is it because he has eyes only for Semadar? Because Delilah has not yet perfected her *femme fatale* arts?

79. Again I want to emphasize that I am speaking of classical Hollywood cinema, where heterosexuality is the norm.

fantasy world of film. A desire so intense that it consumes itself along with its object is a heady aphrodisiac.[80]

For the female spectator both the focus on the woman's point of view and the portrayal of Delilah as a strong, independent woman may have some appeal. Showing the heroine's point of view makes contradictory demands on women spectators.[81] We may derive satisfaction from Delilah's self-sacrifice for the sake of love. On the other hand, we may wonder, Why was this sacrifice narratively and cinematically necessary? The answer to this question lies not within the biblical story, which offers no closure where Delilah is concerned, but within the film itself, which reflects, as Kaplan has shown for classical cinema, the positioning of woman within patriarchy.[82]

As for Delilah's independence, it is more apparent in this film than real, and in this respect De Mille's Delilah resembles the Delilah of the biblical story, who is a pawn of the Philistines. In the Bible the Philistines gain Delilah's cooperation through bribery and use her power for their own ends. In the film, Delilah is not the pawn of the Philistines; seducing Samson in order to learn the secret of his strength is her idea. But even though the betrayal is her idea, she needs the Saran's permission in order to undertake it. The *femme fatale* needs permission to seduce! She manipulates the Saran through the one way available to her, her sexuality. Her power, like her only visible means of support, comes from him, and she has quite an extravagant life-style, as witnessed by her gowns, jewels, and valuable possessions ('The woman that rules the ruler of the five cities must have great wealth', says Samson as he plunders her rich caravan). Delilah's independence, then, is based on manipulation, greed, and betrayal. This is not a very happy model for the woman spectator. In classical narrative cinema perhaps the female spectator, like the *femme fatale*, cannot win.

Delilah is her own person in at least one respect. She, like Samson, follows where her heart leads her. In the final scene she turns her back on the Saran and all he has to offer. But where does her heart

80. The pun is intended.

81. Kaplan, *Women and Film*, p. 49; Doane, *The Desire to Desire*, pp. 157, 168-69.

82. Kaplan (*Women and Film*, p. 49) compares the function of such films to soap operas today: 'To the extent that women see reflected in the films dilemmas that are indeed theirs (as the result of their positioning within patriarchy), the works speak to them'.

lead her? The film has an ending typical of melodrama, with the woman sacrificing her happiness and herself, which Delilah does literally by remaining with Samson in the temple, for 'higher' male ends.[83] Delilah sacrifices herself so that Samson, and ultimately his god, can triumph over tyranny and evil.

The *femme fatale*, like any representation, is never fully under the control of its creators. Kaplan suggests how a female spectator may read the fetishized female as a resisting image through a kind of complicity with the actress, who knows herself to be an object and plays with her own objectification.[84] What Kaplan says about Marlene Dietrich in *Blond Venus* applies to Hedy Lamarr in *Samson and Delilah* as well. She self-consciously uses her body as spectacle, positioning herself as object of the male gaze and making the female spectator aware of this placing (fig. 6.5).[85] She knows men are watching her and she is confident of the effect she will have on them ('Do you know a better bait, Samson? Men always respond'). Lamarr as Delilah looks directly at the camera, sure of her beauty and its impact on the viewer. The way she plays for the camera inhibits our immediate identification with her and causes us to identify instead with the gazing camera. Her self-conscious positioning defamiliarizes us with the image before us, making us aware that we are watching spectacle and that we are watching from a distance.[86] Through becoming more conscious of the film's mechanisms for masking the anxiety the *femme fatale* produces (investigation, fetishism), the female viewer can accept, and even enjoy, the illusion of the *femme fatale* for what it is.

Deconstructing the *femme fatale* trope, either by asking what motivates it, as Horney's work encouraged us to do, or by looking for ways to appropriate it for a female audience, as Kaplan's approach suggests, does not mean doing away with it. What deconstructing the trope does is expose the paradox that male self-esteem depends upon the image of the *femme fatale*. Men need the *femme fatale* and women will play her for the power she has over men. She is here to stay as long as gender relations remain fundamentally unchallenged. That may not be such a bad thing, if we can learn to recognize the figure

83. Kaplan, *Women and Film*, p. 38.

84. Kaplan, *Women and Film*, pp. 50-59; similarly, Doane, *The Desire to Desire*, pp. 180-83.

85. Kaplan, *Women and Film*, p. 51.

86. Kaplan, *Women and Film*, p. 58.

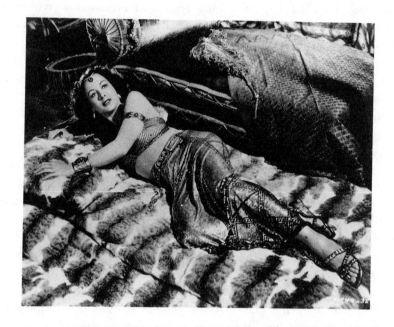

Figure 6.5. Hedy Lamarr as Delilah, in *Samson and Delilah*

for the construct it is and imagine new ways of seeing the trope.
Doane suggests using fantasy 'as a space for work on and against the
familiar tropes of femininity'. Everything depends, she points out, on
how we see ourselves. 'And it is now possible to *look elsewhere.*'[87]

It will be interesting to see what happens to the story of Delilah and
Samson in its next cinematic incarnation, starring Liz Hurley as Delilah
(so far no one is disclosing what *this* Delilah is being paid). Will it
offer steamy sex scenes, as do other films by its director, Nicolas
Roeg? Or will it provide family entertainment 'with high production
values' befitting its biblical subject, as a spokesperson for its producer,
Turner Network Television, has claimed?[88] If Martin Scorsese in *The
Last Temptation of Christ* could make Judas a hero of sorts, could
something similar be done for Delilah? That is a version I would like
to see. Whatever way Roeg decides to tell this old story yet again, it
will be difficult for the new *Samson and Delilah* to approach the
cinematic power and interpretive genius of De Mille's version. Since

---

87. Doane, *The Desire to Desire*, p. 183; italics hers.
88. *The Evening Standard* (London), Wednesday, 24 January 1996.

I am ending my investigation of Delilah with discussion of film, I would like to let De Mille's version have the last word. Readers who know the film will recognize its aptness as a final comment on one of film's most remarkable *femmes fatales*. When Victor Mature as Samson topples the colossal image of Dagon and the temple comes crashing down on the Philistines in a spectacular finale, George Sanders, the urbane, unflappable, and worldly-wise Saran, lifts his cup in a toast of admiration and says, simply: 'Delilah'.

Bibliography

Ackerman, James S.
1974   'The Literary Context of the Moses Birth Story (Exodus 1-2)', in *Literary Interpretations of Biblical Narratives* (ed. K.R.R. Gros Louis, with J.S. Ackerman and T.S. Warshaw; Nashville: Abingdon Press), pp. 74-119.

Ackerman, Susan
1992   'Isaiah', in Newsom and Ringe (eds.), *The Women's Bible Commentary*, pp. 161-68.

Alpert, Rebecca
1994   'Finding Our Past: A Lesbian Interpretation of the Book of Ruth', in Kates and Reimer (eds.), *Reading Ruth: Contemporary Women Reclaim a Sacred Story*, pp. 91-96.

Alter, Robert
1981   *The Art of Biblical Narrative* (New York: Basic Books).

Andersen, Francis I., and David Noel Freedman
1980   *Hosea* (Anchor Bible, 24; Garden City, NY: Doubleday).

Anderson, Bernhard W.
1978   *The Eighth Century Prophets* (Proclamation Commentaries; Philadelphia: Fortress Press).

Apfel, Roberta, and Lise Grondahl
1994   'Feminine Plurals', in Kates and Reimer (eds.), *Reading Ruth: Contemporary Women Reclaim a Sacred Story*, pp. 55-64.

Aschkenasy, Nehama
1986   *Eve's Journey: Feminine Images in Hebraic Literary Tradition* (Philadelphia: University of Pennsylvania Press).

Babington, Bruce, and Peter William Evans
1993   *Biblical Epics: Sacred Narrative in the Hollywood Cinema* (Manchester: Manchester University Press).

Bach, Alice
1993   'Good to the Last Drop: Viewing the Sotah (Numbers 5.11-31) as the Glass Half Empty and Wondering How to View It Half Full', in *The New Literary Criticism and the Hebrew Bible* (Journal for the Study of the Old Testament Supplement Series, 143; ed. J. Cheryl Exum and David J.A. Clines; Sheffield: JSOT Press), pp. 26-54.
1993   'Reading Allowed: Feminist Biblical Criticism Approaching the Millennium', *Currents in Research: Biblical Studies* 1, pp. 191-215.
1993   'Signs of the Flesh: Observations on Characterization in the Bible', *Semeia* 63, pp. 61-79.

1994   'With a Song in Her Heart: Listening to Scholars Listening for Miriam', in
            Brenner (ed.), *A Feminist Companion to Exodus to Deuteronomy*, pp. 243-54.

Bailey, Randall C.
1990   *David in Love and War: The Pursuit of Power in 2 Samuel 10-12* (Journal for
            the Study of the Old Testament Supplement Series, 75; Sheffield: JSOT
            Press).

Bal, Mieke
1987   *Lethal Love: Feminist Literary Readings of Biblical Love Stories* (Bloomington:
            Indiana University Press).
1988   *Murder and Difference: Gender, Genre, and Scholarship on Sisera's Death*
            (Bloomington: Indiana University Press).
1988   *Death and Dissymmetry: The Politics of Coherence in the Book of Judges*
            (Chicago: University of Chicago Press).
1991   *Reading 'Rembrandt': Beyond the Word-Image Opposition* (Cambridge:
            Cambridge University Press).
1993   'The Elders and Susanna', *Biblical Interpretation* 1, pp. 1-19.
1993   'Metaphors He Lives By', *Semeia* 61, pp. 185-207.

Barr, James
1981   'A New Look at Kethibh-Qere', in *Remembering All the Way* (ed. A.S. van
            der Woude; Oudtestamentische Studiën, 21; Leiden: Brill), pp. 19-37.

Beattie, D. R.
1978   'Ruth III', *Journal for the Study of the Old Testament* 5, pp. 39-48.

Benjamin, Walter
1969   *Illuminations* (ed. with an introduction by Hannah Arendt; New York:
            Schocken Books).

Berger, John
1972   *Ways of Seeing* (London: Penguin Books).

Berlin, Adele
1983   *Poetics and Interpretation of Biblical Narrative* (Sheffield: Almond Press).
1994   'Ruth and the Continuity of Israel', in Kates and Reimer (eds.), *Reading
            Ruth: Contemporary Women Reclaim a Sacred Story*, pp. 255-60.

Bernstein, Moshe J.
1991   'Two Multivalent Readings in the Ruth Narrative', *Journal for the Study of
            the Old Testament* 50, pp. 15-26.

Berquist, Jon L.
1993   'Role Dedifferentiation in the Book of Ruth', *Journal for the Study of the
            Old Testament* 57, pp. 23-37.

Bertman, Stephen
1965   'Symmetrical Design in the Book of Ruth', *Journal of Biblical Literature* 84,
            pp. 165-68.

Bird, Phyllis
1974   'Images of Women in the Old Testament', in *Religion and Sexism* (ed.
            R.R. Ruether; New York: Simon & Schuster), pp. 41-88.
1989   '"To Play the Harlot": An Inquiry into an Old Testament Metaphor', in
            Gender and Difference in Ancient Israel (ed. Peggy Day; Minneapolis: Fortress
            Press), pp. 75-94.

Blenkinsopp, Joseph
 1990   *Ezekiel* (Interpretation, A Bible Commentary for Teaching and Preaching; Louisville: John Knox Press).

Bloom, Harold
 1973   *The Anxiety of Influence: A Theory of Poetry* (New York: Oxford University Press).
 1975   *A Map of Misreading* (New York: Oxford University Press).

Borges, Jorge Luis
 1984   *Seven Nights* (trans. Eliot Weinberger; New York: New Directions).

Bos, Johanna W.H.
 1988   'Out of the Shadows: Genesis 38; Judges 4.17-22; Ruth 3', *Semeia* 42, pp. 37-67.

Brenner, Athalya
 1983   'Naomi and Ruth', *Vetus Testamentum* 23, pp. 385-97 [repr. in Brenner (ed.), *A Feminist Companion to Ruth*, pp. 70-84].
 1985   *The Israelite Woman: Social Role and Literary Type in Biblical Narrative* (Sheffield: JSOT Press).
 1993   'Naomi and Ruth: Further Reflections', in Brenner (ed.), *A Feminist Companion to Ruth*, pp. 140-44.
 1993   'On "Jeremiah" and the Poetics of (Prophetic?) Pornography', in Brenner and van Dijk-Hemmes, *On Gendering Texts*, pp. 177-93.
 1994   'An Afterword: The Decalogue—Am I an Addressee?', in Brenner (ed.), *A Feminist Companion to Exodus to Deuteronomy*, pp. 255-58.
 1996   'Pornoprophetics Revisited: Some Additional Reflections', *Journal for the Study of the Old Testament* 70, pp. 63-86.

Brenner, Athalya (ed.)
 1993   *A Feminist Companion to Ruth* (The Feminist Companion to the Bible, 3; Sheffield: Sheffield Academic Press).
 1994   *A Feminist Companion to Exodus to Deuteronomy* (The Feminist Companion to the Bible, 6; Sheffield: Sheffield Academic Press).
 1995   *A Feminist Companion to the Latter Prophets* (The Feminist Companion to the Bible, 8; Sheffield: Sheffield Academic Press).

Brenner, Athalya, and Fokkelien van Dijk-Hemmes
 1993   *On Gendering Texts: Female and Male Voices in the Hebrew Bible* (Biblical Interpretation Series, 1; Leiden: Brill).

Brenner, Gerry
 1990   'Readers Responding: An Interview with Biblical Ruth', *Soundings* 73, pp. 233-55.

Bright, John
 1965   *Jeremiah* (Anchor Bible, 21; Garden City, NY: Doubleday).

Brooks, Peter
 1987   'The Idea of a Psychoanalytic Literary Criticism', in *Discourse in Psychoanalysis and Literature* (ed. Shlomith Rimmon-Kenan; London: Methuen), pp. 1-18.
 1993   *Body Work: Objects of Desire in Modern Narrative* (Cambridge, MA: Harvard University Press).

Brownlee, William H.
 1986   *Ezekiel 1–19* (Word Biblical Commentary, 28; Waco, TX: Word Books).

Brueggemann, Walter
  1988   *To Pluck Up, to Tear Down: A Commentary on the Book of Jeremiah 1–25*
            (Grand Rapids: Eerdmans).
  1990   *First and Second Samuel* (Interpretation: A Bible Commentary for Teaching
            and Preaching; Louisville: John Knox Press).
Butler, Judith
  1990   *Gender Trouble: Feminism and the Subversion of Identity* (New York:
            Routledge).
Cady Stanton, Elizabeth
  1993 [1898]   'The Book of Ruth', in Brenner (ed.), *A Feminist Companion to Ruth*,
            pp. 20-25.
Camp, Claudia V.
  1993   'Metaphor in Feminist Biblical Interpretation: Theoretical Perspectives',
            Semeia 61, pp. 3-36.
Camp, Claudia V., and Carole R. Fontaine (eds.)
  1993   *Women, War, and Metaphor: Language and Society in the Study of the Hebrew
            Bible* (Semeia, 61; Atlanta: Scholars Press).
Campbell, Edward F., Jr
  1975   *Ruth* (Anchor Bible, 7; Garden City, NY: Doubleday).
Carlson, R. A.
  1964   *David, the Chosen King* (Stockholm: Almqvist & Wiksell).
Carroll, Robert P.
  1986   *Jeremiah* (Old Testament Library; Philadelphia: Westminster Press).
  1995   'Desire under the Terebinths: On Pornographic Representation in the
            Prophets—A Response', in Brenner (ed.), *A Feminist Companion to the
            Latter Prophets*, pp. 275-307.
Caws, Mary Ann
  1986   'Ladies Shot and Painted: Female Embodiment in Surrealist Art', in *The
            Female Body in Western Culture: Contemporary Perspectives* (ed. S.R.
            Suleiman; Cambridge, MA: Harvard University Press), pp. 262-87.
Cixous, Hélène, and Catherine Clément
  1986   *The Newly Born Woman* (trans. Betsy Wing; foreword by Sandra M.
            Gilbert; Minneapolis: University of Minnesota Press).
Clark, Gordon A.
  1993   *The Word* Hesed *in the Hebrew Bible* (Journal for the Study of the Old
            Testament Supplement Series, 157; Sheffield: JSOT Press).
Clements, R.E.
  1980   *Isaiah 1–39* (New Century Bible Commentary; Grand Rapids:
            Eerdmans).
  1988   *Jeremiah* (Interpretation, A Bible Commentary for Teaching and Preaching;
            Louisville: John Knox Press).
Clines, David J.A.
  1991   'Michal Observed: An Introduction', in Clines and Eskenazi (eds.), *Telling
            Queen Michal's Story*, pp. 24-63.
  1991   'The Story of Michal, Wife of David, in its Sequential Unfolding', in Clines
            and Eskenazi (eds.), *Telling Queen Michal's Story*, pp. 129-40.
  1995   'Ethics as Deconstruction, and, the Ethics of Deconstruction', in *The Bible
            in Ethics: The Second Sheffield Colloquium* (ed. John W. Rogerson,

Margaret Davies and M. Daniel Carroll R.; Journal for the Study of the Old Testament Supplement Series, 207; Sheffield: Sheffield Academic Press, 1995), pp. 77–106.

1995   *Interested Parties: The Ideology of Writers and Readers of the Hebrew Bible* ((Journal for the Study of the Old Testament Supplement Series, 205; Gender, Culture, Theory, 1; Sheffield: Sheffield Academic Press).

Clines, David J.A., and Tamara C. Eskenazi (eds.)

1991   *Telling Queen Michal's Story: An Experiment in Comparative Interpretation* (Journal for the Study of the Old Testament Supplement Series, 119; Sheffield: JSOT Press).

Cogan, M.

1968   'A Technical Term for Exposure', *Journal for Near Eastern Studies* 27, pp. 133–35.

Conroy, Pat

1996   *Beach Music* (New York: Bantam).

Coogan, Michal David

'The Woman at the Window: An Artistic and Literary Motif.' Unpublished paper.

Culler, Jonathan

1975   *Structuralist Poetics: Structuralism, Linguistics, and the Study of Literature* (Ithaca, NY: Cornell University Press).

Daly, Mary

1973   *Beyond God the Father: Toward a Philosophy of Women's Liberation* (Boston: Beacon Press).

Darr, Katheryn Pfisterer

1992   'Ezekiel', in Newsom and Ringe (eds.), *The Women's Bible Commentary*, pp. 183–90.

1992   'Ezekiel's Justifications of God: Teaching Troubling Texts', *Journal for the Study of the Old Testament* 55, pp. 97–117.

Davies, Gordon F.

1992   *Israel in Egypt: Reading Exodus 1–2* (Journal for the Study of the Old Testament Supplement Series, 135; Sheffield: JSOT Press).

Deen, Edith

1955   *All of the Women of the Bible* (New York: Harper & Row).

De Lauretis, Teresa

1984   *Alice Doesn't: Feminism, Semiotics, Cinema* (London: Macmillan).

Derrida, Jacques

1976   *Of Grammatology* (trans. Gayatri Chakravorty Spivak; Baltimore: Johns Hopkins University Press).

1978   *Writing and Difference* (trans., with introduction and notes by Alan Bass; Chicago: University of Chicago Press).

1981   *Dissemination* (trans., with introduction and notes by Barbara Johnson; Chicago: University of Chicago Press).

Diamond, A.R. Pete, and Kathleen M. O'Connor

1996   'Unfaithful Passions: Coding Women Coding Men in Jeremiah 2-3 (4.2)', *Biblical Interpretation* 4, pp. 288–310.

Dijk-Hemmes, Fokkelien van

1993   'The Metaphorization of Woman in Prophetic Speech: An Analysis of

Ezekiel 23', in Brenner and van Dijk-Hemmes, *On Gendering Texts*, pp. 167-76.

1994   'Some Recent Views on the Presentation of the Song of Miriam', in Brenner (ed.), *A Feminist Companion to Exodus to Deuteronomy*, pp. 200-206.

Dillenberger, Jane

1990   *Image and Spirit in Sacred and Secular Art* (New York: Crossroad).

Doane, Mary Ann

1987   *The Desire to Desire: The Woman's Film of the 1940s* (Houndmills: Macmillan).

1991   *Femmes Fatales: Feminism, Film Theory, Psychoanalysis* (London: Routledge).

Duffy, Maureen

1985   Collected Poems *1949–1984* (London: Hamish Hamilton).

Durcan, Paul

1994   'Talking Pictures', *The Independent Magazine*, 12 March 1994, pp. 24-31.

Ebach, Jürgen

1996   'Die Schwester des Mose: Anmerkungen zu einem "Widerspruch" in Exodus 2, 1-10', in *'Mit unsrer Macht ist nichts getan…': Festschrift für Dieter Schellong zum 65. Geburtstag* (ed. Jörg Mertin, Dietrich Neuhaus, and Michael Weinrich; Herchen Verlag), pp. 101-15.

Eichrodt, Walther

1965   *Der Prophet Hesekiel. Kapitel 1-18* (Das Alte Testament Deutsch, 22.1; Göttingen: Vandenhoeck & Ruprecht).

1970   *Ezekiel* (trans. C. Quin; Old Testament Library; Philadelphia: Westminster Press).

Elley, Derek

1984   *The Epic Film: Myth and History* (London: Routledge & Kegan Paul).

Ellwood, Gracia Fay

1988   *Batter My Heart* (Pendle Hill Pamphlet, 282; Wallingford, PA: Pendle Hill).

Exum, J. Cheryl

1983   'The Theological Dimension of the Samson Saga', *Vetus Testamentum* 33, pp. 30-45.

1983   '"You Shall Let Every Daughter Live": A Study of Exodus 1.8-2.10', *Semeia* 28, pp. 63-82 (reprinted in Brenner [ed.], *A Feminist Companion to Exodus to Deuteronomy*, pp. 37-61).

1985   '"Mother in Israel": A Familiar Figure Reconsidered', in *Feminist Interpretation of the Bible* (ed. Letty M. Russell; Philadelphia: Westminster Press), pp. 73-85.

1990   'The Centre Cannot Hold: Thematic and Textual Instabilities in Judges', *Catholic Biblical Quarterly* 52, pp. 410-31.

1992   *Tragedy and Biblical Narrative: Arrows of the Almighty* (Cambridge: Cambridge University Press).

1993   *Fragmented Women: Feminist (Sub)versions of Biblical Narratives* (Journal for the Study of the Old Testament Supplement Series, 163; Sheffield: JSOT Press; Valley Forge, PA: Trinity Press International).

1994   'Second Thoughts about Secondary Characters: Women in Exodus 1.8–2.10', in Brenner (ed.), *A Feminist Companion to Exodus to Deuteronomy*, pp. 75-87.

1995   'Michal at the Movies', in *The Bible in Human Society: Essays in Honour of John Rogerson* (ed. M. Daniel Carroll R., David J.A. Clines and Philip R. Davies; Journal for the Study of the Old Testament Supplement Series, 200; Sheffield: Sheffield Academic Press), pp. 273-92.

1995   'The Ethics of Biblical Violence against Women', in *The Bible in Ethics: The Second Sheffield Colloquium* (ed. John W. Rogerson, Margaret Davies and M. Daniel Carroll R.; Journal for the Study of the Old Testament Supplement Series, 207; Sheffield: Sheffield Academic Press), pp. 248-71.

Fetterley, Judith

1991   'Palpable Designs: An American Dream: "Rip Van Winkle"', in *Feminisms: An Anthology of Literary Theory and Criticism* (ed. R.R. Warhol and D. Price Herndl; New Brunswick, NJ: Rutgers University Press), pp. 502-508 (reprinted from *The Resisting Reader* [Bloomington: Indiana University Press, 1977]).

Fewell, Danna Nolan, and David Miller Gunn

1990   *Compromising Redemption: Relating Characters in the Book of Ruth* (Louisville: Westminster/John Knox Press).

1991   'Tipping the Balance: Sternberg's Reader and the Rape of Dinah', *Journal of Biblical Literature* 110, pp. 193-211.

Fisch, Harold

1982   'Ruth and the Structure of Covenant History', *Vetus Testamentum* 32, pp. 425-37.

Flagg, Fannie

1987   *Fried Green Tomatoes at the Whistle Stop Cafe* (London: Vintage).

Fokkelman, J. P.

1981   *Narrative Art and Poetry in the Books of Samuel.* I. *King David* (Assen: van Gorcum).

1986   *Narrative Art and Poetry in the Books of Samuel.* II. *The Crossing Fates* (Assen: van Gorcum).

1986   *Narrative Art and Poetry in the Books of Samuel.* III. *Throne and City* (Assen: van Gorcum).

Foucault, Michel

1990 [1976]   *The History of Sexuality: An Introduction*, I (New York: Vintage Books).

Fowl, Stephen

1995   'Texts Don't Have Ideologies', *Biblical Interpretation* 3, pp. 15-34.

Frye, Northrop

1966   *Anatomy of Criticism* (New York: Atheneum).

Frymer-Kensky, Tikva

1992   *In the Wake of the Goddesses: Women, Culture, and the Biblical Transformation of Pagan Myth* (New York: Free Press).

Fuchs, Esther

1985   'The Literary Characterization of Mothers and Sexual Politics in the Hebrew Bible', in *Feminist Perspectives on Biblical Scholarship* (ed. Adela Yarbro Collins; Chico, CA: Scholars Press), pp. 117-36.

1987   *Israeli Mythogynies: Women in Contemporary Hebrew Fiction* (Albany: State University of New York Press).

Galambush, Julie
1992 *Jerusalem in the Book of Ezekiel: The City as Yahweh's Wife* (Society of Biblical Literature Dissertation Series, 130; Atlanta: Scholars Press).
Gamman, Lorraine, and Margaret Marshment (eds.)
1988 *The Female Gaze: Women as Viewers of Popular Culture* (London: The Women's Press).
Gaster, Theodor H.
1981 *Myth, Legend, and Custom in the Old Testament*, II (Gloucester, MA: Peter Smith).
Gilbert, Sandra M., and Susan Gubar
1979 *The Madwoman in the Attic: The Woman Writer and the Nineteenth-Century Literary Imagination* (New Haven: Yale University Press).
Glancy, Jennifer A.
1994 'Unveiling Masculinity: The Construction of Gender in Mark 6.17-29', *Biblical Interpretation* 2, pp. 34-50.
Goldreich, Gloria
1994 'Ruth, Naomi, and Orpah: A Parable of Friendship', in Kates and Reimer (eds.), *Reading Ruth: Contemporary Women Reclaim a Sacred Story*, pp. 33-43.
Gordon, Pamela, and Harold C. Washington
1995 'Rape as a Military Metaphor in the Hebrew Bible', in Brenner (ed.), *A Feminist Companion to the Latter Prophets*, pp. 308-25.
Greenberg, Moshe
1983 *Ezekiel, 1–20* (Anchor Bible, 22; Garden City, NY: Doubleday).
Greenstein, Edward L.
forthcoming *Reader Responsibility: The Shaping of Meaning in Biblical Narrative* (Journal for the Study of the Old Testament Supplement Series; Gender, Culture, Theory, 6; Sheffield: Sheffield Academic Press).
Griffin, Susan
1981 *Pornography and Silence: Culture's Revenge against Nature* (New York: Harper & Row).
Guillory, John
1986 'Dalila's House: *Samson Agonistes* and the Sexual Division of Labor', in *Rewriting the Renaissance: The Discourses of Sexual Difference in Early Modern Europe* (ed. Margaret Ferguson, Maureen Quilligan and Nancy Vickers; Chicago: University of Chicago Press), pp. 106-22.
Gunkel, Hermann
1913 *Reden und Aufsätze* (Göttingen: Vandenhoeck & Ruprecht).
Halperin, David M., John J. Winkler, and Froma I. Zeitlin (eds.)
1990 *Before Sexuality: The Construction of Erotic Experience in the Ancient Greek World* (Princeton, NJ: Princeton University Press).
Hals, Ronald M.
1969 *The Theology of the Book of Ruth* (Philadelphia: Fortress Press).
Hardy, Thomas
1994 [1874] *Far from the Madding Crowd* (London: Penguin Popular Classics).
Harvey, D.
1962 'Ruth', *The Interpreter's Dictionary of the Bible*, IV, pp. 131-34.

Hertzberg, Hans Wilhelm

1960   *Die Samuelbücher* (Das Alte Testament Deutsch, 10; 2nd rev. edn; Göttingen: Vandenhoeck & Ruprecht).

1964   *I & II Samuel* (trans. J. S. Bowden; Old Testament Library; Philadelphia: Westminster Press).

1969   *Die Bücher Josua, Richter, Ruth* (Das Alte Testament Deutsch, 9; Göttingen: Vandenhoeck & Ruprecht).

Hillers, Delbert R.

1972   *Lamentations* (Anchor Bible, 7A; Garden City, NY: Doubleday).

Holladay, William L.

1986   *Jeremiah 1* (Hermeneia; Philadelphia: Fortress Press).

Horney, Karen

1967   *Feminine Psychology* (London: Routledge and Kegan Paul).

Hubbard, Robert L., Jr

1988   *The Book of Ruth* (Grand Rapids: Eerdmans).

Humbert, Paul

1958   'Art et leçon de l'histoire de Ruth', in *Opuscules d'un hébraïsant* (Neuchatel: University of Neuchatel), pp. 83-110.

Hyman, Ronald T.

1984   'Questions and Changing Identity in the Book of Ruth', *Union Seminary Quarterly Review* 39, pp. 189-201.

Janzen, J. Gerald

1992   'Song of Moses, Song of Miriam: Who Is Seconding Whom?', *Catholic Biblical Quarterly* 54, pp. 211-20 (reprinted in Brenner [ed.], *A Feminist Companion to Exodus to Deuteronomy*, pp. 187-99).

Joüon, Paul

1986   *Ruth: Commentaire philologique et exégétique* (Subsidia Biblica, 9; 2nd edn; Rome: Biblical Institute Press).

Kaiser, Otto

1972   *Isaiah 1–12* (trans. R. A. Wilson; Old Testament Library; Philadelphia: Westminster Press).

Kaplan, E. Ann

1983   *Women and Film: Both Sides of the Camera* (London: Routledge).

Kates, Judith A., and Gail Twersky Reimer (eds.)

1994   *Reading Ruth: Contemporary Women Reclaim a Sacred Story* (New York: Ballantine Books, 1994).

Kilpatrick, G.G.D.

1956   'Exposition to the Book of Isaiah', in *The Interpreter's Bible*, V (New York: Abingdon Press), pp. 165-381.

Kim, Jichan

1993   *The Structure of the Samson Cycle* (Kampen: Kok Pharos).

King, Philip J.

1988   *Amos, Hosea, Micah—An Archaeological Commentary* (Philadelphia: Westminster Press).

Kolodny, Annette

1985   'A Map for Rereading: Gender and the Interpretation of Literary Texts', in *The New Feminist Criticism: Essays on Women, Literature, and Theory* (ed. Elaine Showalter; New York: Pantheon Books), pp. 46-62.

Kreitzer, Larry J.
1993   *The New Testament in Fiction and Film: On Reversing the Hermeneutical Flow* (The Biblical Seminar, 17; Sheffield: JSOT Press).
1994   *The Old Testament in Fiction and Film: On Reversing the Hermeneutical Flow* (The Biblical Seminar, 24; Sheffield: Sheffield Academic Press).

Kristeva, Julia
1986   'Stabat Mater', in *The Female Body in Western Culture: Contemporary Perspectives* (ed. S. R. Suleiman; Cambridge, MA: Harvard University Press), pp. 99-118.

Kunsthistorisches Museum Wien
1995   *Eros und Mythos: Begleitheft zur Ausstellung des Kunsthistorischen Museums, Wien 1995.*

LaCocque, André
1990   *The Feminine Unconventional: Four Subversive Figures in Israel's Tradition* (Minneapolis: Fortress Press).

Lamphere, Louise
1974   'Strategies, Cooperation, and Conflict among Women in Domestic Groups', in *Woman, Culture, and Society* (ed. Michelle Zimbalist Rosaldo and Louise Lamphere; Stanford: Stanford University Press, 1974), pp. 97-112.

Landy, Francis
1994   'Ruth and the Romance of Realism, or Deconstructing History', *Journal of the American Academy of Religion* 62, pp. 285-317.

Langmuir, Erika
1994   *The National Gallery Companion Guide* (London: National Gallery Publications).

Laqueur, Thomas
1990   *Making Sex: Body and Gender from the Greeks to Freud* (Cambridge, MA: Harvard University Press).

Lasker-Schüler, Else
1966   *Sämtliche Gedichte* (Munich: Kösel Verlag).

Leach, Edmund
1983   'Why Did Moses Have a Sister?', in Edmund Leach and D. Alan Aycock, *Structuralist Interpretations of Biblical Myth* (Cambridge: Cambridge University Press).

Lerner, Gerda
1986   *The Creation of Patriarchy* (New York: Oxford University Press).

Levine, Amy-Jill
1992   'Ruth', in Newsom and Ringe (eds.), *The Women's Bible Commentary*, pp. 78-84.

Levine, Étan
1973   *The Aramaic Version of Ruth* (Analecta Biblica, 58; Rome: Biblical Institute Press).

Lewalski, Barbara K.
1990   'Milton on Women—Yet Again', in *Problems for Feminist Criticism* (ed. Sally Minogue; London: Routledge).

Magdalene, F. Rachel
1995   'Ancient Near Eastern Treaty-Curses and the Ultimate Texts of Terror: A

Study of the Language of Divine Sexual Abuse in the Prophetic Corpus', in Brenner (ed.), *A Feminist Companion to the Latter Prophets*, pp. 326-52.

Magonet, Jonathan

1991   *A Rabbi's Bible* (London: SCM Press).

Martin, Dale B.

1995   'Heterosexism and the Interpretation of Romans 1.18-32', *Biblical Interpretation* 3, pp. 332-55.

McColley, Diane K.

1989   'Milton and the Sexes', in *The Cambridge Companion to Milton* (ed. D. Danielson; Cambridge: Cambridge University Press), pp. 147-66.

Meyers, Carol

1988   *Discovering Eve: Ancient Israelite Women in Context* (New York: Oxford University Press).

1991   '"To Her Mother's House": Considering a Counterpart to the Israelite *Bet 'ab*', in *The Bible and the Politics of Exegesis: Essays in Honor of Norman K. Gottwald on His Sixty-fifth Birthday* (ed. D. Jobling, P.L. Day and G.T. Sheppard; Cleveland: Pilgrim Press), pp. 39-51.

1994   'Miriam the Musician', in Brenner (ed.), *A Feminist Companion to Exodus to Deuteronomy*, pp. 207-30.

Midrash Rabbah: Ruth

1939   (trans. L. Rabinowitz; London: Soncino).

Miles, Margaret R.

1989   *Carnal Knowing: Female Nakedness and Religious Meaning in the Christian West* (New York: Vintage Books).

Mintz, Alan

1982   'The Rhetoric of Lamentations and the Representation of Catastrophe', *Prooftexts* 2, pp. 1-17.

Moi, Toril

1985   *Sexual/Textual Politics: Feminist Literary Theory* (London: Methuen).

Mollenkott, Virginia

1970   'Relativism in *Samson Agonistes*', *Studies in Philosophy* 67, pp. 89-102.

Morris, Leon

1968   *Ruth* (Tyndale Old Testament Commentaries; London: Tyndale Press).

Muilenburg, James

1969   'Form Criticism and Beyond', *Journal of Biblical Literature* 88, pp. 1-18.

Müllner, Ilse

1996   'Tödliche Differenzen: Sexuelle Gewalt als Gewalt gegen Andere in Ri 19', in *Von der Wurzel Getragen: Christlich-feministische Exegese in Auseinandersetzung mit Antijudaismus* (ed. Luise Schottroff and Marie-Theres Wacker; Leiden: Brill), pp. 81-100.

Mulvey, Laura

1989   *Visual and Other Pleasures* (Houndmills: Macmillan).

Nead, Lynda

1992   *The Female Nude: Art, Obscenity and Sexuality* (London: Routledge).

Newsom, Carol A.

1989   'Woman and the Discourse of Patriarchal Wisdom: A Study of Proverbs 1-9', in *Gender and Difference in Ancient Israel* (ed. Peggy Day; Minneapolis: Fortress Press), pp. 142-60.

Newsom, Carol A., and Sharon H. Ringe (eds.)
1992   *The Women's Bible Commentary* (Louisville: Westminster/John Knox Press).

Nicol, George G.
1988   'Bathsheba, a Clever Woman?' *Expository Times* 99, pp. 360-63.

Niditch, Susan
1990   'Samson As Culture Hero, Trickster, and Bandit: The Empowerment of the Weak', *Catholic Biblical Quarterly* 52, pp. 608-24.

Nielsen, Kirsten
1985   'La choix contre de droit dans le livre de Ruth: De l'aire de battage au tribunal', *Vetus Testamentum* 35, pp. 201-12.

Norris, Christopher
1982   *Deconstruction: Theory and Practice* (London: Metheun).

Ochshorn, Judith
1981   *The Female Experience and the Nature of the Divine* (Bloomington: Indiana University Press).

O'Connor, Kathleen M.
1992   'Jeremiah', in Newsom and Ringe (eds.), *The Women's Bible Commentary* , pp. 169-77.

Oz, Amos
1978   'The Hill of Evil Counsel', in *The Hill of Evil Counsel: Three Stories* (trans. Nicholas de Lange; Glasgow: Fontana/Collins).

Paglia, Camille
1990   *Sexual Personae: Art and Decadence from Nefertiti to Emily Dickinson* (New York: Vintage Books).

Pardes, Ilana
1992   *Countertraditions in the Bible: A Feminist Approach* (Cambridge, MA: Harvard University Press).

Phillips, Anthony
1986   'The Book of Ruth—Deception and Shame', *Journal of Jewish Studies* 37, pp. 1-17.

Putnam, Ruth Anna
1994   'Friendship', in Kates and Reimer (eds.), *Reading Ruth: Contemporary Women Reclaim a Sacred Story*, pp. 44-54.

Radzinowicz, Mary Ann
1978   *Toward Samson Agonistes: The Growth of Milton's Mind* (Princeton, NJ: Princeton University Press).

Rauber, D. F.
1970   'Literary Values in the Bible: the Book of Ruth', *Journal of Biblical Literature* 89, pp. 27-37.

Rooney, Ellen
1991   '"A Little More than Persuading": Tess and the Subject of Sexual Violence', in *Rape and Representation* (ed. L.A. Higgins and B.R. Silver; New York: Columbia University Press), pp. 87-114.

Rosaldo, Michelle Zimbalist
1974   'Woman, Culture, and Society: A Theoretical Overview', in *Woman, Culture, and Society* (ed. Michelle Zimbalist Rosaldo and Louise Lamphere; Stanford: Stanford University Press, 1974), pp. 97-112.

Rudolph, Wilhelm
1962 *Das Buch Ruth, Das Hohe Lied, Die Klagelieder* (Kommentar zum Alten Testament, XVII, 1-3; Gütersloh: Gerd Mohn).
Rutledge, David
1996 'Faithful Reading: Poststructuralism and the Sacred', *Biblical Interpretation* 4, pp. 270-87.
Sakenfeld, Katherine Doob
1985 *Faithfulness in Action* (Philadelphia: Fortress Press).
Sanderson, Judith E.
1992 'Amos', in Newsom and Ringe (eds.), *The Women's Bible Commentary*, pp. 205-209.
1992 'Micah', in Newsom and Ringe (eds.), *The Women's Bible Commentary*, pp. 215-16.
1992 'Nahum', in Newsom and Ringe (eds.), *The Women's Bible Commentary*, pp. 217-21.
Sasson, Jack M.
1979 *Ruth: A New Translation with a Philological Commentary and a Formalist-Folklorist Interpretation* (Baltimore: Johns Hopkins University Press).
1988 'Who Cut Samson's Hair? (And Other Trifling Issues Raised by Judges 16)', *Prooftexts* 8, pp. 333-39.
Schüngel-Straumann, Helen
1995 'God as Mother in Hosea 11', in Brenner (ed.), *A Feminist Companion to the Latter Prophets*, pp. 194-218.
Scott, Bernard Brandon
1994 *Hollywood Dreams and Biblical Stories* (Minneapolis: Fortress Press).
Seow, C. L.
1989 *Myth, Drama, and the Politics of David's Dance* (Harvard Semitic Monographs, 44; Atlanta: Scholars Press).
Setel, T. Drorah
1985 'Prophets and Pornography: Female Sexual Imagery in Hosea', in *Feminist Interpretation of the Bible* (ed. Letty M. Russell; Philadelphia: Westminster Press), pp. 86-95.
Sherwood, Yvonne
1996 *The Prostitute and the Prophet: Hosea's Marriage in Literary-Theoretical Perspective* (Journal for the Study of the Old Testament Supplement Series, 212; Gender, Culture, Theory, 2; Sheffield: Sheffield Academic Press).
Shields, Mary E.
1995 'Circumcision of the Prostitute: Gender, Sexuality and the Call to Repentance in Jer. 3.1-4.4', *Biblical Interpretation* 3, pp. 61-74.
forthcoming 'Ezekiel 16: Body Rhetoric and Gender', *Journal of Feminist Studies in Religion*.
Siebert-Hommes, Jopie
1988 'Twelve Women in Exodus 1 and 2: The Role of Daughters and Sons in the Stories Concerning Moses', *Amsterdamse Cahiers voor Exegese en Bijbelse Theologie* 12, pp. 47-58.
1992 'Die Geburtsgeschichte des Mose innerhalb des Erzählungszusammenhangs von Exodus i und ii', *Vetus Testamentum* 42, pp. 398-403.

Silverman, Kaja
1988   *The Acoustic Mirror: The Female Voice in Psychoanalysis and Cinema* (Bloomington: Indiana University Press).
Smith, Ruth
1995   *Handel's Oratorios and Eighteenth-Century Thought* (Cambridge: Cambridge University Press).
Sölle, Dorothée, Joe H. Kirchberger, and Herbert Haag
1994   *Great Women of the Bible in Art and Literature* (Grand Rapids: Eerdmans).
Stacey, Jackie
1994   *Star Gazing: Hollywood Cinema and Female Spectatorship* (London: Routledge).
Sternberg, Meir
1985   *The Poetics of Biblical Narrative: Ideological Literature and the Drama of Reading* (Bloomington: Indiana University Press).
1992   'Biblical Poetics and Sexual Politics: From Reading to Counterreading', *Journal of Biblical Literature* 111, pp. 463-88.
Stoddard, Eve Walsh
1991   'The Genealogy of Ruth: From Harvester to Fallen Woman in Nineteenth-Century England', in *Old Testament Women in Western Literature* (ed. Raymond-Jean Frontain and Jan Wojcik; Conway, AR: UCA Press), pp. 205-36.
Thistlethwaite, Susan Brooks
1985   'Every Two Minutes: Battered Women and Feminist Interpretation', in *Feminist Interpretation of the Bible* (ed. Letty M. Russell; Philadelphia: Westminster Press), pp. 96-107.
1993   '"You May Enjoy the Spoil of Your Enemies": Rape as a Biblical Metaphor for War', *Semeia* 61, pp. 59-75.
Todorov, Tzvetan
1977   *The Poetics of Prose* (trans. Richard Howard; Ithaca, NY: Cornell University Press).
Trible, Phyllis
1978   *God and the Rhetoric of Sexuality* (Philadelphia: Fortress Press).
1994   'Bringing Miriam out of the Shadows', in Brenner (ed.), *A Feminist Companion to Exodus to Deuteronomy*, pp. 166-86.
Ulreich, John C., Jr
1988   '"Incident to All Our Sex": the Tragedy of Dalila', in *Milton and the Idea of Woman* (ed. Julia M. Walker; Urbana: University of Illinois Press), pp. 185-210.
Weems, Renita J.
1989   'Gomer: Victim of Violence or Victim of Metaphor?', *Semeia* 47, pp. 87-104.
1992   'The Hebrew Women Are Not like the Egyptian Women: The Ideology of Race, Gender and Sexual Reproduction in Exodus 1', *Semeia* 59, pp. 25-34.
1995   *Battered Love: Marriage, Sex, and Violence in the Hebrew Prophets* (Minneapolis: Fortress Press).
Westbrook, Raymond
1990   'Adultery in Ancient Near Eastern Law', *Revue Biblique* 97, pp. 542-80.

Williams, James G.
  1982   *Women Recounted: Narrative Thinking and the God of Israel* (Sheffield: Almond Press).
Winkler, John J.
  1990   *The Constraints of Desire: The Anthropology of Sex and Gender in Ancient Greece* (New York: Routledge).
Wolde, Ellen van
  1997   'Texts in Dialogue with Texts: Intertextuality in the Ruth and Tamar Narratives', *Biblical Interpretation* 5, forthcoming.
Wolff, Hans Walter
  1974   *Hosea* (trans. Gary Stansell; Hermeneia; Philadelphia: Fortress Press).
Yee, Gale A.
  1992   'Hosea', in Newsom and Ringe (eds.), *The Women's Bible Commentary* , pp. 195-202.
Zakovitch, Yair
  1990   *Ruth: Introduction and Commentary* (Tel Aviv: Am Oved [Hebrew]).
Zenger, Erich
  1986   *Das Buch Ruth* (Zürcher Bibelkommentare AT, 8; Zürich: Theologischer Verlag).

INDEXES

INDEX OF REFERENCES

OLD TESTAMENT

NEW TESTAMENT

INDEX OF AUTHORS